THE HERO,
AMERICAN STYLE

THE HERO,
AMERICAN STYLE

Marshall Fishwick

DAVID McKAY COMPANY, INC.
New York

Library of Congress Catalog Card Number: 69–13472

MANUFACTURED IN THE UNITED STATES OF AMERICA

VAN REES PRESS • NEW YORK

To

Jeff, Ellie, Sue, and Lou

Contents

"Who cares what the fact was, when we have made a constellation of it to hang in heaven, an immortal sign?"

RALPH WALDO EMERSON

"America is a country which has grown by the leap of one hero past another."

NORMAN MAILER

"Presidential hopefuls in 1968 are being judged primarily on style or what passes for style as projected by TV."

PENN KIMBALL

"God, I'm glad I'm not me."

BOB DYLAN

THE HERO,
AMERICAN STYLE

Point of Departure

HISTORY is meaningless without heroes; there is no score before they come to bat. "It is natural to believe in great men," Emerson wrote. "All mythology opens with demigods." Our job is to examine America's great men, by name and type—swashbucklers, squires, cavaliers, natural men, self-made men, jolly giants, smooth roughnecks, poor whites, hot shots, cool ones, celebrities, pop princes. Our concern is lifestyle and leadership in the evolution of America.

Hence we seek not only data but understanding. Behind the *who* and the *what* is the all-important *why*. Library shelves are full of books naming heroes and telling what they did. But why are they heroes? What process elevated and, later, deflated them? Why do they come in clusters, like grapes; and why do some of the grapes turn sour? As we tell about our heroes, what do they tell us about ourselves?

We set out to study the changing contours of greatness from John Smith to John Kennedy.

Recognizing heroes is one thing, theorizing about them another. We confront a monomyth [1] whose nucleus is a magnification of the ageless steps in the rites of passage— separation, initiation, return. Having served folk culture

---

[1] James Joyce coined the term "monomyth" to encompass various aspects of mythic belief which converge into popular usage.

1

so well, will the monomyth adapt to pop culture? Has it already done so, without our recognizing it?

Western man lives at a time when many old myths have lost their power. When an old mythology disintegrates, a new one originates. To survive is to remythologize. That process is well under way in the 1960s. We not only discover new myths; we participate in them. That is why we have so much trouble understanding what is going on all around us. What is *behind* the student uprisings, LSD, hippies, anti-heroes? What are the young, the black, and the poor trying to tell us? How shall we respond?

Why do they put go-go girls in cages? The question sounds silly, but it is substantive. The dynamic, voluptuous symbols of freedom, even anarchy, behind bars—go-go nowhere. "The land of the free" up-tight with authority and inhibitions. The land of celebrities, riddled with cynicism. The greatest military power in history, bogged down in Asian rice paddies. History turned into a happening. One nation, very divisible, jaded and jailed.

What happens to go-go girls? Suddenly they don't make the scene. Just when they found a place on the tube they don't have a sponsor. We can't find that old copy of *Playboy* with their photographs. Bye-bye, go-go.

Heroes are mirrors of the times. Like cars, can openers, and miniskirts, they endure enforced obsolescence. Lindbergh still lives; yet how can we tell our children what his 1927 flight meant to our parents? Tell them how the "Lone Eagle" was "close to inhabitants of a universe closed to mortal men?" Come on, Dad, you're putting me on.

And what about "old" celebrities—under twenty—who are out before we are sure they are in? Was Elvis Presley turned out to pasture in Bluegrass Country? Who doused the candles at the James Dean Shrine? Where did you go, Joe DiMaggio? "No one can take the place of the superstars of the last decade. I'll never forget what's-his-name."

Who decreed that Abstract Expressionist painters and Absurd dramatists were part of the Establishment? What does Marshall McLuhan mean when he says, "If it works it's obsolete"? Heroes (pro, anti, non) rise and fall too quickly for analysis; they blow away like yesterday's newspaper and fourth-class mail. Who, under these circumstances, dares write about *The Hero, American Style?*

I do. The hero provides a knothole through which to scan the whole ball park. Behind today's confusion and hypertension the game proceeds; the drama of one of history's vital cultures unfolds. We will neither see it all nor understand all that we see. Still, we shall try. What a game!

Ours is the era of figure-it-out-yourself movies (Joseph Losey's *Accident,* Michelangelo Antonioni's *Blow Up*) and heroes. The historian must resist the lure of presentism. He must always insist that we look back before looking around. Discover where we have been before deciding where we are, or where we are going. Of course, lifestyles change, and generation gaps widen; but heroes never go out of style. Myths shape the man; style shows how it has shaped him.

My book is about men, myths, and styles in America. It searches for universal meaning in our national pattern. We start by looking at the hero in history, but we soon move to the hero in America.

1

The Hero in History

"It is natural to believe in great men. All mythology opens
with demigods."

RALPH WALDO EMERSON

"Great men seem to have only one purpose in life—getting
into history. That may be all they are good for."

WILL CUPPY

STYLES in heroes, as in everything else, change; but heroes
never go out of style. History was blind when the first great
men prevailed. Demigods opened the first act. Scores of
centuries later, the drama continues.

In classic times heroes were god-men; in the Middle
Ages, God's men; in the Renaissance, universal men; in the
eighteenth century, gentlemen; in the nineteenth, self-made
men. Our century has seen the common man and the outsider become heroic. In keeping with the times they have
reacted to our social and scientific revolutions. Some of
them now go where once only gods could dwell—in outer
space. Heroes must act their ages. History is not meaningful
without people, and people are ineffective without leaders.
The search for paragons is inherent in human nature. In
remote areas of the world men are still deified in their own
lifetimes. The idea of aloofness in super-human power
comes late in history.

Just as there are many roles, so are there many meanings. Historians see heroes as shaping the flow of events, philosophers as altering thought patterns, social scientists as evoking attitudes of behavior, folklorists as evoking legends and ballads, politicians as winning elections. Messiah, emancipator, founding father, preserver, creative genius are related terms for one whose influence or personality captivates the people. Emerging at a moment when men's emotions are deeply stirred, the hero appeals to both imagination and reason. No one knows just when and why he comes. The gift of heaven, he is a force and a rallying point.

Like a stream, history moves in one direction for a time, then veers off in another. Gaining momentum it washes away old banks and gouges out new channels. Those who perceive and justify this, altering with the flow of events, are heroes.

Some men flash into prominence—one-issue politicians, matinee idols, sports champions—only to disappear like a flash flood. During their golden moments, however, the maxim is "Winner take all." We quote and misquote them with equal ease. At this juncture no one knows if they are true culture heroes or faddish meteors. (As we shall see, Marshall McLuhan, oracle of today's media revolution, is a contemporary example.) Every age has thousands of aspiring heroes. Some carry through to the second generation, which feels the hero's power in stories told by their fathers. By the third generation his exploits take on a certain remoteness. Always susceptible to legend, a hero becomes superhistorical in myth.

The Greeks had a word for it—*heros,*—the superior man deified after death. In him men's values and dreams were epitomized. This magic of leadership the Greeks called charisma. They imagined that the peaks of Mount Olympus were reserved for the men-gods who showed charismatic leadership. Such a figure was Heracles, called Hercules by the Romans. Beginning as a petty ruler subject to the order of a more powerful king at Argos, Heracles benefited from known exploits plus mythical stories attributed to him. Finally, he emerged as the Greek Happy Warrior, meeting (as Socrates points out in the *Gorgias*) deep psychological needs of his people. The Athenians, craving a hero of their own, elevated the soldier-seducer Theseus, strong in battle "for rich-haired Helen's sake." Ionian in spirit, he was fond of dancing and music, though city fathers toned down his amorous stories. They deleted Hesiod's references to Theseus's passion for Aegle. Bolstered by his role in plays by Aeschylus, Sophocles, and Euripides, Theseus become more deliberate, lofty, and Olympian over the centuries. Cimon brought Theseus's bones to Athens from Scyros, buried them in the heart of the city, and established his cult.[1] History has blotted out this particular shrine; but one can visit Francis's bones in Assisi, Lenin's in Moscow, or Kennedy's in Washington and see the same phenomenon at work.

In contemplating Theseus (or Francis, or Lenin, or Kennedy), his admirer found courage and faith. On Hadrian's Arch was inscribed *Athens, formerly the City of Theseus*. Athenians did not respect him because he was Theseus; he was Theseus because they respected him.

Still a third Greek hero was chosen by Homer to tower over his great epic poem—Odysseus. His ten-year wandering after the Trojan War not only provided the material for one of the world's greatest stories; it also gave us the notion of odyssey—the long wandering marked by many changes of fortune. Adventurer-warriors all—but how different are Heracles, with his prowess and brute strength; Theseus, with his balanced personality; and Odysseus, with

[1] See Walter R. Agard, *Classical Myths in Sculpture* (Madison, Wisc.: University of Wisconsin Press, 1953).

7

his craftiness and political sagacity. In neither Greek nor American culture is the heroic style monolithic. Perhaps, as Emerson suggests, the one characteristic of a genuine heroism is its persistency.[2]

So impressive, in fact, is this persistency that lesser men are convinced that the hero is a chosen one. The deaths of Roland, Heracles, and Kennedy all drew forth that opinion. The Greeks were certain that their mighty men were part gods and part men. "Those Greeks were probably best advised," Kerenyi writes in *The Heroes of the Greeks,* "who, like the inhabitants of the Island of Kos, burned a sheep at evening as a hero's offering and next morning sacrificed a bull to him as a God."

In Roman times the old gods declined and new ones quickly emerged. Pagan Olympus was supplanted by Christian heaven, where heroes dwelled in everlasting glory. During Christ's lifetime Messiahs could be found on every street corner; but by the second century, with the martyrdom of Saint Polycarp, the method of Christian veneration was generally accepted in a sizable portion of Europe.[3] Europeans would eventually export these saints to the far corners of the earth. Working in the same terms as primitive mythology, saints perform the same heroic offices as did classical gods. They render the services of intercession and prediction, providing the focus for relic worship and canonization. Style, but not substance, changed. Heroes got haloes.

Then and now the operative aura for heroes was *golden.* They sat on golden thrones, had golden haloes, dreamed of heaven with its streets of gold. Today they project their

[2] See Emerson's piece on "Heroism" in *Essays and Poems* (1844), p. 205. The matter is also explored in Harold Lubin's "Introduction" to *Heroes and Anti-Heroes* (San Francisco: Chandler Press, 1968), pp. 9 f.

[3] See D. Ribble's *The Martyrs, A Study in Social Control* (Chicago: University of Chicago Press, 1931) and J. M. Mecklin's *The Passing of the Saint* (Chicago: University of Chicago Press, 1941).

golden glow in film and polychrome advertisements, for which they are given bags of gold which enable them to follow the golden sun in all seasons.

Every hero mirrors the time and place in which he lives. He must reflect men's innermost hopes and beliefs in a public way. No easy task this. First he will benefit from excess adulation then fall prey to the hysteria of depreciation. The rise and fall of heroes is closely tied in with a culture's ultimate purposes.

The hero is always a barometer to the national "climate of opinion." For years the Radical Republicans and Abolitionists of the 1860s were condemned for their abuse and scurrility by American historians. But in the civil-rights revolution of the 1950s they form the nucleus of a New Left hero class.[4] Soviet idols today are unlike those venerated by Czarist Russia or in Stalinist war years. The "climate of opinion" reflected in 1967 celebrations of Communism's Fiftieth Anniversary bore little resemblance to the outlook of Lenin's day.

Eventually great men are accepted as acts of faith. No Dead Sea scroll could alter Jesus' place in the Christian hierarchy. No historical document could stop Pocahontas from flinging herself on the block and saving Captain John Smith's head. No retelling of the events of the Long March could detract from the heroism of Mao Tse-tung. Monomyths do not bow to the tyranny of facts.

Each hero is emphatically himself, but there are recognizable heroic themes and counterthemes. Time and again one runs into variants of Cinderella and the antithetical Sly Fox. The Persevering Tortoise is the antithesis of the Futile Searcher; the Escapist of the Returning Prodigal; the Golden Fly of the Ugly Duckling; Patient Griselda of the Inconstant

---

[4] Arnold A. Rogow, "The Revolt Against Social Equality," *Dissent*, IV (Autumn 1957).

Lover. Heroic fairy tales are universal and primary stirrings of the human soul, and all heroic reputations seem to swing between two poles—the saint (Buddha, Paul, Malcolm X) and the conqueror (Alexander, Napoleon, Eisenhower). The former stresses meekness and renunciation, the latter aggressiveness and affirmation. Both groups require missions, martyrs, and disciples.[5]

In fact, a full-fledged culture hero must develop his own mystique and empower a whole array of hero-makers to propound it. Napoleon's empire has crumbled, his code is outmoded, but his legend flourishes. He did not hesitate to order the Pope to Paris for his coronation as Emperor, or to substitute his name for the divinity in the school catechism. His appearance on battlefields, which he methodically documented, was a masterpiece of image-making. French poets, patriots, and dramatists helped him to create and spread the Napoleonic legend, as A. J. Guerard shows in his *Reflection on the Napoleonic Legend*. Nor can we blame this on the gullibility of nineteenth-century man. There has probably never been a more effective hero-making device in history than the propaganda machine perfected by Hitler and his associates during the days of the Third Reich. We are forced to update Emerson's contention that "Reputations of the nineteenth century will one day be quoted to prove its barbarism."

To master the macrocosm one must first overcome the microcosm. The source of true heroic power is internal. When he tackles the outer world, the hero faces the inertia of his fellow men; upsetting the social equilibrium brings

[5] For a full discussion of these matters see Otto Rank, *The Birth of the Hero, and Other Essays* (New York: Vintage Books, 1964); David Malcolmson, *Ten Heroes* (New York: Duell, 1939); and Joseph Campbell, *The Hero with a Thousand Faces* (New York: Pantheon, 1949) (paperback ed., Meridian, 1956).

10

conflict. Either his triumph or defeat restores the social equilibrium. His importance stems from perceiving the enduring significance of daily flux. Creative leaders are a leaven in the lump of ordinary humanity. They run out threads of relation through everything, fluid and solid, material and elemental.

When this occurs, man becomes symbol. Caesar symbolized the power of Rome, Kubla Khan the cruelty of Asian hordes, Saint Thomas the wisdom of Christianity, Descartes the method of science. Realizing this, scholars have long sought patterns and typologies in the heroic story. That there are similarities in such matters as birth, youth, and death has long been recognized. Johann Georg von Hahn advanced his "Aryan Expulsion and Return Theory" in 1864, expanded later by Alfred Nutt and Otto Rank. Antti Aarne proposed a tale-type system in 1910, and Vladimir Propp published his *Morphology of the Folktale* in 1928. All this paved the way for Lord Raglan's monumental book called *The Hero: A Study in Tradition, Myth, and Drama* (1936).[6] Raglan named 22 elements in the heroic saga, covering origin, early struggles, marriage, reign, death, and burial, opening the door to comparative study of content and internal structure. The stories of Oedipus, Theseus, Moses, Christ, and King Arthur have marked similarities; all are rooted more in myth than in history. Raglan's formula can be applied with interesting results to the leading American hero of my generation, John F. Kennedy. His father was called to a royal court (as Ambassador to the Court of Saint James) and the son was educated by (presumably) wise men (at Harvard). Then he went off to fight an evil dragon

---

[6] Details on these books, and the general growth of comparative methods, are presented by Alan Dundes, editor, *The Study of Folklore* (Englewood, N.J.: Prentice-Hall, Inc., 1965).

11

(the Japanese navy) and after a bloody fracas (PT 109) triumphed and returned to marry the beautiful princess (Jackie). Having inherited his father's kingdom (politics) he fought and defeated a second contender (Nixon) before taking over as ruler (President). For a time he reigned smoothly and prescribed laws. Then he suddenly lost favor (the Bay of Pigs crisis), tried to rally his people, and died a sudden and mysterious death (did Oswald really shoot Kennedy?). Amidst great mourning (the first worldwide television funeral) he was buried on a sacred hillside (Arlington). Now he has many shrines (a cultural center, airport, library, highway, and a space launching site).

The single factor that links all Raglan and non-Raglan paragons together is heroic style. Style—a characteristic mode, manner, or method of expression, skill or grace. Umph. Zing.[7]

Ancient Egypt had style. From simple cubic masses they constructed buildings and monuments which were uniquely their own. Strong and refined, the Egyptian style was canonized, and changed little for thirty generations. The Greeks had style, and imposed it on much of the eastern Mediterranean. In the Renaissance, single cities in Italy (Siena, Florence, Venice) developed such distinctive styles that centuries later they are still the platform upon which much of the history of Western painting is based.

People as different as Socrates, Nero, St. Francis, Kubla Khan, Robin Hood, Julius Caesar, and William Shakespeare all had style. Very good men, and very bad men, too,

[7] The literature of style is extensive, the work of Heinrich Wilfflin, Joseph Margolis, Carl Friedrich, and John Rupert Martin being important. Wylie Syper's *Four Stages of Renaissance Style* (New York: Peter Smith, 1955) suggests an approach which can be applied to other periods. See also Meyer Schapiro's essay on "Style" in A. L. Kroeber's *Anthropology Today* (Chicago: Phoenix, 1953) and George Kubler's *The Shape of Time* (New Haven: Yale University Press, 1962).

never seem to lack it. Take Henry VIII, for example. Whether he was launching a ship, gnawing on a mutton bone, or ogling a bosom, he was superbly himself. The same could be said of his daughter, Elizabeth; and it is to her reign that we shall turn when our analysis of America's heroes begins. In her name men explored and subdued a New World in which nature herself was a major adversary.

From the first, lifestyle has been the dye which colors the total fabric of culture and the lives of all heroes.

Style, like nature, despite all our study and probing, remains a mystery. Not only the folkstyle of the peasants, with its earthly eternal flavor, but also that of people in all contexts reflects an *élan vital* which no simple or complex formula can encompass. Most of this book will deal with people, not formulas. First we must establish some criteria for choosing these people, ordering their stories, and linking them into a single chain. Even if this inner civilization style, like Walt Whitman's poetry, eludes us, we must continue to search for its meaning.

One finds the term "style" attached to almost everything—cultures, nations, dynasties, regions, periods, crafts. The voluminous literature of art is rooted in the labyrinthine network of the notion of style. Style always means more when it describes one specific figure in space than when it deals with a type of existence in time. Style is bound up with sequence—but who can determine what the sequence should be?

Fumbling for an answer, we end up with models or metaphors. In our minds we form a mental image or pattern that represents for us the "style" of a painter, writer, or period. Then we realize that pratically all metaphors for style place matter on the inside, style on the outside. Jean Cocteau notes that decorative style has never existed. "Style is the soul, and unfortunately with us the soul assumes the form of the body." [8]

Styles belong to a time and place, and so do heroes. Our great men are not only eventful; they are event-making. They determine issues or events whose consequences would have been profoundly different if they had not acted. The event-making man not only finds a fork in the historical road—he helps to create it.[9] Just as myth is a charter for society, the hero is the personification of the ethos.

If he means much to many, he must, nevertheless, go his own lonely way. In addition to nobility, courage, and persistency, the hero confronts inevitable loneliness. When the great task comes, he must do it alone. Like Heracles, he must die in lonely agony on a mountain funeral pyre, or like Old Bill Williams, die in the snow with his feet pointing toward the fire. This is the quality in their lives that no man can explain or interpret for another.

The arrangement and interpretation of American heroes that follows is, therefore, partly subjective. Whether or not there is an American style, in heroes or anything else, is a moot question. We can date our political independence precisely. Whether the United States ever has been, or will be, culturally independent and unique is not clear. It was one thing for Emerson to insist that we had "listened too long to the courtly muses of Europe," and quite another to do anything about it. When it comes to the James boys, we have more to say about Henry than Jesse. Leatherbound books, pseudo-palaces, and baroque opera houses remain monuments to Culture with a capital C.

[8] Quoted by Susan Sontag, whose essay "On Style" in *Against Interpretation* (New York: Farrar, Strauss and Giroux, 1966) casts new light on this difficult subject.

[9] These words paraphrase Sidney Hooks's in chapter IX ("The Eventful and the Event-Making Man") of his study of *The Hero in History* (New York: Humanities Press, Inc., 1943).

14

Despite this cultural schizophrenia, heroes of many types and colors have flourished on our land—oldstyle, folkstyle, fakestyle, popstyle—white, red, and black. First we shall sketch the general boundaries of the hero in America; then seek out the generic types that have flourished here, and the men whose names have so thrilled us that we have not hesitated to hang them in heaven.

2

The Hero in America

"Oh, how Americans have wanted heroes, wanted brave simple fine men!"

SHERWOOD ANDERSON

THE United States is not so much a nation or a people as a search. For red men it began when history was blind, when they left the outer reaches of Asia, and spilled across into a land of ice and pain. For white men it began four centuries ago, when sailors on tiny ships ventured into outer waters. Today the search continues in outer space.

In the spring of 1565 an Englishman gave Richard Hakluyt a Geneva Bible and said, "Read Psalm 107." "They that go down to the sea in ships, that do business in great waters," he read, "these see the works of the Lord, and His wonders in the deep."

Men did go down to sea, many inspired by Hakluyt's books. They broke the mental gates of brass and reached the realms of gold. They sailed, slaughtered, scooped up treasure; these were the first Europeans who qualified as American heroes.

But other heroes were already in that vast, scarcely occupied continent. Explorers soon noted that the aboriginal could and did have complex and beautiful hero tales and legends of his own. Generations later, white tourists would come to his reservation, watch him dance, and throw him a

16

coin for his effort. But they would neither comprehend nor accept his heroic premises; they would not hang in heaven an aboriginal who blocked the road west.

Actual Indian massacres and atrocities bolstered Anglo-Saxon ideology in which the goods (white) triumphed inevitably over the bads (red). Everyone knew that the only good Indian was a dead Indian. Arthur Guiterman picked up the flavor in his "Ballard of Dime Novels":

> Take up the long-neglected pen
> Redeem its valiant steel from rust
> And write those magic words again:
> Another redskin bit the dust!

Even small children can close their eyes and see it all—spotted ponies, faces smeared with war paint, the savage attack, the brave defense, the miraculous cavalry charge. Punishment is meted out with Old Testament swiftness, and we can breathe easier again.

Differently educated and oriented, the natives whom President Johnson called in 1968 "the most neglected and needful minority group" clung to their folkstyle in the Age of Circuitry. They preferred ancient ways, which had been established when the first white men arrived on horses, when their descendants now whizzed overhead in jet planes. Indians' approach to landscape was and is basically religious, while that of the white man is economic. This irreconcilable difference has all but deprived the red man of his right to exist on his prehistoric homeland. It also prohibited the white man from making peace with the American earth; there has always been something demonic in his exploitation of it.

Poor in legal tender, America's Indians have always been rich in ceremony. Bold colors and primordial gestures point to their spiritual drama; wisdom and experience are distilled

17

in the hunt and the sacrifice. "They have what our world has lost," writes John Collier in a probing study of the ancient gods that still hover over our land of mod culture. In *Indians of the Americas* he writes, "They have it now. What the world has lost, the world must have again, lest it die. Now many years are left to have or not have, to recapture the lost ingredient."

For Indians corn (maize) is central, just as is wheat for Europe and rice for Asia. Corn cannot reproduce itself; there is no such thing as a "wild" ear of corn. If the tiller dies, the corn decays with him.

But in the Americas corn lives, sustaining an ever increasing population, and a new giant world power. We have not built on sand, but on loam. Stand in an American cornfield in August. Listen to the corn rustling and growing in the blazing sun. Then say, *"This* is America."

Europeans adopted Indian crops and methods to survive on the land. When broadcast planting failed, for example, they learned the hill-planting method from the natives. More accurately, some learned; others died for their errors or intractability. All had to learn that the American earth is sovereign—a power to be reckoned with and feared.

Over this earth is a hot sun that scorches a hole in the imagination. Beside it, the English sun looks like a faded shilling. Again, consider the ugly hurricanes that masquerade behind feminine names like Bertha, Dora, or Evelyn. America is plagued by the continental waywardness of rampaging nature; by violence and paradox; by the cold blue wind in the day and the hot human blues in the night. Here nature can rumble, and roar, and gurgle, or be majestically silent. Only Daniel Boone's cunning, Jimmy Bludso's cussedness, and Paul Bunyan's power could cope with it. Men as good as John Henry have broken their poor hearts trying to hammer it to death.

18

West of the Mississippi is a wild, bone-breaking landscape, fit for uncouth exiled gods.

In the East, civilization rests on water, timber, and land. Beyond the Mississippi the first two props are missing. A whole line of inventions, ranging from barbed wire and six-shooters to combines and cotton sleds, have made it possible for men to live there—live, but never conquer.

From the beginning America's story has been one of painful separation and slow adjustment, the saga of caravans venturing from the citadels. What set the caravans rolling? A curious, satanic restlessness; some blind glory of the human soul which leaped into the darkness.

Beyond the coastal plains were hardwood forests and smooth-topped mountains stretching to lakes that were inland oceans. But that was not the half of it. There were great grieving plains, cactus-crusted deserts, canyons, valleys, the Rockies, then another green forest, stretching northward indefinitely. Here was too much land to cover with place names. So they slapped a slogan on it—Manifest Destiny.

Generation after generation, the American earth has been sacred to the red men, irresistible to the white. Whatever their race or heroic dreams, Americans have loved the road. Today's thruways merely widen and extend the buffalo trails, wagon paths, and toll pikes that were there earlier. We want to get there, then keep going. One feels the tribal stirring in his blood—buy it, try it, leave it—the road, man. Go-go lives in the heart of American mythology.

Ours is a new nation with old memories. Europeans carried folktales and legends with them, and admired oldstyle heroes long before there were new ones. A strong oldstyle streak remains in our heroes. Mother Europe will never completely abandon her offspring.

Seventeenth-century swashbucklers and squires did not

want to be "American." They were carrying their flags to the far corners of the earth—expecting to make their fortunes in the process. Then they could go "home" to Europe, in ease and triumph.

By the eighteenth century, however, many Americans were ready to risk their lives, fortunes, and sacred honor to cut the sturdy European umbilical cord. Most of them were also willing to discard what was left of Europe's time-crusted mythology, symbolism, and ceremony. Being rid of it was a benefit, rather than a penalty, of active rebellion.[1]

A successful revolution is always a nation's finest hour; the time that tries men's souls. Nothing historians find or say can dampen the "Spirit of '76" and 1976 will only enhance it. For generations it has been all but impossible to criticize the Patriots, or defend the Tories, without bringing down censure on one's head. Sydney Fisher found ample material for a book called *The Legendary and Mythmaking Process in Histories of the American Revolution.*

If heroes come, can hero-makers be far behind? The struggle that produced George Washington also produced Parson Weems. An itinerant bookseller and permanent hero-worshipper, Weems was ready with a sermon, a stump speech, or a jig on short notice. Studying great men made his bosom "heave with emotion unutterable, while the tear of delicious admiration swelled in my eyes." Anyone interested in the hero, American style, should study Weems's *History of the Life, Death, Virtues, and Exploits of General Washington,* published in 1800. The hero of a new nation is revealed as an oldstyle paragon. Seldom a hard book to

[1] The literature on this topic is extensive, as various categories in the *Harvard Guide to American History,* Oscar Handlin, *et al.* (Cambridge, Mass.: Harvard University Press, 1963) indicate. Ralph H. Gabriel's chapter on "Pre-Sumter Symbolism" in *Course of American Democratic Thought* (New York: Ronald Press, 1956) is an excellent short introduction.

come by, Weems's *History* was frequently revised and fattened. In 1921 the seventy-ninth successful edition appeared.

Anticipating Horatio Alger, his only peer in American heroics, Weems turned Washington's life into a fairy-tale success story. "Here was a proper rise for you!" he gloated when Washington snared the rich widow Custis. In the fifth edition he introduced the cherry tree story (the most persistent single legend in American history), the cabbage story, and the wild colt story. He mixed mythology and musketballs, and proved conclusively that all the old clichés could be adapted to the new democratic environment. Weems made intelligible the type of hero young America craved, in terms that most Americans could understand.[2]

Poets and novelists had a much harder time adapting the European idiom to America. Not until Herman Melville's *Moby Dick* could the nation boast of a major literary masterpiece indigenous to the American scene. The hero, Captain Ahab, is a sort of anti-hero. The white whale, Moby Dick, is a symbol of evil. Melville himself had no illusions about Americans' comprehending his voyages through strange symbolic seas. "I will be remembered," he predicted, "as the man who lived with cannibals."

Melville was only one of those who found it hard to create adequate symbols and myths in a culture dedicated to fact-finding. Songs, eagles, and liberty bells have been conjured up, but have proven to be inadequate personifications for such abstractions as liberty and justice. Unfortunately, Americans worship nothing in common; few objects possess *mana*—supernatural and mystical power. There is a world of difference between Athena's owl and

---

[2] The matter is well covered by Dixon Wecter, *The Hero in America* (New York: Charles Scribner's Sons, 1941), and Marcus Cunliffe, *George Washington, Man and Monument* (Boston: Little, Brown and Co., 1958). Other titles dealing with the hero in America are listed in the Bibliographical Note at the end of this volume.

Uncle Sam's eagle, between the Oracle at Delphi and Liberty holding a mob cap on a stick.

Only externally has the American "melting pot" really melted. We understand external gestures and words, and can to this degree communicate. But we do not share with each other the symbols, rituals, and ceremony by which thought is compressed, emotion conveyed, and true unity of spirit achieved. Not only have we been unable to invent such things for ourselves; we have even despoiled those we inherited.

Easter is for most Americans the time of the "Easter Parade," chocolate eggs, and cuddly bunnies. (Just what function the bunny serves, no one seems to know.) Before the Civil War, the Fourth of July had some claim on the communal imagination. But the Confederate States have never regained their fervor for the "glorious Fourth." Even Yankees insist that it be "safe and sane." With changes in lifestyle, observances of holidays change, too. The folk quality of Independence Day and the birthdays of early patriots has gone. Now we spend holidays watching professional athletes race across our television screens—for a price.

The inauguration of the President of the United States, the world's most powerful executive, should be a high point of national ritual. In fact, it is a short, drab occasion. Compared with the coronation of a European king or a Polynesian prince, the twenty-minute affair in Washington seems empty and pointless. Who knows what ritual should go with all other major public officials—senators, governors, mayors? Who knows, and all too often, who cares?

There is Thanksgiving, of course—that day of heavy meals and long naps. Few churches, and almost no homes, hold Thanksgiving services. Even the date depends on legislative action. Usually it falls on the fourth Thursday in

November: except in Texas, where the date depends on when the Texas–Texas A & M football game is played.

At such games we have cheerleaders and "queens," who parallel our agricultural royalty (Orange Queen, Onion Queen, etc.). This is, in a manner of speaking, ceremonial America, with flamboyant publicity and perverse nostalgia for the European monarchy disowned in the eighteenth century. Cultural schizophrenia continues to reveal itself as one studies the hero in America.

Other traits which are strong in America's heroes are exaggeration and eccentricity. To exaggerate is to simplify, to make grotesque. This little ditty about a fight in Texas illustrates the point:

> They fit and fit, and gouged and bit
> And struggled in the mud
> Until the ground for miles around
> Was kivered with their blood;
> And a pile of noses, ears, and eyes
> Large and massive, reached the skies.

In our heroes, and in our thinking, one finds too much of the Roman and too little of the Greek.[3] Love of bigness and regularity often betrays us. Every classical order tends to pave the way for a mechanical order and, eventually, a mechanical trap. This is the message we get from studying the all too-human Henry Ford and the not-human-enough Paul Bunyan.

Eccentricity flared up long before the beats, hippies, and yippies. Consider that colonial New Englander Timothy Dexter, made a "Lord" by his own say. He made his fortune selling warming pans to the West Indians at an enormous profit.Then he wrote *A Pickle for the Knowing Ones,* which

[3] For further details see Leo Gurko, *Heroes, Highbrows and the Popular Mind* (Indianapolis, Ind.: Bobbs-Merrill, 1953) and Orrin Klapp, *Heroes, Villains and Fools* (Englewood, N.J.: Prentice-Hall, Inc., 1962).

23

had no punctuation. Criticized on this score, Lord Timothy got out a second edition with a page of punctuation marks at the end, so readers could "pep[p]er and solt it as they plese." Davy Crockett, Old Bill Williams, Huck Finn, Mr. Dooley, Will Rogers, and Bob Dylan all followed his cue, and did as they damn well pleased.

Imposing a grid pattern on American culture or heroes is an impossible task. Ours is a land of tense turbulent cities, with long fingers of power; plantations warmed over by glowing memories; stinking ghettoes and soaring penthouses. It abounds with atomic reactors, foot-long hotdogs, nomadic Indians, sedentary bureaucrats, guided missiles, block slums, glass domes, mud huts, little magazines, big sells, wetbacks, flashbacks, comebacks. Who would claim to be the hero of all these people in all these crevices of American culture?

Hence the tendency to divide and conquer—to classify heroes by regions, generations, ethnic groups. Into little boxes witth them—Old Stormalong and Daniel Webster for New England, Daniel Boone and Davy Crockett for the mountains, Jeff Davis and Robert E. Lee for the South, Bigfoot Wallace and Lyndon Johnson for the Southwest. Or else move chronologically, as most historians like to do, from John Smith to John Kennedy.

I shall attempt to find the common denominator not in regions (which have been made meaningless by technological change) or periods (they are all arbitrary), but in lifestyle. One can play with definitions ("all that people are, do, believe, and dream"), but understand lifestyle fully only in flesh-and-blood manifestations. Lifestyles have meanings that cannot be reduced to words, death and resurrection cycles of their own. This will be demonstrated, I hope, by examining archetypal heroes in America: swashbuckler, squire, cavalier, natural man, self-made man, jolly giant, smooth roughneck, poor white, cool one, celebrity, media

24

man. Variations on these themes make up the symphony of America.

There are other themes we will not play—and variations within major themes which we will not hear. We will not hear the lovable "Aw, shucks!" of the modest Lou Gehrig, or the strident "Burn, baby, burn!" of Stokely Carmichael. The cacophony of Joe Hill and Geronimo will be muted, as will the plight of graceful losers, like Adlai Stevenson. We will not take sides on Aaron Burr, or join those who want to "upgrade" Thaddeus Stephens or "Vinegar Joe" Stilwell. These omissions are not intentional slights, but simple recognitions that we are selecting, rather than summarizing.

The selection gets ever harder as we move closer to the present. Every generation thinks that the "towering personalities" of their childhood have not been replaced—and indeed, the particular tower of which they speak goes out of style. In any event, the hero is not so much a person as a mirror held up to a culture, a flesh-and-blood embodiment of style. Despite obvious European precedents, American folk heroes are startlingly different from most Old World heroes of myths or of *Märchen*. The aristocratic patterns discovered by European scholars didn't describe the careers of our plebeian peddlers, brawlers, and con men.[4] American folk heroes are generic expressions of the youthful culture which produced them. Get-ahead Poor Richard and go-ahead Davy Crockett carried the American stamp.

So did fakestyle and popstyle heroes who followed them. Though they emerged from what Dwight Macdonald liked to call "the dead sea of masscult," there was nothing moribund about their contribution and revolutionary impact.[5]

[4] This matter is developed by Daniel Hoffman, *Form and Fable in American Fiction* (New York: Oxford University Press, 1961).

[5] In a pivotal essay called "A Theory of Popular Culture" (*Politics*, 1944), Macdonald wanted to integrate the masses into high culture. In a 1953 version (*Diogenes*), he was wavering. By 1962, in a book called

This point will be proved, I hope, in some of my later chapters which follow Bob Dylan's meteorology:

> You don't need a weather man
> To know which way the wind blows.

Wallace Stevens's statement was more elegant and evocative:

> The hero is a feeling, a man seen
> As if the eye was an emotion,
> As if in seeing we saw our feeling
> In the object seen and saved that mystic
> Against the sight, the penetrating,
> Pure eye.[6]

One who penetrates that feeling might discover new clusters of meaning, new information on the hero, American style. This is our quest. Thus we become part of the continuing American search, agonizing and never-ending. Like Richard Hakluyt, we too must go down to the sea in ships. There we sense the spray that chilled Drake, Raleigh, and Smith—bold heroes for the brave new world.

Against the American Grain (New York: Random House, 1962), he called for two cultures: one for the masses, the other for the classes. Mr. Macdonald is very stimulating, and his ideas tend toward what we have called "oldstyle."

[6] "To a Hero in a Time of Crisis," in *Collected Poems of Wallace Stevens* (New York: Knopf, 1954). Reprinted by permission of Alfred A. Knopf, Inc.

3

Swashbucklers

"AMERICANS," Horatio Greenough wrote, "have no half-fabulous, legendary wealth, no misty, cloud-enveloped background." Not so. No land has ever evoked more legends or more heroic efforts to create them. We have craved and found heroes in every generation. Modeled on European patterns, the first of these were adventurers and swashbucklers. The action begins with them.

Swash: to make violent noisy movements, and move with a splashing sound. *Swashbuckler:* a boasting soldier or blustering daredevil. Yes, these are the right words to evoke those early knights-errant who came to our shores, full of impossible yet sometimes successful schemes. They set our heroic style. To examine that style and the men who have typified it is to ask what it means to be an American.

The swashbucklers' program can be summed up in a single line: they sailed, slaughtered, and scooped up treasure. They were activists and agitators, on stage even when there was no audience, victims of old medieval dreams and superstitions, conquerors of the brave new world. Yet "conquer" is a big word; the new land was strong medicine. Europeans wanted to know: "What shall we do to the land?" History

27

replied: "What will the land do to you?" Man and land interacted to produce American lifestyles.

Begin, then, with Sir Francis Drake staring at the Pacific from the heights of Panama in 1573, beseeching God for life and leave "to sail once in an English ship upon that sea." Sail he did, rounding Cape Horn, pillaging Spanish ports, moving north on the *Golden Hind,* reaching California in 1579. As if this didn't assure his place as father of the new world swashbucklers, he continued west around the globe and reached England in 1580.

While Drake girdled the earth his countrymen dreamed of a northwest passage to America—men like Humphrey Gilbert and his half brother, Walter Raleigh. Granted a patent for the "inhabiting and planting of our people in America," Gilbert landed his little force on Newfoundland, pushed forward in foul weather with three ships, and reluctantly turned back, to try again the next spring. A strange monster appeared, "in shape, hair and color like a very lion, sliding upon the water with his whole body (excepting his legs) in sight." The wooden timbers groaned; the heavens opened up. Gilbert's tiny *Squirrel* was capsized. "We are as near to heaven by sea as by land!" he shouted as he disappeared from view. The line, like the life, was heroic.

Inheriting Gilbert's patent, Raleigh sent out two ships (the Queen would not allow him to go), which reached the Carolina coast in 1584. They found a wonderful grass whose pod could be used for clothes (cotton), a strange vegetable that grew underground (potato), and an herb that could be pulverized, burned, and inhaled (tobacco). In 1585 ten ships returned to Roanoke Island, but eventually the hard-pressed colonists persuaded Sir Francis Drake to take them home when he appeared. In 1587 Raleigh sent out another small fleet, whose governor, John White, was to found "the Citie of Raleigh in Virginia." On Roanoke Island, where they landed, White's granddaughter Virginia Dare was born—the first English child in the New World. That same month John White sailed to England for supplies, leaving behind 89 men, 17 women, and hopes for an enduring city.

All England's strength was needed for the invading Armada; John White was not able to return until 1591. Then he and his sailors confronted one of the enduring mysteries of American history. Only the word CROATOAN on a stockade post suggested what might have happened to the Lost Colony.

Raleigh fared better than his ill-fated colonists. Betrayed by enemies and abandoned by friends, he endured long years imprisoned in the Tower of London. Once Elizabeth was gone, his enemies prevailed. To the wife of the new king, James I, Raleigh wrote, "I long since presumed to offer your Majesty my service. . . . I would rather die in serving the King and my country than to perish here." But perish he did, having noted that the executioner's axe was a sharp medicine that cured all ills. On October 29, 1618, a cry went out from the crowd that has yet to be answered: "Where shall we find another such head to cut off?" [1]

Drake, Gilbert, Raleigh—even short vignettes catch reflections of bright, boundless lives. These were, in fact, swashbucklers, and those who prefer them in fancy can read Elizabethan literature.

That literature sets the stage for the hero, American style. As E. M. W. Tillyard shows, the Elizabethan cosmos is grounded in medieval thought.[2] The central metaphor was

[1] For Raleigh's life see Philip Edwards, *Sir Walter Raleigh* (Toronto: Longmans, 1953); for his colonies, D. B. Quinn's *The Roanoke Voyages,* 2 vols. (Cambridge, England: Cambridge University Press, 1956); for his trial, Margaret Irwin's *That Great Lucifer: A Portrait of Sir Walter Raleigh* (New York: Harcourt, Brace and World, Inc., 1960).

[2] E. M. W. Tillyard, *The Elizabethan World Picture* (New York: Paperback ed., Vintage, 1959). The Elizabethan quality of seventeenth-century American heroes has been documented by many scholars.

a great chain of being, stretching from the foot of God's throne to the meanest of inanimate objects. Everything in creation was linked. The writings of Shakespeare, Jonson, Marvell, and many others were posited on this notion, so were the actions of Drake, Frobisher, Raleigh, and Smith.

Men always act out their times—they have no alternative. The Elizabethan beau ideal was compounded of elements as diverse and extarordinary as the society in which he moved. In the rapid expansion of English trade and influence, a pyramid of power developed. If monarchs were the hands of God, gentlemen were the fingers of the king. They ran the mechanism of state and set the tone. They were exemplars in style and manners. No wonder the first American heroes were English gentlemen.

In this time of tumult, danger, and intensity, by some metaphysical alchemy, opposites were fused. The Elizabethan hero was a man with a foot (sometimes a cloak) in the mud, an eye on the heavens, a dagger up his sleeve. Over the age hovers William Shakespeare. "He is," Jan Kott writes, "violent, cruel and brutal; earthly and hellish; evokes terror as well as dreams and poetry; is most true and improbable, dramatic and passionate, rational and mad." [3]

Drake skirted and looted the New World. Gilbert died trying to colonize it. Raleigh landed colonists, saw fate devour them, faced the headsman for his own intrigue and ambition. Despite these connections with America, none can be called a truly *American* hero. They belong to England and made their reputations on water rather than on land. One of their contemporaries—temperamentally their brother, cut from the same bolt of cloth—would first act out the heroic idea on American soil.

Captain John Smith's life (which forms a separate chap-

[3] Jan Kott, *Shakespeare Our Contemporary* (London: Methuen and Co. Ltd., 1964), p. 223.

ter in American Historiography)[4] so mixed myth and malaria that no one can ever hope to disentangle the truth. He was the son of a prosperous tenant farmer and left home in 1596 at age 16 to seek Adventure, with a capital A. Then followed deeds beyond believing in the "debatable lands" of Poland, Muscovy, Hungary, and Turkey. He was sold into slavery, goaded into personal combat, and pushed into the sea before winning from the English College of Heralds a coat of arms inscribed "Vincere est vivere" (To conquer is to live). If we label John Smith our first authentic American hero, prototype of later swashbucklers, we face this blunt question at the outset—was he a liar? [5]

For years historians, following the lead of Henry Adams, Edward T. Channing, and Edward D. Neill, dismissed Smith's claims as published exaggerations. In the 1950s a Hungarian scholar, Dr. Laura Polyanyi Striker, came to Smith's rescue. Meticulous and ingenious, she located the places Smith mentioned in his accounts by studying Hungarian sources. "He would not possibly have written as he did without having lived through the events he described," Dr. Striker concluded. "It is time we gave him full credit for being not only a valiant fighter, but an acute historian and chronicler as well." [6]

[4] See Jarvis M. Morse, "John Smith and His Critics: A chapter in Colonial Historiography," in the *Journal of Southern History*, Vol. L, 1935. The main source for the life and exploits of Smith is to be found in his own works; his prose was as colorful as his actions. The first complete edition of his work was edited by Edward Arber and published in Birmingham, England, in 1884. This was reprinted, with an additional introduction by A. G. Bradley, in 1910. The best recent accounts are Philip L. Barbour's *The Three Worlds of Captain John Smith* (New York: Houghton Mifflin Co., 1964), and Paul Lewis's *The Great Rogue* (New York: McKay, 1966).
[5] See Marshall Fishwick, "Was John Smith a Liar?" in *American Heritage*, IX, No. 6 (October 1958), pp. 28 f.
[6] See Dr. Striker's "Lewis L. Kropf on Captain John Smith's True Travels," *Virginia Magazine of History and Biography* (January 1958);

Smith was back in England in 1604, ready to invest a thousand ducats and his sacred honor in the New World. He was on board when three tiny ships of the London Company set sail for Virginia—the ships that landed at Jamestown to effect the first permanent English settlement in the New World.

Smith arrived in chains, having been accused of mutiny en route; but his knowledge of fortifications was so great that he was released and put to work. Soon he was a Council member and Indian trader. In the winter of 1608 he went up the Chickahominy River to bargain for food. Hostile Indians killed two companions and captured Smith. He took a compass from his pocket and proceeded to give a lesson in navigation. Fascinated by Smith's accounts of "how the sunne did chase the night about the world continually," they presented him to Chief Powhatan. The Chief was not impressed enough to stay the execution, and the hapless Captain was taken to the stones where his brains were to be beaten out. Our first potential hero was about to become a martyr.

Enter our first heroine—Powhatan's lovely child Pocahontas. She allegedly put his head in her arms and laid her own upon his to save Smith. Much impressed, Powhatan released Smith and sent him back to Jamestown under escort. Some authorities have rejected this story. Still, the rescue incident is in keeping with Indian customs of the time. And if the story were not true, how then did Smith return loaded with presents when other prisoners were killed? And why did Pocahontas visit Jamestown afterward, showing a new friendliness to the intruders? True or false, nobody doubted the story in Smith's lifetime.

and her "Preface" to Bradford Smith's *Captain John Smith, His Life and Legend* (Philadelphia: J. B. Lippincott Co., 1956).

Back in Jamestown, Smith was caught in the arguments of a bickering Council. There was even talk of hanging him to atone for the death of his two comrades. All was forgotten when long-awaited ships were sighted, bringing the first supplies from England.

Smith continued to advance inland. He explored Chesapeake Bay, discovered the Susquehanna River, and named New England. Elected Council President in 1608, he countered the London investors' demand for immediate profit with his "Rude Reply":

Send but thirty carpenters, husbandmen, gardiners, fishermen, blacksmiths, masons and diggers up of trees, roots, well provided; than a thousand of such we have. For except we be able to lodge and feed them, the most will consume with want of necessities before they can be made good for anything.

A year later the outspoken Smith was grievously wounded when a powder keg ignited and seared his flesh. There was no surgeon, so he returned to London. He was only thirty at the time, but would never see Virginia again—"my wyfe, to whom I have given all." [7]

Back home he put his pen to work. His *Generall Historie of Virginia* (1624) went through six editions in eight years; *True Travels* (1631) came out shortly before his death. A quarter of his fortune, twenty pounds, was left for his funeral. London's Great Fire of 1666 wiped out St. Sepulchre's Church, where Smith's body was buried, and his epitaph with it. The last earthly trace of our first swashbuckler was gone forever.

History has rewarded him with fame though it denied him gold. This unique blend of English knight and Ameri-

---

[7] For further details see Paul Lewis's *The Great Rogue* (New York: McKay, 1966). Smith, Lewis concludes, fell in love with the New World. "America enthralled him as long as he lived."

can pragmatist typifies the oldstyle seventeenth-century hero. Despite his faults, he deserves this reputation. Captain Smith never doubted that he could accomplish the impossible; and sometimes he did. Old soldiers like Richard Potts and William Phettiplace adored him. "Upon no danger would he send men where he would not lead them himself," Potts wrote. "He loved actions more than words, and hated falsehood. His adventures were our lives, and his loss our deaths."

Gentlemen continued to set out for the land named for Good Queen Bess. None made a deeper mark than Sir William Berkeley. There was *another* man with style. A graduate of Oxford and the Inns of Court, he left behind a successful life in London at thirty-four to become Virginia's governor and serve in that post for twenty-five years. So successful was Berkeley's campaign against unfriendly Indians that his treaty kept the peace for three decades. So vigorous was he in rejecting the government of Cromwell and the Puritans that he won for Virginia the flattering royalist nickname of "Old Dominion." Temporarily retired in his lordly Virginia manor, Berkeley returned to the Governor's House when the Stuarts were restored in 1660. He ordered the sheriffs to proclaim the new monarch, and to issue writs and warrants in His Majesty's name. At a time when modern Europe was getting ever more democratic, Berkeley favored a divine rights king. He even thanked God that there were no public schools and printing presses in his colony.

He met his match in Nathaniel Bacon, another Oxford graduate who became the center of protest against royal authority. Berkeley's threat that he would hang anyone who proceeded against the Indians without royal commission did not faze hot-blooded Bacon. "If the redskins meddle with me, damn my blood but I'll harry them, commission or no commission!" he shouted. They meddled, and he harried.

Berkeley branded the Baconites traitors. An open break followed.

Evaluating Bacon's Rebellion is a difficult task and is one which is not central to our purposes.[8] But the style of the rebels is. They dashed back and forth on horseback, brandished their swords, and performed as King Arthur might have done under similar circumstances. Eyewitness accounts and bits of dialogue have come down to us. On June 23, 1767, the Rebels marched to the State House where Berkeley and the House of Burgesses were meeting. The Governor knew what to do under those circumstances. He walked out to the Rebels, denounced Bacon, and ripped open his own shirt.

"Here! Shoot me—'fore God, fair mark. Shoot!" Sir William cried.

"We are not murderers," Bacon replied.

The next move was Berkeley's. He drew his sword from the scabbard and challenged Bacon to a personal duel.

"Sir," Bacon replied, "I came not, nor intend, to hurt a hair on your Honor's head. And as for your sword, your Honor may please to put it up; it shall rust in its scabbard before ever I shall desire you to draw it. I come for a commission against the heathen who daily inhumanly murder us and spill our brethren's blood. And a commission I will have before I go!"

No reply from Berkeley. "Prime your guns!" Bacon ordered. The hopelessly outnumbered burgesses granted the commission. But the final word had not yet been spoken. Before the rebellion's conclusion, speeches by both leaders mirrored the heroic style of that era and place. Here is an example by Nathaniel Bacon:

[8] The studies of Wesley Frank Craven, Thomas Jefferson Wertenbaker, and Wilcomb E. Washburn cover the matter. For a summary, see my *Virginia: A New Look at the Old Dominion* (New York: Harper and Row, 1959), chap. 2.

If ever you have fought well and bravely, you must do so now. They call us rebels and traitors, but we will see whether their courage is as great as their pretended loyalty. Come on, my hearts of gold! He who dies in the field of battle dies in the bed of honor!

The speech worked. Bacon drove Berkeley into exile, burned Jamestown, and went off to gather more support. When he became "sick of a flux" and died unexpectedly, the rebellion disintegrated. Governor Berkeley reassumed control and meted out terrible vengeance. He executed more men than had been killed in the entire Rebellion, and prompted Charles II to say, "That old fool has hanged more men in that naked country than I did for the murder of my father."

Whatever Sir William did was in line with his oldstyle vision. He never knew why the English court failed to honor and applaud him. At first he refused to stand aside when Herbert Jeffreys came to replace him as governor. Sir William sailed back to England, an embittered old man and arrived too sick to appear at court. Only fifteen months after Bacon's Rebellion began, Berkeley died, disillusioned and discouraged. But he had been true to his own heroic image, to the very end.

So had his contemporary Peter Stuyvesant, governing a prosperous Dutch colony to the north. Like Captain John Smith, Stuyvesant was a soldier who went to the Leeward Islands as governor in Curacao. Whereas Smith had almost lost his head, Stuyvesant actually lost a leg in battle; but he still managed to come to New Amsterdam as governor in 1646. Again like the Virginia swashbucklers, Stuyvesant restored order, tightened regulations, and made friends with the Indians. In storybook fashion he captured all New Sweden, including the present state of Delaware. With an arrogance paralleling that of Berkeley, he dismissed citizens who demanded a share in the government; later he was forced to surrender by an English fleet. Americans have found him a fascinating figure. To Washington Irving, Stuyvesant was not a hero, but a combination of heroes—"a rawboned male like Ajax, with a pair of shoulders like Hercules . . . and with Coriolanus's sovereign contempt for the people." [9] Oldstyle references all, going back not only to Europe, but to ancient Greece.

This idea of the American hero lingered on into the eighteenth century. In the fall of 1716 Virginia's Governor Alexander Spotswood stood atop the Blue Ridge Mountains, his peacock plume poking a hole in the sky, his green velvet cape flapping in the breeze, his silver spurs jangling. He was claiming land for England, and doing homage to his sovereign King George. We have a list of the provisions the party carried: "several sorts of liquor, viz: Virginia red wine and white wine, Irish usquebaugh, brandy, shrub, two sorts of rum, champagne, canary, cherry punch, cider, etc., etc." Apparently these merry-makers intended to float the Shenandoah Valley into the British Empire.

Spotswood definitely favored heroic gestures. Having been "dangerously wounded" at Blenheim, he refused to seek medical aid; instead he dashed off to retrieve the offending cannonball as a souvenir. For this and other feats he was made a quartermaster general at the age of twenty-eight. He could and did "swear like our army in Flanders," as his subjects discovered when he became Governor of Virginia. He also set up iron works, imported artisans, and advanced the flag westward. On this particular day, he buried a paper in one of the innumerable empty bottles. The document claimed all the territory to the west for his King.

[9] Washington Irving, *A History of New York* . . . (New York: n.p., 1848), p. 134.

Back in Williamsburg, Spotswood had miniature gold horseshoes made for all those who had gone to the Blue Ridge with him. On them was inscribed "Sic Juvat Transcendere Montes." Those gentlemen have been known ever since as the Knights of the Golden Horseshoe. What more proof does one need of the flowering of the Elizabethan metaphor? Stretching back beyond that style was the medieval influence, seen in such items as peasants' homes and sheds, pegged-board furniture, and European copybook items of every sort. The durability of oldstyle in a new environment is remarkable. It carries over into twentieth-century literature and art. What Arnold Toynbee calls the idolization of an ephemeral past is constantly revealing itself.

Even the movies reveal the irresistible charm of the never-never land past. Consider the career of Douglas Fairbanks, a swashbuckler who, like the Elizabethans, won fame by heading west, sword in hand. His emphasis on physical prowess became a phobia. Like Charlie Chaplin, he created a new heroic type in a new media; but whereas Chaplin's genius for pantomine was destroyed by sound, Fairbanks was able to carry his swashbuckling Robin Hood into the age of sound.[10]

To show the "predominant passion of America" he developed a comic-acrobat pose. He was the prankish roughneck, the scamp who held up trains just to get the conductor's ticket-punch. By marrying Mary Pickford, "America's Sweetheart," he completed the character-building. To quote the dust jacket of *Douglas Fairbanks: The Fourth Musketeer:* "It was inevitable that one of America's heroes should fall madly in love with America's Sweetheart, and marriage was

[10] See Alistair Cooke, *Douglas Fairbanks: The Making of a Screen Character* (New York: Museum of Modern Art, Film Library series No. 2, 1945).

the only course possible.[11] It seemed equally inevitable that this Musketeer should make films called *The Mark of Zorro* and *The Thief of Bagdad*. For like the swashbucklers before him, Doug's was a world of make-believe, unashamed and joyous. Balustrades were made to be vaulted, chandeliers to swing from, walls to be scaled. Oldstyle heroics continued to fascinate Americans in their highly industrialized New World.

There were still Americans in isolated culture-pockets who lived their lives along oldstyle lines. Some were and are caught in the primordial misery of the poor and bypassed. Others are quite happy (thank you) to look to the swash-buckling past, to live essentially feudal lives in the Jet Age. Hero-types never really die. Instead they move off the main highways into the back country.

The infinite and intricate threads that tie us to oldstyle Europe will never be entirely cut. My great-great aunt, who came to America from England fifty years ago, still speaks a Yorkshire dialect that many neighbors cannot understand and tells medieval tales of the moors. In "progressive" Wisconsin, Swiss immigrants around New Glarus put on an annual Wilhelm Tell Festival in seventeenth-century German. Who knows what dreams the Basques dream, as they watch their herds high in the mountains of Montana?

The first widespread American lifestyle—a European transplant—has survived best at the two extremes of the social scale: at the top where people can afford anachronisms, and at the bottom where they are too poor to modernize. Poverty pockets of Appalachia are, literally, another world. Their past does not entice or delight us. But the past that we encounter on film or the stage does. The attraction of the swashbuckler is latent in us all. Deep in the heart of

[11] Ralph Hancock and Letitia Fairbanks, *Douglas Fairbanks: The Fourth Musketeer* (New York: Dial Press, 1956), p. 114.

suburbia, we dream of Camelot. Deep in the White House, too, when John F. Kennedy was there. He made no effort to conceal his love for the musical *Camelot,* nor the lines which urged:

> Don't let it be forgot
> That once there was a spot
> For one brief shining moment
> That was known as Camelot.

4

Squires

". . . first in the hearts of his countrymen."

HENRY LEE

SEVENTEENTH-CENTURY knights were displaced in America by eighteenth-century squires. Again there were European precedents—the English lord, German Junker, French marquis, Italian count. American models reflected, but did not imitate these. They invaded not only the physical frontier, but the mental frontier that divides old from new, acceptable from dangerous.[1]

Behold the squire, on the banks of his river—Connecticut, Hudson, Susquehanna, Potomac, James; proud of his class privileges, even in a dynamic, fluid society; naming his slaves Pompey, Cato, and Caesar; ready to ride a horse, defend a fort, dance a minuet, or form a government as circumstances required.

Give him a local habitation and a name, like William Byrd of Westover. Explorer, writer, bon vivant, linguist, scientist, pattern-setter, he saw and thought as much as any American who died before the Revolution. A man of two worlds, Will spent all but eight of his first thirty-one years in Europe. Witty and urbane, the young aristocrat cultivated

---

[1] Isaiah Berlin, "A Marvelous Decade," *Encounter*, VI, No. 5 (May 1956), p. 21.

London's literary and social lions. At twenty-two he was invited to join the Royal Society, to which he submitted a paper on an albino Negro who was "dappled." Ribald plays, masquerade balls, coffeehouse gossip, clandestine trysts—all these played a part in young Will Byrd's life.

Lawyer and man-about-town, he returned to Virginia in 1696 to begin a political career that would see him serve in the House of Burgesses, as Councilor and Auditor-General of the colony, and as Virginia's representative before the Board of Trade. After less than a year at home, he returned to England as legal representative of the Virginia Assembly. The job was not so serious that young Will didn't manage to have a considerable amount of pleasure.

On his favorite ladies he lavished neoclassical pseudonyms and amorous solicitations. One such lady (called "Facetia" and believed to have been Lady Elizabeth Cromwell) was his preoccupation during 1703. When she left for a trip to Ireland, her frustrated lover wrote an impassioned letter:

The instant your coach drove away, madam, my heart felt as if it had been torn up by the very roots, and the rest of my body as if severed limb from limb . . .

Already Byrd was learning what it meant to be a Renaissance man, poured in the English mold. Polished speech, graceful manners, heroic poses were cultivated. He would take the oldstyle home, to flourish on American soil.

The sudden death of his father in 1704 terminated his London venture. Will Byrd, who had lived so irresponsibly in cosmopolitan London, returned to assume the responsibilities of a provincial planter. The colony to which he returned was a place of both comfort and crudity, sophistication and supersitition. Not far from homes modeled after the finest London manors was the cutting edge of the New

World frontier. Some of Byrd's neighbors discussed the most advanced ideas of Enlightenment. Others argued about how to dispose of a witch who crossed Currituck Sound in an eggshell. Poor Grace Sherwood, against whom the charge was made, was subjected to rough treatment, and for many months languished in "ye common gaol." Finally released, she lived to be eighty and died a natural death.

Other colonial ladies faced problems (including Will Byrd) that were less ephemeral than witchcraft. A good example was Martha Burwell, a Williamsburg belle, who rejected the suit of Sir Francis Nicholson, the governor, so she might marry a man more to her liking. If she did so, swore the enraged Nicholson, he would cut the throat of the bridegroom, the clergyman, and the issuing justice. Martha refused to give in, even when Nicholson threw in more throats, including those of her father and brothers. She married her true love. No throats were cut. But visitors to the Governor's palace in Williamsburg observed that His Excellency made "a Roaring Noise."

Colonial America was governed by a system of benevolent paternalism. Aristocrats intermarried, and essential jobs— sheriff, vestryman, justice of the peace, colonel of militia— stayed in the family. Support of the gentry was the prerequisite to social and political advancement. Wealth, status, and privilege were interlocked. Wealth guaranteed status; status conveyed privilege; and privilege insured wealth.

Will Byrd both understood and mastered the colonial world. Retaining the seat in the House of Burgesses which he had won before going to England, he married the fiery Lucy Parke and became a squire. Burdened all his life with the responsibility of hundreds of slaves and thousands of acres, he never became bitter or provincial. His diaries, incredibly frank and detailed, were written in shorthand and not published until the mid-twentieth century. He also left a large group of essays, poems, character sketches, translations, and satires. There were 3600 volumes in his library, dealing with philosophy, history, divinity, law, travel, and literature. His love of learning, and especially the classics, was genuine. His first wife died; his second he admired hardly less for her money (an absolute essential) than for her knowledge of Greek (an admirable achievement). The new mother-in-law was promptly nicknamed Medusa.

The country squire, American style, stood in the shadow of Europeans who sprang from the rhetorical tradition—back to Aristotle and Socrates, on to Cicero and Castiglione, across the Atlantic with the Elizabethans. In the Age of Conversation, manor house talk might touch on heroes and horses, faraway loves or runaway slaves, Bacon (the philosopher) or bacon (hickory-cured). There would be talk of the latest English writers, after which planters might recite a few lines themselves.

William Byrd thrived on talk and relished local gossip. He loved to meet good conversationalists at his door and hated to see them depart. He wanted them back, with all the news they could remember. Meanwhile, he had his own daily schedule to keep him intellectually alert. As soon as the master of Westover awoke, he commenced his study of Latin, Greek, or Hebrew before breakfast. His favorite room was not the parlor, but the library.

Of his own works, none except his diary surpasses his *History of the Dividing Line.* On his fifty-third birthday Byrd was appointed one of the Virginia commissioners to survey the disputed Virginia-North Carolina boundary. Byrd's *History* proves him one of the day's ablest masters of English prose. For days comedy and tragedy alternated for supremacy. Indians stole their food. Bad weather and poor luck caused Byrd to swear like a trooper in His Majesty's Guards. To mend matters, Byrd's companions arranged a party around a cheerful bowl and invited a country bumpkin to attend. She must have remembered the party for a long time. "They examined all her hidden Charms and play'd great many gay Pranks," noted Byrd, who disapproved of the whole affair. "The poor Damsel was disabled from making any resistance by the Lameness of her Hand." A few years later Byrd was on the frontier again, this time surveying 20,000 acres of bottom land. On September 19, 1733, he staked out two cities—"one at Shacco's to be called Richmond, and the other at the point of the Appomattuck River, to be called Petersburg." At that moment a baby was trying out his infant lungs on a Northern Neck plantation. How could Byrd have known that this child, George Washington, would grow up to be not only the master of Mount Vernon, but the father of a country that rebelled against mother England?

No squire has better credentials, nor fits the accepted pattern, better than Washington. Born in the country where his great-grandfather had settled, land was the continuing passion of his life. Few people knew as much about the physical and human dimensions of America. A veteran surveyor in his teens, an experienced fighter in his twenties, Washington was the unanimous choice to command the American army in 1775. John Adams was impressed by one who would leave "his delicious retirement, his family, and his friends, sacrificing his ease, and hazarding all in the cause of his country." The aristocratic lifestyle which he exemplified so well had a Newtonian neatness and precision. Virtue, idealism, patriotism, and piety were well-defined and understood terms, found in men like Washington, Adams, Jefferson, Penn, Franklin, Jay, and Madison. In account after account we read how impressed men were on meeting Washington, how well he symbolized the cause which he championed. Yet the spoils of victory never interested him.

"How much more delightful to an undebauched mind," Washington wrote to his friend Arthur Young, "is the task of making improvements on the earth than all the vain glory which can be acquired from ravaging it."

As lifestyles change, so does our sympathy with those who best exemplify them. Over the years George Washington has been turned from a man into a monument—a man in the white marble toga. To contemporary poet Robert Lowell he seems as distant and aloof as his monument. These lines from Lowell's "The March," commemorate the October 23, 1967, sortie by peace demonstrators on Washington:

> Under the too white marmoreal Lincoln Memorial
> the too tall marmoreal Washington obelisk,
> gazing into the too long reflecting pool,
> the reddish trees, the withering autumn sky,
> the remorseless, amplified harangues for peace . . .

Why dismiss the George Washington in whom there burned a mad hell which, on the few occasions when it was freed, seared the souls of those who stood in its path? There was hotter blood in his veins than the D.A.R. dreamed of. Five small vignettes indicate how human the man they never called George really was.

The young teen-ager, hickory-tough and backwoods-minded, was forced to copy off *Rules of Civility and Decent Behavior* from an English adaptation of a French guide— the kind of assignment that sent a latter-day kindred spirit, Huck Finn, onto a raft and down the river. But George gritted his teeth and copied:

Put not another bit into your Mouth til the former be Swallowed.

Cleanse not your teeth with the Table Cloth, Napkin, Fork or Knife.

Kill no Vermin as Fleas, lice ticks, &c. in the Sight of others.

46

What interested him deeply as he grew into manhood was not pithy thoughts, but pretty girls. We know some of their names: Betsie Fountleroy, Frances Alexander, Lucy Grymes, Mary Cary, Mary Philipse. When he showed interest in Sally Cary her father thundered, "Remember! You are accustomed to your coach and six!" She chose wealthy coach-conscious George Fairfax. Could Sally have been scared off by young Washington's poetry, of which this is a painful sample:

> Xerxes wasn't free from Cupid's Dart
> And all the greatest heroes felt the smart.

Or was she, like Lucinda Lee, more afraid of his actions than his words? One day Lucinda was walking in the garden with her sisters, Nancy and Milly. "We were cutting thistles to try our sweethearts," she wrote in her *Journal,* "when Mr. Washington caught us, and you can't conceive how he plagued us—chased us all over the garden and was quite impertinent." On another occasion: "While we were eating the apple pye in bed, God bless you! Making a great noise, in came Mr. Washington, dressed in Hannah's short gown and petticoat, and seazed me and kissed me twenty times, in spite of all the resisteance I could make; and then Cousin Molly." What sort of marble man is this?

Now that few can or want to be squires, it is easy to dismiss the copybook world of George Washington. But we do so at the peril of not understanding how our country came into being and what it stood for. Simply to learn a few eighteenth-century phrases, "Give me liberty or give me death . . . life, liberty, and the pursuit of happiness . . . a government of laws, not men," will not suffice in the revolutionary electronic twentieth-century world. When we look back we should see not only abstract phrases, but real men, real events. Lifestyles are not the products of airy nothings and high rhetoric. They are made out of mud, blood, and sweat.

So look again at the General Washington who wanted "news on the spur, for I am all impatience," and who found New Englanders "an exceedingly dirty and nasty people." Hearing that a sword had been broken over the head of a deserting officer, Washington deemed it "a mild punishment"; Bismarck was not the first leader to think blood and iron were the only national foundations.

Recall what the painter Gilbert Stuart saw when he studied the weathered face of Washington: "All his features were strong, indicative of the most ungovernable basic passions, and had he been born in the forest he would have been the fiercest man among the savage tribes."

This is the Washington who suffered and squirmed under the symbolic trappings as first President of the Republic. Look at him at an afternoon reception, wearing his black-velvet suit with silver knee and shoe buckles, yellow gloves, a glittering silver sword in a scabbard of polished white leather. An old Revolutionary soldier approaches in buckskin. He has walked from Kentucky to Philadelphia for the meeting. Both the President and his lady recognize him from the window and hurry to the door to greet him cordially.

"I never was better treated," the veteran reported. "I hadn't believed a word against him. I found out that he was still Old Hoss."

As he grew old (Martha called him her "Old Man") Washington could be tender as well as tart. In 1783 the tired warrior was confronted with an inflammable document from young officers rebelling against the bungling Continental Congress. If justice were not done, they insisted, they would march to Philadelphia and take matters in their own hands.

"Gentlemen, you will permit me to put on my spectacles," Washington said gently, "for I have not only grown gray but almost blind in service to my country." That was all he said. No one marched on Philadelphia.

Look with me, finally, as a visitor approaches Washington's step-grandson, anxious to see the squire of Mount Vernon after his retirement. "You will meet with an old gentleman riding alone," he is told, "in plain, drab clothes, a broad-brimmed white hat, a hickory switch in his hand, and carrying an umbrella with a long staff, which is attached to his saddle bow. That is General Washington."

I was thinking of this old gentleman while watching thousands of Peace Marchers mill around his monument in October, 1967. Some may have remembered him as a rebel, who turned in his British uniform rather than fight against what he believed in. Others might have been remembering him as the official who put down Shays's Rebellion and had no patience with citizens who take the law into their own hands. Thus he may have been a solace to both contending sides—just as he appeared on the great Confederate seal, when Southern states left the Union which Washington had made possible. Like any demigod, he means all things to all men.

This will be made clearer in the 1970s, when we celebrate the bicentennial of the Revolution. A blue-ribbon committee is planning the celebrations. Writers and publishers are researching and reloading every piece of eighteenth-century artillery. The tiny colonies that "fired the shot heard round the world" are, two centuries later, the strongest nation on earth. But the nature of revolutions has changed. In this accidental century, we face the revolution of rising expectations. Our environment is in revolt. Things are plugged in, turned on, juiced up. Time and space have been fused into space-time. Beginning and end-points of actions are indeterminate; intervals between actions are infinitely varied in content and duration. Electronic media are creating new myths,

49

providing new mental and emotional frameworks in which to live. We are forced to refocus on reality.

And that is what Washington was constantly doing—why he was, and remains, the greatest of the great Americans. On the dance floor, the frontier, the battlefield, the conference room, the podium, or the plantation veranda, he focused on what he saw and acted accordingly. He still focuses—on stamps, dollar bills, school notebooks, mountainsides. "Look this fellow straight in the eye," a currently popular insurance ad that features Washington's portrait suggests. "Now honestly say, 'I have not smoked a cigarette in at least a year.' " Would *you* lie to George Washington?

He fascinates us by presenting the mystery of no mystery. Like Yahweh, Washington was what he was—like a primitive king unearthed by archeologists, who reigned majestically until killed ritually. His life is all of a piece; he is together. That is why he can be turned into a monument.

From time to time writers, exasperated by the wholeness, attack that monument. Debunkers of the 1920s pronounced Washington vain, ordinary, undemocratic—"almost as impersonal (to quote William E. Woodward) at the top of the government as a statue on top of a monument would have been." Word of such attacks reached the White House and the monosyllabic Calvin Coolidge. Would Washington's reputation topple, he was asked? Coolidge walked slowly to the White House window and gazed across the Mall. "The Monument's still there," he said.

That "big chimney on the Potomac," as *The New York Tribune* dubbed it, is still there, shining and white. Its lofty simplicity and soaring strength bring meaning to the stone, as they did to the man.

Across the Mall people still enter the Lincoln Memorial to view the king-sized marble statue of the Great Emancipator and to wipe the corners of their eyes. The Washington

50

Monument does not encourage you to moisten your eyes. It demands that you lift them up.

Thirty-four Presidents later, another General became President—the best prepared for high civil office since George Washington. Dwight D. Eisenhower had not only commanded Operation Overlord, the largest single military operation in history; he had proven so fine a diplomat and coordinator that he was swept into office in 1952. Like Washington, he was a country boy, who knew the smell of the barnyard and the pitch of the plow. He too had leap-frogged over the "old aristocrats" and the "leisure class" to win his fame. Only in the military, where rank still has its privilege, could an Atomic Age squire exist. That, in essence, is what Eisenhower was.

Born near Denison, Texas, in 1890, Eisenhower (a sturdy name—in German, *iron striker*) grew up in the Kansas hinterlands. Turned down when he applied to Annapolis in 1910, he went to West Point. Not in the classroom, but on the football field, did he gain attention. When an injury benched him, he announced he "wanted to get out of here and back to the plains of Kansas." But he held on, to graduate 61st in a class of 150 and serve as a Captain in World War I. Desk jobs followed, with infrequent promotions. Major Eisenhower might have been lucky to end up a Colonel had not World War II erupted. In 1942 he became Chief of the Army's Operation Division in Washington. Soon afterwards General George Marshall promoted him over 366 senior officers to make him head of America's armed forces in Europe. After that his rise was meteoric. When the invasion of Europe came in June, 1944, the final decision was his. "O.K., let's go," he said on June 6. With all the fanfare, he was still the simple Kansas farm boy. A year later, with victory in Europe, Ike was widely acclaimed "one of the

51

great heroes of our time." Then, after 37 years of military service, he went into politics.

Like Washington, and many a squire before him, he found civilian bureaucracy unbearable and the ways of politicians incomprehensible. Still he hung on for two terms, taking out his frustration on golf balls, and so bungling the U-2 spy plane episode in May, 1960, that he canceled out the gains for which he had worked so hard for years. Having turned over the reins of government to John F. Kennedy in 1961, he retired to a splendid estate near Gettysburg. The squire had found a permanent home for himself at last. Soon he would seem out of date, penning platitudes for the *Reader's Digest;* but he had won an honorable place in the squirearchy, and few Americans begrudged him his role of senior statesman.

Less of a public figure, but more of a squire, was the man who opened up the door for Eisenhower's advance, and quietly oversaw the whole military scene in Washington—George Marshall. In his veins flowed the blood of the Taliaferros, Randolphs, Carters, and Marshalls—squires all. He completed the rigorous four-year course at the Virginia Military Institute without a single demerit, and went on to serve brilliantly in World War I. Still, in 1933 the fifty-two-year-old colonel did not seem marked for fame. Compulsory retirement was only thirteen years away, and he had not won his first star as brigadier. In 1939 President Roosevelt appointed Marshall Chief of Staff, promoting him over the head of dozens of senior officers, just as Marshall would soon promote Eisenhower.

In 1940 the Marshalls bought Dodona Manor, a Georgian mansion near Leesburg, Virginia. There he went whenever he could, and there, after enunciating the Marshall Plan as Secretary of State, he died. This reticent squire's love of moderation, his abiding concern for rationality and balance, and distaste for public acclaim, made him seem out of date in the Age of Celebrities. An aristocrat, steeped in tradition, with a courtly devotion to traits no longer in style, he was also living proof that heroic stereotypes are never out of style, once the right man comes along.

5

Cavaliers

"There are unplumed knights in the American saddle."

CHARLES FURLONG

"WE of the South," boasted Robert Toombs as the Civil War approached, "are a race of gentlemen." "We are," William Caruthers added, "a generous, fox-hunting, wine-drinking, duelling and reckless race of men." These were death-gasps of the last phase of oldstyle—the sound of cavaliers riding off into the European-dominated past.

Cavalier: a gentleman trained in arms and manège; a mounted soldier; a latter-day plumed knight. Historically, our thoughts return to seventeenth-century England, and the cavalier's vain attempt to keep the Stuarts in power; the ancient horse opposing the newly installed horsepower; a Van Dyke portrait; ostrich plumes; and pithy lines by Herrick or Crashaw. After their defeat, we see the cavaliers escaping to Virginia, the Old Dominion, after the other dominions of Charles I deserted him. And we know how quickly the sturdy legend grew from a slim trickle of historical truth: "They gave Virginians their passion for handsome houses and fast horses, and brought to public life something more than it had before of the English notion that offices should be held for the benefit of the gentry." [1]

---

[1] John S. Bassett, *The Writings of Colonel William Byrd of Westover in Virginia, Esq.* (Richmond: Garrett and Massie, 1901), p. xi. The offi-

Horses came early to the English colonies—along with cavalier legends and aspirations. Though the first seven horses arriving in Jamestown were disposed of in a summary fashion (they were eaten), later ones got more consideration. Horses actually raced through the streets of Jamestown and Williamsburg. The first president of the College of William and Mary, the Reverend Dr. James Blair, was also "father of the Virginia Turf." Bulle Rock, imported by James Patton in 1730, was America's first thoroughbred. By 1800, a hundred (nearly half of all thoroughbreds in the land) were in Virginia, owned by men like George Washington, Thomas Jefferson, Benjamin Harrison, and Arch Randolph. Thus did the squires double as cavaliers, confirming their oldstyle status and Fairfax Harrison's contention (in *The Equine F.F.V.'s*) that the best families owned the best horses—good blood, all around.

The dependence on European models and images was confirmed time and again, as in William Caruther's nineteenth-century study of *The Cavaliers of Virginia.* "We thank God," he wrote, "that we have lived in the days when those tales of romance were sent forth from Abbotsford, to cheer the desponding hearts of thousands, and tens of thousands." Men saddled their horses and rode miles to get Sir Walter Scott's latest novel. If you want to know how the rural aristocracy thought in the mid-century—and why Mark Twain accused Scott of starting America's Civil War —read some of those novels for yourself.

The archetypal importance of this last phase of a derivative lifestyle is documented in William Taylor's *Cavalier and Yankee,* which shows how these two impressive figures grew

---

cial history text for the state of Virginia, commissioned by the General Assembly in 1950 and used ever since, is entitled *Cavalier Commonwealth* (New York: McGraw-Hill, 1957).

out of a split cultural pattern. When that split actually occurred, under the banner of secession and open rebellion, the cavalier made his last glorious stand—defenders of a hopelessly outnumbered agrarian South, substituting speed and courage for strength and supplies, following the Bonnie Blue Flag into defeat.

A century after that bloody, futile war ended—that romantic, reckless, unforgivable war—bits of color lodge in our minds, like pieces of a smashed mosaic.

"Jeb" Stuart, jangling and glittering as he mounts "Skylark" or "Star of the East;" ostrich feathers, gold spurs, red-lined cape, pure effrontery. On a bright June morning he set out with 1200 men, rode around McClellan's whole army, and returned short only one man. Then, young and golden, he fell in the dust of Yellow Tavern.

Senator Louis Trezevant Wigfall, eyes like a Bengal tiger's, self-appointed colonel on Beauregard's staff, clad in a blue frock coat and a red silk sash. When Fort Sumter is in flames he sails from Morris Island, without orders from anyone, demanding the surrender of the Fort.

Major Chatham Roberdeau Wheat, leader of the tough Louisiana Tigers, waiting for the battle of Gaines's Mill, which will claim his life. In one hand is a tall glass of whisky, in the other his mother's prayer book. He partakes deeply of both. "Sure am glad I got a fast horse," he says. "Thanks, Lord."

General "Stonewall' Jackson, twice-a-Sunday churchgoer, "desert-fox" of the rebellion, hell on horseback. In 32 days, with less than 15,000 men, he marched 400 miles, fought five major battles, completely routed two armies, crushed a third, and took 4000 prisoners.

Yet looming above them all, last of the cavaliers, Robert E. Lee—in the middle of a crimson field, with no blood on his hands. In this figure of concealed and controlled fire

56

we see the archetypal cavalier—the only major hero in American history of whom we can say, loser take all.[2]

Robert E. Lee was, in a sense, an anachronism. The new folkstyle had (as we shall see) taken root before his time. Only hopeless nostalgia could have made the rural South fight against the industrializing North; only grace and style could have caused Lee so to lead the South as to emerge a national, rather than a sectional, hero. He is the cavalier in the rear-view mirror, who acted out his life as if he were his own grandfather.

Most of his early life was removed from the mainstream of American life. He was raised on a patrician plantation and educated at West Point—both strongholds of oldstyle. In the best cavalier tradition, he was obsessively fond of horses. Product of one of America's distinguished families, Lee had a profound love of nature and the land. His greatest pleasure was to ride in the country, on horseback. The code by which Lee lived was marked by directness and simplicity. The God venerated was the anthropomorphic deity of the Old Testament; Lee was humble before such a God all his life. He began and ended every day on his knees, believing literally in the Scriptures and God's participation in human affairs. Next to God came the family. To his wife and children Lee gave full devotion; he never tired of visiting and entertaining his many kinsmen. At parties he always preferred the company of women to men, and of daughters to mothers. Like Lord Chesterfield, he believed so much in the society around him that his acts not only followed, but set, the style.

Those who believe in roots and family continuity naturally make much of Lee. His family record, stretching back even before Thomas Lee was appointed the only native Vir-

[2] Of the many biographies, Douglas Southall Freeman's four-volume *R. E. Lee* (New York: Scribner, 1935) remains the standard.

ginian to serve as Royal Governor, is impressive. When Robert E. Lee IV graduated from Washington and Lee in 1949, the family traditions still survived. Yet more than most American heroes, Robert E. Lee reached Olympus by accident. We do not feel that he would have been idolized had not the Civil War occurred. The war made the man and not visa versa. Having studied the personality of Washington, Jefferson, or Lincoln, we can scarcely conceive of their not having altered their age. Certainly Lee would have lived a good life, and like so many Lees before him, won his niche in history. But it was the military secession and especially the South's inability to consummate it, that made him a pivotal figure.

Not only the cavalier Robert E. Lee, but the horse who bore him into battle, emerged from the struggle with an aura of immortality. Ribbon winner in the 1859 and 1860 Lewisburg fairs, "Jeff Davis" was purchased first by Thomas L. Broun, then by Lee, who rechristened him Traveller. In the years ahead the gray horse and his rider were under constant fire, but miraculously they were never scratched. Around campfires at night Johnny Rebs told tales about "Marse Robert" and his steed, whose mane and tail were tweaked out by soldiers and souvenir hunters. Traveller was at Appomattox for the surrender; he carried Lee to Richmond afterwards and then westward to Lexington, where Lee became president of Washington College. One of the students there, John B. Collyar, noted: "General Lee was more demonstrative toward Traveller than he was to any man. They bore a common grief in their memory of the past." [3]

"Traveller is my only companion, I may say my only

[3] Traveller outlived Lee, and died on a mattress supplied by ladies of Lexington. In 1907 his bones were exhumed, mounted, and placed on display in Lee Chapel, where they may still be seen.

pleasure," Lee wrote. "He and I, whenever practicable, wander in the mountains and enjoy sweet confidences." This is the scene to recall as we move from the world of the horse to that of the machine—from oldstyle to folkstyle, and an America that learned (in Emerson's words) to speak her own language, stand on her own feet.

From the standpoint of general interest, Lee was too good to make a universal hero. If only he had displayed more of the tragic flaws or emotional outbursts that make men fascinating to study! Even Douglas Southall Freeman, Lee's leading apologist, said that Washington is more interesting than Lee, simply because he seems more human. We know what Lee did on the battlefield, and as a college administrator. Most of the rest, as with Hamlet, is silence. He did not write books or make speeches to justify himself. He did not exploit his appeal or reputation; he refused to act consciously in the heroic manner.

Edwin Alderman, a perceptive student of Southern character, wrote of Lee's appeal:

Some wonder why Virginia and the South give to General Lee a sort of intensity of love that they do not give even to Washington . . . Lee is a type and an embodiment of all the best of the state. Its triumphs, defeats, joys, sufferings, rebirths, pride, patience center to him. In that regnant figure of quiet strength may be discerned the complete drama of a great stock.[4]

Every hero has local shrines preserved and visited by admirers. Arlington and Stratford, Lee homes, head the list, which also includes the Lee House in Richmond, various battlefields, bridges, and structures connected with Lee's military exploits, the Appomattox area, and the Lexington area. Lee Chapel, on the campus of Washington and Lee University, is his sanctuary. In this Victorian edifice,

[4] Edwin Alderman, *Virginia, A Memorial Address* (Charlottesville, Va.: University of Virginia, 1909), p. 10.

which Lee was responsible for building, his body is interred, and his office and keepsakes are displayed. Valentine's recumbent statue of Lee was placed in the front of the chapel in 1883. Wherever one sits he gazes at the serene marble face of the General asleep on the field of battle. On either side stand venerated emblems of the Lost Cause, Confederate battle flags. Underneath the statue is the Lee family crypt. Whenever cadets from the adjoining Virginia Military Institute pass, they cease talking and salute the dead leader of the Army of Northern Virginia.

The real sanctuary of Robert E. Lee is the hearts and minds of the people. He has appealed to many types of Americans. For the average citizen he is the great soldier, the General on a white charger who defended the South. For the historian he is a key figure of middle-American history, whose decision to lead the Southern army and later to surrender that army and urge reconciliation, helped shape the national destiny. For the intellectual and philosopher he symbolizes an unmachined, agrarian way of life, which trusted in a simplicity later abandoned in an age of technology. For the aristocrat he is the model planter and gentleman, an American embodiment of *noblesse oblige*. For the poet and novelist Lee is the silent enigma, the romantic cavalier who said little, but did much. For the educator Lee is the college president whose innovations rejuvenated Southern education. For the churchman Lee is the undeviating Christian, whose trust in his God never faltered. For the genealogist he is the flower of a great American family, the best proof that blood will tell. For the soldier, he is a military genius who said that duty is the most sublime word in the English language.

Five years after Appomattox, General Lee was dead. His fabled Army of Northern Virginia would ride again only in fiction and on film. There was no more place for cavaliers in the North *vs.* South struggle, so they went west. The Golden Age of the cowboy was about to begin. The novel which first reflected this was named *The Virginian.* In place of the plantation was the ranch; now the cavalier was a cowpoke. The myth rode on.[5]

"Cowboy" dates back to the American Revolution, a term applied to Tories who raided Whig cattle. The term, derisive like "Yankee Doodle," spread westward, to be applied to workmen who rounded up stray cattle in the Rio Grande country. Development in the cattle business was ended abruptly by the Civil War, and Lincoln's blockade on Southern ports. When Lee was leading Confederate troops there were few professional American cowboys, no recognizable stereotype. Most of the cowboys of this period were Mexicans.

Then came the cattle boom. Between 1860 and 1870 the number of head jumped from 11,000 to 520,000 in Wyoming, from 26,000 to 430,000 in Montana and from 71,000 to 791,000 in Colorado. For the Great American Barbecue, cattlemen wanted to have plenty of beef on hand. That meant putting more workers in the saddle. The cavalier was about to be resurrected.[6]

Since he stares out at us from movie screen and television, we know him well—tall, tanned, sinewy, weather-beaten, heroic. Never far away is his horse, Old Paint, with almost human intelligence. They form the most enduring team in American mythology, our closest link with a lifestyle that

[5] No book describes it so brilliantly as W. J. Cash's *The Mind of the South* (New York: Knopf, 1941). For a more scholarly analysis, see Edgar T. Thompson, editor, *Perspectives on the South: Agenda for Research* (Durham, N.C.: Duke University Press, 1967).

[6] Good historical summaries may be found in Frederick L. Paxson, *History of the American Frontier* (New York: Houghton Mifflin Co., 1924); Douglas Branch, *The Cowboy and his Interpreters* (New York: Appleton-Century-Crofts, 1926); and Walter P. Webb, *The Great Plains* (New York: Blaisdell, 1950).

stretches back for centuries. In the Computer Age the farmer is pathetic, but the cowboy is still heroic.

Like many hell-raising cavaliers before him, the cowboy presents a discouraging field for missionaries. He is more Darwinian than Christian; turning the other cheek is out of the question. The Freudian overtones of his stereotype are unmistakable. Brandishing his gun and shooting from the hip, he advertises his gender in much the same way as the male fiddler crab who, during courtship, waves his extra claw in the air to advise the female crab of what texts insist on calling "the reproductive situation." A cowboy specialty, once the long drive was over, was raising hell. Some excuse had to be made in a blue-law nation where the ghost of John Calvin still stalked the land. The obvious one was his isolation and "natural manliness." The unbroken quiet of the plains, a perpetual solitary confinement, could become unbearable. Like a heavy weight, the silent space bore down upon the mind. Men cried aloud to break through the padded loneliness. Not all of them could stand it. Some cracked.

When they got to town, they broke loose. To the usual vices were added such new ones as conditions would permit. In his *Sketches of the Cattle Trail* (1874), McCoy pictured the cowboys reveling in dens of iniquity with "men who lived a soulless, aimless life, dependent upon the turn of a card for a living; blear-eyed and dissipated, worse than a total blank." What could be more shocking—and enticing —to law-abiding Eastern urbanites? The beautiful bibulous Babylons of the Plains came to symbolize freedom and escape. Many a tourist dollar was, and is, spent on Babylon. Las Vegas, Tombstone, and Reno prosper. Oh, to be a cowboy and let off a little steam without ending up in police court!

Not all cowboy exploits are fictitious. Nelson Story, Oliver Loving, Ike Pryor, and Charles Goodnight led lives that would make the TV producer's dream spectacular. In 1866, Story, with a handful of cowboys, drove a thousand cattle all the way from Fort Worth to Montana, right through the heart of the Indian country, despite opposition from the Sioux, Cheyennes, and the United States Cavalry. But what schoolbook mentions Story? What politicians eulogize him?

The first man to utilize the cowboy in dime novels was Prentiss Ingraham. His model was Buck Taylor, who performed in Buffalo Bill's Wild West Show. In an 1887 novel, Ingraham told how Taylor had "won his spurs" and became a Texas Ranger. The hero was a Nordic, carrying the White Man's Burden around in Mexican-infested country. This racism has persisted in the cowboy stereotype. The editor of a large cowboy pulp magazine recently wrote: "We are dealing with a stereotype. The white race has always been noted for being hard-drinking, hard-fighting, and fearless. The heroes of our stories are all like this."

The cowboy world, which invades our living room every night of the week, is one in which everyone knows what he is supposed to do, and does it. Cowboys lead us away from the complexities of civilization, into a world of simple feeling and direct emotion.

Our hero on horseback is a safety valve for our souls. When tension mounts, we turn on the TV and vicariously hit the trail, protecting innocent schoolteachers and gunning down heavy-bearded rustlers. Sherwood Anderson enjoyed this kind of reverie:

There goes Sherwood Anderson. Treat him with respect. He's a bad man when he is aroused. But treat him kindly, and he will be as gentle with you as any cooing dove.

As Walter P. Webb points out, the cowboy novel presents a peculiar difficulty for the author. He must write about a pastoral and half-nomadic group for settled readers in an urban environment; he must describe a lifestyle for readers who can only experience it vicariously. Since his 1902 novel *The Virginian* was the first to solve the problem, Owen Wister set the tone for the "realistic western libel" which has persisted ever since.

Wister's hero was related to other oldstyle heroes like John Smith, William Byrd, and Jeb Stuart. He could ride a horse, solve a mystery, entertain a crowd, and infatuate a girl with equal facility. Gary Cooper re-created the role (Trampas) in a 1929 movie, wooing and winning Molly Wood, the pretty schoolteacher from Vermont. Cavalierly he replies to villains' taunts: "When you call me that, smile." Twenty years later the same Gary Cooper starred in *High Noon*. Once again the dusty and unplumed knight "does what he has to do," despite townspeople's cowardice. There was no absolute victory, no simplistic ending. For the Swedish critic Harry Schein *High Noon* had an "urgent political message," and was "the most honest explanation of American foreign policy." [7] In the interlude between *The Virginian* and *High Noon* the cowboy hero had evoked a literature, a mythology, and graphic symbolism of his own.

All sorts of people had examined and documented this— historians, sociologists, economists, theologians, folklorists, psychologists, and novelists. Symbol, myth, image, style, and influence had been explored. A deep theological yearning was uncovered. To quote Alexander Miller:

If just once I could stand in the dust of the frontier main street facing an indubitably bad man who really deserved exter-

[7] Harry Schein, "The Olympian Cowboy," *American Scholar* (Winter 1955). See also Philip Durham, "The Cowboy and the Mythmakers," *Journal of Popular Culture*, I, No. 1 (Summer 1967).

mination, and with smoking six-gun actually exterminate him—shoot once and see him drop. Just once to face real and unqualified evil, plug it and see it drop.[8]

Since hero-stories demand a rigid form, and repetition is necessary to feel the power of the Gods, Western readers never tire of the stereotypes. Experiencing the same thing in a number of Westerns is like going to the same religious service every Sunday. The hero gains immeasurably from repetition. We can never have too much of our cavalier on horseback.

This explains the success of writers as different, and as prolific, as Zane Grey, Andy Adams, Emerson Hough, Eugene Manlove Rhodes, Clarence Mulford, Stephen Payne, and Omar Barker, as well as the fascination of psychiatrists and socio-psychologists with cowboy culture. Dr. Warren J. Barker finds the cowboy hero "invested with egosyntonic characteristics of the child who aspires to pseudo adulthood." Dr. Kenneth Munden of the Menninger Foundation thinks "the cowboy myth in its form of manifest denial of the female or mother figure represents the intense childhood desires for her and the fears attending these desires." The six-gun has become a sex-gun; even the cowboy's horse is a phallic symbol.

Being "Western" is not confined to books and theories. The pose spills over into economics, promotion, and recreation. Cities like Prescott, Arizona, and Cheyenne, Wyoming, have turned rodeos into big business; cowboys are the cash register's best friend. Yet no genuine cowboy folk hero, in the terms folklorists employ, has yet appeared in America. Our paragon is faceless, despite the considerable efforts to make him a "personality." Much was done for Pecos Bill, who first got into print in 1923, the brainchild of Edward

[8] Durham, *op. cit.,* p. 61.

65

("Tex") O'Reilly.[9] He belongs to a phony type we shall call the jolly giants, and leave for a later chapter. The same can be said for Alkalai Ike, One Lung Lyon, Bean-Hole Brown, Bullfrog Doyle, and Bronco Jones. With Pecos comes the fabulous horse Widow Maker who has 27 gaits (23 forward and 4 reverse), and Slue Foot Sue, who rides the Rio Grande on a catfish, demonstrating that she is "a true girl of the West."

Several far-from-phony Easterners have helped the Western mythology along. One of them, a sickly young Harvard student named Owen Wister, we have already met as the author of *The Virginian*. Another refugee for health reasons was Theodore Roosevelt, who came, saw, and wrote a book on *Ranch Life and the Hunting Trail* (1888). He swallowed the cowboy legend without question:

He prepared the way for the civilization from before whose face he must himself disappear. Hard and dangerous though his existence is, it has yet a wild attraction that strangely draws to it his bold, free spirit.

Catching some of this spirit, Roosevelt used it to lead his Rough Riders up San Juan hill during the bully Spanish-American War; and that in turn helped him enter the White House. There was more than a little of the oldstyle in this advocate of the strenuous life. Could not the same thing be said, as late as World War II, about General George Patton, who traded in the saddle of a horse for the turret of a tank?

The main trait of the oldstyle hero is that he is unilinear. He stands for one single pattern, one cluster of ideas. There is no turning away from them. He can, and does, defend them with his very life. As wholesome and trustworthy as homogenized milk, he is virile and simplistic. With him the

[9] See Edward O'Reilly, "The Saga of Pecos Bill," *Century Magazine,* 106:827–833 (October 1923).

love of open spaces is a passion, the willingness to accept responsibility a dogma. To his style, his code, and his horse he is always faithful.

"The Westerner," Robert Warshow has pointed out, "seeks not to extend his dominion but only to assert his personal value. Always prepared for defeat, he retains his inner invulnerability." [10]

Cowboy stories are little courses in Americanism. Only in this sense do they transcend the oldstyle framework in which they are inevitably cast. Virtue triumphs and evil is undone, against a genuinely American background. In this reincarnation the hero on a horse provides the framework for an expression of common ideals of morality and behavior. Our nation and others that have come under our cultural influence have a cowboy complex. The cowboy may well have more influence as a social force now that his ethos has been destroyed than he did a century ago.

This helps explain why a National Cowboy Hall of Fame was opened at Oklahoma City in November, 1955, amid a Hollywood-like blend of galloping horses, cavalier capers, and electronic music. Twelve hundred horsemen, a full platform of founders, and thousands of spectators gathered on Persimmon Hill for the ceremonies. "This reminds me of a Hollywood super-western," commented Will Rogers, Jr., son of the late Oklahoma cowboy-humorist who had gone from the open plains to Ziegfeld's Follies in New York, following the oldstyle-fakestyle path that Buffalo Bill had blazed before him. "The legend of the American cowboy, no matter how phoney, no matter how much Hollywood horses it up, still is the great symbol of America," Rogers told the large audience. "What the knight in armor is to Europe, what the legend of Robin Hood is to England, so the story of the

[10] Robert Warshow, "Movie Chronicle: The Westerner," *Partisan Review* (April 1954), p. 196.

Western cowboy is to America." Men who worked in local factories and airplane assembly lines—clad, of course, in cowboy boots and ten-gallon hats—applauded and approved.[11]

Not only the citizens of Oklahoma, but groups in and out of cowboyland have discovered the economic, psychological, and symbolic importance of the cowboy in contemporary America. Militant Negroes have made a point of stressing the role of black men in the cowboy's history. In 1967 a Negro veterinarian named Whit Dawkins rode 450 miles across the state of Nebraska on horseback "in commemoration of the Negro cowboy." One did not have to look far to see how editors of *Ebony* tried to tie in the event with early American folklore:

Paul Revere dashed from Boston to Lexington. The Headless Horseman galloped through Sleepy Hollow. Now Whit Dawkins is credited with the "ride of the century" in his ride to commemorate the Negro cowboy.[12]

"I didn't get much sleep," Dawkins reported. "They never got enough of those stories about the Negro buckaroo, the rider and roper and wrangler who was as good—and as bad —as the white cowboy."

Not on the highway, but on the television screen has the cowboy image—the last vestigial remain of folkstyle America—made its indelible mark. It is because of electronics that the endlessly fascinating knight-turned-cowpuncher has ridden across the open range, right into our living rooms. He stares at us during breakfast, from the back of the cereal box, from shelves and stands in bookstores, drugstores, and supermarkets from Miami to Seattle. Travel where we will,

11 See David Davis, "Ten-Gallon Hero," *American Quarterly*, VI, No. 2 (Summer 1954), for other aspects of cultural role-playing in the West.
12 *Ebony*, XXIII, No. 4 (February 1968), p. 75.

he awaits us in local movie houses in Budapest, Dar es Salaam, Bogotá, and Saigon. America's *Bonanza* has become the world's leading television show, featured in over sixty lands—not because it was good history or drama, but because it was good mythology. People who had not yet entered the modern world could look forward to the days when such justice, purpose, and order prevailed; people who were trapped in twentieth-century complexities could look back at the "good old days" of the nineteenth century. For thousands of urbanites, the past went thataway; and they could visit it in Disneyland or Bonanzaland.

"With TV," Marshall McLuhan writes in *Understanding Media,* "the Western acquired new importance, since its theme is always: 'Let's make a town.'" In the existential world of alienation and *angst,* it is a heart-warming prospect.

Bonanza is not oldstyle, but fakestyle; more accurately, it is a blending of the two. Both gained from the fusion. This kind of remythologizing is at the heart of any creative renaissance, perhaps, eventually, of survival. Faced with a new situation, we inevitably attach ourselves to the objects and the aura of the most recent past. In McLuhan's metaphor, "We look at the present through a rear-view mirror. We march backwards into the future. Suburbia lives imaginatively in Bonanzaland." [13]

Who says cowboys are kid stuff?

[13] Marshall McLuhan and Quentin Fiore, *The Medium Is the Massage* (New York: Random House, 1967), p. 74.

6

Natural Men

"We're as happy as can be,
Doing the what-comes-Naturally."

IRVING BERLIN, *Annie Get Your Gun*

"WE have listened too long to the courtly muses of Europe,"
Ralph Waldo Emerson complained in 1837. "I embrace the
common, I explore and sit at the feet of the familiar, the
low." Nine years later Englishman William Thomas coined
a word which encompassed the things that concerned Emerson—folklore. Designed to replace such labels as "Popular
Antiquities and Popular Literature," Thomas's "good Saxon
compound" would study manners, customs, superstitions,
ballads, and proverbs. It would deal with the actual life of
the people, and the way wisdom was transmitted orally from
one generation to another.

The New World to which the swashbucklers came was
not a vacuum, but the home of complex Indian cultures, in
which folklore abounded. White immigrants brought their
own folklore across the ocean with them. Well into the
twentieth century it flourished in America. English folklorist
Cecil J. Sharp tramped around the Southern Highlands in
1918, collecting over 4000 surviving ballads.

In the late eighteenth century, the golden age of American yarns and tall tales opened, involving the Yankee
peddlar, Hudson River Dutchman, Kentucky rifleman, ring-

tailed roarer, Negro banjo-picker. In the hands of Abe Lincoln, pioneer farm anecdotes would become a deadly political weapon, embracing the common and sitting at the feet of the low. Before Lincoln, folkstyle heroes like Daniel Boone, Davy Crockett, Kit Carson, and Old Bill Williams came into their own. Lincoln himself would carry the tradition into the White House. With his assassination the tradition and the nation took a different tack. Between the time Daniel Boone entered Kentucky and Abraham Lincoln entered the Ford Theater—folklife America.

Scholars will accept no short definition of folklore. The *Standard Dictionary of Folklore, Mythology, and Legend* lists 21. Key words in the 21 "standard" definitions are oral, transmission, tradition, survival, and communal.[1] Folklore is found among isolated groups who have developed their own distinctions and stability. This isolation may be not only spacial, but occupational, religious, racial, or linguistic. The enclave of provincial culture may be in the Kentucky mountains, among sailors, the Pennsylvania Dutch, Gullah Negroes, or French-Canadians. A family might be the crucial unit, as with certain ballads. Folk cultures are essentially rural and religious. Behavior is traditional, spontaneous, and personal. The sacred prevails over the secular. Status determines the economy, rather than the open market. All folklore is orally transmitted, but not all that is orally transmitted is folklore.

The connections between European folklore and American variations are well-documented. One of the best-known examples is "Barbara Allen," a ballad that crossed oceans

[1] For recent summaries of these continuing dilemmas, see R. M. Dorson's *Folklore Research Around the World* (Bloomington: Indiana University Press, 1961), Kenneth S. Goldstein's *A Guide For Field Workers in Folklore* (Austin, Texas: University of Texas Press, 1964), and Alan Dundes, *The Study of Folklore* (Englewood, N.J.: Prentice-Hall, 1965).

71

and mountains with ease. A young girl scorns her lover, Sweet William (or Willie, Sweet Jimmy, Young Johnny, or Jimmy Grove). Pepys praised a rendition by the celebrated London actress, Mrs. Knipp, in 1666. He would have been surprised to know that generations later Americans were singing:

> Way down South where I come from
> Is where I got my learning.
> I fell in love with a pretty little girl
> And her name is Barbey Ellen.

"The Two Sisters" became "Sister Kate" in the New World. In "The Gypsy Laddie," a fair lady gives herself to a roving gypsy. Her lord returns, finds her gone, chases after her, and rescues her, and hangs fifteen of the gypsies. In adaptations that have come to light in America, retribution and hanging are omitted. Instead, the lady casts her lot with the roaming vagabonds—a decision that might well have appealed to hard-pressed trailblazers moving westward:

> She was used to a feather bed
> And servants all around her,
> And now she has come to a bed of hay
> With gypsies all around her.

What had been "The Three Ravens" in England became "The Three Crows" in America. In all aspects of folk life the tendency is to exalt the natural and immediate over the artificial and distant. Nature was not only a factor, but a cult, in the young Republic. Cooper's novels, Bryant's poems, and Hudson River paintings verify this. The cult was not exclusively American—remember Marie Antoinette playing milkmaid at Versailles. But because of the actual presence of the wilderness, there was a particular relevance to the doctrine in the New World. What the European romantic dreamed the American actually experienced.[2]

The folk hero was a mirror reflecting this cultural truth. Daniel Boone entered the backwoods where folk songs were sung—long, lean, tough, full of unquenchable fire. The human embodiment of the natural man, his was one of the most fully realized American lives.

He was the American Ulysses who inspired James Fenimore Cooper's fictional Natty Bumppo—who typified the Adamic, independent qualities which belong to the frontiersman. In him we have the first outline of what eventually became the amalgam hero of America, the man of the West.[3]

The noble savage and the natural man merge in Boone. The savage Indian was Boone's greatest master, and he adapted himself to the forest, Indian-like. Like the aboriginals, Boone was filled with the wild beauty of America. He felt the ecstasy of complete possession of the new country. This ecstasy he enjoyed through unbending devotion to the wilderness. William Carlos Williams calls him, "A great voluptuary born to the American settlements against the niggardliness of the damning puritanical tradition." [4]

Boone was a modest man who claimed to have killed only one Indian in his long career, a semi-literate who had trouble writing his own name, an unsocial fellow who couldn't stand "those damned Yankees" who took from him, by the chicanery of the law, every last acre of his home-

[2] Perry Miller, "The Romantic Dilemma in American Nationalism and the Concept of Nature," *Harvard Theological Review,* XLVIII (October 1955), p. 188.

[3] This point is developed in Henry Nash Smith's *Virgin Land: The American-West as Symbol and Myth* (Magnolia, Mass.: Peter Smith, 1950). See also John Seelye, "Buckskin and Ballistics," in *Journal of Popular Culture,* I, No. 1 (Summer 1967).

[4] William Carlos Williams, *In the American Grain* (New York: New Directions, 1967), p. 134.

stead—these confirm rather than deny genuine folk origins and style.

Boone was a simple-hearted man, always inclined to defend rather than attack. The peace he wanted was the peace of solitude; so he pushed on to those places where later his name became a talisman. Three years younger than Washington, he was the squire turned savage, his manor house the virgin forest. Yet no one should see him as sentimental or poetic. Like the Indians around him, Boone offered himself to his world, hunting, killing with a great appetite, taking the lives of the beasts into his hands as they or their masters, the savages, might take his own. Compact and capable of tremendous activity, symmetrical and instinctive in understanding, he is an awe-inspiring American hero.

The cult object is the long rifle which tamed the frontier. The word "frontier" has come to symbolize any urgent national need, any program a Jefferson, Roosevelt, or Kennedy initiates. New frontiers obsess us. When the virgin land ran out, the city, the Negro, and the moon became "new frontiers." Coonskinners from the West are always ready to challenge Redcoats of the East. The congealed idea of "frontier" sustains them—rite words in rote order. Leading the settlers onto the frontier is the sinewy figure of Daniel Boone. We are planters without roots, settlers who can't settle down. Edna St. Vincent Millay summed it up:

> My heart is warm with the friends I make
> And better friends I'll not be knowing;
> But there isn't a train I wouldn't take
> No matter where it's going.

Path, rail, airway—American obsessions. Boone was "American" in a way that John Smith, William Byrd, Cotton Mather, and George Washington could not match or understand. Yet Boone's heroic image was molded by oldstyle thinkers, springing from the Romantic Revolution, based more on feeling than logic or reason. Entranced by Rousseau, Americans dreamed of the natural man and the noble savage, free from society's shackles. This explains why Boone had a literary following in Europe long before many Americans heard of him. Here was another rustic Ben Franklin, of whom Byron wrote in *Don Juan:*

> Boone lived hunting up to ninety;
> And what's still stranger, left behind a name . . .
> Not only famous, but of that good fame
> Without which glory's but a tavern song.

Boone was a born wanderer, always answering the call of that something just over the ridge. His world was full of folklore, superstitions, and action. "Let the girls do the spelling," his father said, "Dan will do the shooting." The long rifle was soon in his young hands, and he used it well for years. At twenty-two Daniel married the daughter of a farmer, a girl he almost shot while "fire-hunting" for deer. The object was to flash a torch and see the animal's eyes reflected in the night. Catching sight of gleaming eyes, Daniel raised his rifle to shoot—discovering just in time a young girl. She rushed home to report she'd been chased by a panther.

In 1773 the Boones and six other families set out for Kentucky. Indians attacked near Cumberland Gap, killing six, including Boone's son James. Such tragedies added to Boone's widespread appeal. Boone was sent by Virginia's governor to warn the surveyors in Kentucky of the impending danger of an uprising. Accompanied by "Big Mike" Stone, he covered eight hundred miles in sixty-two days, going as far as the Falls of the Ohio. In 1775, he was commissioned by Colonel Richard Henderson to hack out the Wilderness Road to Boonesborough, where he built a fort.

Here he and his companions resisted attacks on Fort Boone. He was the leader in the rescue of his daughter, Jemima, and the Calloway girls, who had been kidnapped by the Indians. Captured by Indians at Blue Licks and adopted as a son by the Shawnee Chief, Blackfish, Boone received the tribal name "Big Turtle." He escaped in time to warn his comrades at Fort Boone of an Indian attack. These were ideal episodes for legend-makers.

Boone did little of historical importance in his later life. His chief concern was contesting the loss of various pieces of land. Ejectment suits eventually deprived him of all his holdings. Dismayed, the old hunter left the Kentucky which was later to consider him a special saint, pushing on to present-day Missouri, where his son lived. There he became magistrate of the district. Once again his holding was voided, this time by the United States land commissioner. He traveled back to Kentucky to pay off his debts and ended up with fifty cents to his name. He stayed only long enough to transact his business. Then he headed west.

Men wondered why he preferred to live on the cutting edge of the frontier. "It was too crowded back East," Boone is supposed to have replied. "I had to have more elbow-room." The tranquility of his later years did not diminish Boone's earlier achievements, nor the respect with which Americans viewed him. James Audubon said that the stature and general appearance of this wanderer of the Western forests approached the gigantic. "The very motion of his lips brought the impression that whatever he uttered could not be otherwise than strictly true." This quotation is remarkable when we recall that Boone was only five feet eight inches tall. Audubon viewed Boone as a symbolic as well as an historical figure.

The component parts of the saga were a demi-paradise west of the mountains; land-hungry families who pictured

76

it as a new Eden; a stalwart leader to lead the people west-ward; a lone wanderer guiding his generation on a God-sanctioned trek into the virgin forests.

That scores of people had preceded Boone into Kentucky did not damage the legend. Their achievements were laid at Boone's feet; he was the recipient of the esteem due others. Some historians have lamented this and seen it as unjust. This is the usual procedure with heroes. Through their lives contemporaries' feats and accomplishments are funneled. Every major American hero has been as fortunate in this regard as was Boone, about whom "popular fancy was granted opportunity for unrestrained imagination in creating myth, which age so hallowed that even well-trained historians have hesitated to submit it to scientific analysis." [5]

Legend held that the old hunter never relished civilization. Actually Boone got along reasonably well with his neighbors and sought companionship. Boone was no misanthrope. With his native capacity for leadership and decision, his enduring stoicism despite setbacks, and his love of the outdoors, he was one of the unmachined men of our frontier. These qualities appeal to the twentieth century, when science and technology have brought on perplexing problems. Americans look with nostalgia at the image of a man most happy when he was miles from the nearest gadget, factory, or smokestack. An apt epitaph for Boone was penned by Mark Twain at the end of *Huckleberry Finn*. "But I reckon I got to light out for the territory ahead of the rest, because Aunt Sally she's going to adopt me and civilize me, and I can't stand it. I been there before."

Who spread the Boone legend throughout the land? The first man to perceive epic qualities in the Boone story, and

[5] Clarence W. Alvord, "The Daniel Boone Myth," *Journal of the Illinois State Historical Society,* 19:16–30 (April 1926).

to record them, was schoolmaster-explorer John Filson. An appendix of his *Discovery, Settlement and Present State of Kentucky*, called "The Adventures of Col. Daniel Boone," was the first authentic biography. Translated into Chateau-briand-like prose in 1785, Filson's book became popular among French intellectuals and the rage in Germany when it appeared as *Reise nach Kentucke und Nachrichten von dieser Neu Angebauten Landschaft in Nordamerika*. Timothy Flint, another Boone enthusiast, used the scout as a thinly disguised hero in his novel *Shoshonee Valley*. Daniel Bryan's inflated poem *The Mountain Muse, Comprising the Adventures of Daniel Boone; and the Power of Virtuous and Refined Beauty,* contained passages like this:

> O'er all the mazy complicated chain
> Of objects, which are link'd to the grand theme
> That with sublime sensation swell the soul;
> Boone now in all its forceful influence felt.

When in the Bryan saga Boone finally reached the Mississippi, he anticipated the time when "Freedom's Cities and Republics too" would prosper. This theme cropped up in the work of later writers and of the painter George C. Bingham, whose "Emigration of Daniel Boone" (1851) shows the mighty hunter leading folk into the new Eden. These "tan-faced children" dominated the poetry of Walt Whitman, which opened up a new era in American poetry.[6]

In the West other men were duplicating the pioneering of Daniel Boone—moving destiny west, carrying folkstyle into the wilderness. Red-headed, red-bearded Bill Williams walked with a wobble and fought with a fury. Born in Kentucky, he helped survey the Santa Fe Trail, lived with the Hopi Indians, turned up with the expedition Joseph Walker

---

[6] Walt Whitman, "Pioneers! O Pioneers!" in *Leaves of Grass* (New York: Modern Library, 1955), p. 188.

led into California. Ute, Blackfoot, Crow, and Shoshone could never catch up with him. His dialect—as recorded in George F. Ruxton's *Life in the Far West*—was right out of the folk idom:

Do'ee hyar, now, boys, that's Injuns knockin' round, and Blackfoot at that. But that's plenty of beaver, too, and this child mean trappin' any how!

If a greenhorn ruined a piece of meat, he might confront the booming voice of Williams:

Ti-yah, do 'ee hyar, now, darned greenhorn, do 'ee spile fat cow like that wha you was raised? Tham doins' won't shine in this crowd, boy, do 'ee hyar? Whar'll the blood be going to, you precious Spaniard?

Bill trapped alone in unmapped woods—Rousseau's Natural Man—coming in to sell pelts and buy supplies. Once the Indians stole his two pack animals and all his beaver. He followed them, killed them, and returned to Bent's Fort. Then he sold his pelfry, filled up on Taos whisky, spent a day sobering up, and headed for the mountain peaks.

Fate finally overtook Old Bill Williams. In the winter of 1849 six trappers, pursued by Sioux, darted into an isolated canyon sealed by a heavy growth of cedar. They found Williams, propped up against a tree, his feet stretched toward some pine logs half buried in snow. He died just as he had lived—alone.

That same year Kit Carson found a pulp magazine in which he was described as a great hero. His unique distinction among folklife's natural men is that he became famous because of two women whom he had never seen. As John C. Fremont's chief scout, he was lionized in Mrs. Fremont's account of *The Daring Adventures of Kit Carson and Fremont*. Jessie Fremont met Carson, took him home with her,

79

visited newspaper offices. She supervised a sketch of the trapper, which became a standard item in history books. Here was an opportunity to reconcile the savage West and the genteel East. Carson had proved himself indispensable in the triumphant westward march of the natural man.[7]

Faithful retainer to the brilliant Fremont, Carson made an admirable "straight" hero. When Fremont's reputation was clouded by a court-martial for disobedience, Carson's soared upward. How memorable such lines as his answer when Fremont asked did he know the Rockies:

Reckon so. A ten-prong buck warn't done sucking when I last sit on a chair!

Here was the folk idiom geared to heroic purposes. Only five feet six inches tall and weighing 160 pounds, Carson loomed large on the mythic horizon. His story was built on the Boone model; his modest, unassuming ways matched those of old Daniel. Reluctantly, Carson agreed to dictate his story, to which he appended the only word he could write—his name.

Carson admired the Indians, and married two squaws— an Arapaho who died and a Cheyenne who threw dishpans at him. He defended the Indians against unjust charges, and saw that the Navajos were returned to their native region. When Helen Hunt Jackson began her crusade to protect the Indian, she exalted Kit Carson, "The Happy Warrior of the Old West," in the process.[8] What finally happened to Kit? He was too tough to kill. He just wore out.

If Carson had "the merry heart that Shakespeare knew"

[7] Henry Nash Smith, "Kit Carson in Books," *Southwest Review,* XXVIII, No. 2 (Winter 1943).

[8] Mrs. Jackson's book was called *A Century of Dishonor.* See Allan Nevins, "Helen Hunt Jackson, Sentimentalist vs. Realist," in *American Scholar,* X, No. 2 (1956), pp. 269 f.

(one of Mrs. Fremont's claims), he was not a comic figure. Because laughter is an essential ingredient of folk culture, such a hero was bound to appear. Behold Davy Crockett, that "yallar flower of the forest" whose career became a frontier joke. In 1818 there was dwelling near Shoal Creek, Tennessee, a frontier squatter who had "suffered only four days of schooling." When the people of the district decided to set up a temporary government, they elected him justice of the peace. Davy Crockett's career had been launched. He relied on "natural born sense, and not on law learning; for I never read a page in a law-book in all my life." After serving in the state legislature, he accepted (apparently as a joke) the challenge to run for Congress. He won and served two terms. The Whigs adopted him as a tool to win backwoods democracy over to their side. Stressing his eccentricities, humor, and lusty pioneer spirit, they made him into a national buffoon. Party journalists wrote, but attributed to the almost illiterate Crockett, *Sketches and Eccentricities of Col. David Crockett* (1833) and *An Account of Col. Crockett's Tour to the North and Down East* (1835). When Alexis de Tocqueville toured America, he was fascinated by Crockett who "has no education, can read with difficulty, has no property, no fixed residence, but passes his life hunting, selling his game to live, and dwelling continuously in the woods." The Whigs let Davy sit on the platform with Daniel Webster. For a while Tennessee's bear-hunter thought he was going to be nominated for the Presidency. Instead, he failed to be re-elected to Congress. "I told my constituents they might all go to hell, and I would go to Texas," wrote Davy. And go he did, where by dying at the Alamo he put the right finishing touch on his thriving legend.

Crockett Almanacs, issued from 1835 to 1856, attempted to fit humans and animals of adequate proportions into the gigantic, untamed American landscape. The heroic Davy mastered the frontier and the beasts that dwelled in it. Crockett made jokes of situations that in real life were tragic; he mastered the impossible effortlessly, in a backwoods fairyland. Watered with buffalo milk and weaned on whisky, he sprouted so that his Aunt Keziah thought it was "as good as a day's vittles to look at him." The animals learned how useless it was to defy him. "Is that you, Davy?" they would shout when he reached for his gun. "Yes," he would say. "All right, don't shoot. I'm a-comin' down!"

Most Crockett tall tales were based on oral tradition which can be traced back to Daniel Boone. One quality Boone seldom exhibited was humor. Pranks, practical jokes, and boasts seemed beneath him. So Davy Crockett, who made an art of such things, was invented.

Paradoxically, Crockett won fame because of horse sense and immortality because of nonsense. He was the foil for austere and antisocial Boone.

How to pass this natural man on to the youth of an increasingly urbanized America? This question Ohio-born Dan Beard asked himself as the nineteenth century ended. There was still enough of the Wild West left for him to cavort with Yellowstone Kelly, Buffalo Bill, Bat Masterson, and Charlie Russell. A dream began to take shape:

I wanted a society of scouts to be identified with the greatest of all scouts, Daniel Boone, to be known as the Sons of Daniel Boone. Each member would have to be a tenderfoot before attaining the rank of Scout. Eight members would form a stockade, four stockades a fort.[9]

Objects so dear to Boone, Crockett, Carson, and Williams—rifles, traps, buckskin clothes, moccasins, campfires

[9] Dan Beard, *Hardly a Man is Now Alive—An Autobiography* (New York: American Youth Press, 1939), p. 353.

—became symbols for the new Boy Scouts of America. Beard converted President Theodore Roosevelt to the cause. Year after year thousands of Tenderfeet left comfortable homes to trek into piney woods, pitch tents, and eat half-cooked meat to earn Merit Badges. Overnight hikes, jamborees, and canoe trips became an integral part of thousands of childhoods, reflecting the ideals of the far-distant Daniel Boone.

What remained, when no one could find coons for coonskin hats, was the traditional belief that obstacles can be overcome by courageous individual acts. When locations and vocations change, so does heroic style. But the platform on which the hero stands is the nature of man. That endures.

7

Self-Made Men

"Success is men's god."
AESCHYLUS

ALL praise to the country mouse; but admit that city mice have a lifestyle too. The woods of Kentucky were one frontier—the alleys of New York another. Vast changes were wrought when America changed from a rural to an urban civilization. The story of the country boy who made good in the city provided material for a new cultural mythology.

Until the mid-nineteenth century, the natural areas for myth and legend in America were folktales, religion, and an uncontrollable nature. This changed in the new mechanized cities. Once the penny presses and dime novels took over, people could read rather than tell the news. The church moved to the outer fringes of man's life. More and more nature could be controlled by thermostats and indoor work patterns; eventually it would be something visited on vacations, or seen in technicolor movies. Man was no longer a creature in nature, but in society. Not dragons, denominations, and thunderstorms, but depressions, inflation, and racism were his chief fears. Myths and lifestyles of modern America were created primarily in the areas of economics, politics, and sociology. The hero was no longer the hunter or cavalier but the self-made man. Belief in him, Herbert

84

Muller points out in *The Uses of the Past,* "strengthened our faith in ourselves and helped to maintain the habits of enterprise and self-reliance."

The heroic model became the American businessman; his diabolic foil was government interference. There were new clusters of ideas, even myths, for assets, investments, private property, and social institutions, which provided psychological motives for court decisions, inheritance, and philanthropy. All this Thurman Arnold explored in *The Folklore of Capitalism.*

What is more logical than the market place creating its own styles, populating its own Olympus? Had not the church, during a long period of supremacy, done just this? Was not a Robber Baron as bold in his own way as the old-style knights? Was not a man who could bring Model T's out of Detroit as inspiring as an earlier leader who had brought manna out of the wilderness?

Self-help is a theme which runs throughout history. Samuel Smiles was peddling success stories in England long before they overran America; the seventeenth-century Puritans had imported, as an article of faith, the Protestant doctrine of the individual's *calling.* Embodying the quintessence of orthodox Puritanism in America, Cotton Mather spoke effectively for the self-made man and what would become the American Gospel of Success.[1] He is a splendid example of the oldstyle academic writer, who would have been as much at home in Oxford as he was in Boston. Ambitious and pontifical, Mather found one of his key texts in Proverbs 22:29: "Seest thou a man diligent in his business? He shall stand before kings." He endorsed what he called "Particular

---

[1] Moses Rischin, editor, *The American Gospel of Success* (Chicago: Quadrangle Books, 1968). See also A. Whitney Griswold's unpublished doctoral thesis, *The American Cult of Success,* Sterling Library, Yale University.

Employment" not merely for economic advantages, but as a solemn religious duty as well. " 'Tis not honest, nor Christian, that a Christian should have no Business to do," he observed. This stress on self-help and employment in Calvinist teachings linked up nicely with later factors like laissez-faire capitalism, Darwinism, the role of the frontier, and the effect of the man-land ratio in a nearly empty continent.

Long before the British colonies were independent sketches, legends, and paeans to self-made men appeared. Cotton Mather collected some in his *Magnalia Christi Americana;* Benjamin Franklin turned folk wisdom into pithy platitudes in *Poor Richard's Almanack*. They have the earthy texture of the country and the clever turn of the city. "God helps those that help themselves . . . A penny saved is a penny earned . . . He that would catch fish must venture his bait . . . The bird that sits is easily shot." No wonder the *Almanack* sat on the shelf next to the Bible in many an American home. The same down-to-earth shrewdness marked the famous McGuffey readers, from which generations of American schoolchildren learned to read. McGuffey borrowed continuously from Franklin and the accepted standards of folklife America. "Lazy Ned" and "Idle Jane" were the fall guys in McGuffey-land. Terrible was their demise once they defied the accepted capitalistic norms. The homely self-help maxims of Franklin and McGuffey probably influenced the daily life of rural America as much as all the formal philosophies of the period.

Before 1860 American cities mirrored rural ideas and prejudices. In 1830 Boston sponsored the Franklin Lectures "to encourage young men to make the most of their opportunities." City printers learned where the market was. Franklin's biography, "cooked up in a savoury dish" by the master publicist Parson Weems, went through eleven editions. Democracy was made into a secular religion, with self-made man as one of its high priests.

A poor Virginia orphan named Henry Clay first used the term "self-made man" in an 1832 Congressional debate. Five years later Horatio Alger, Jr., was born. He would carry the message onward and upward, telling time and again "the American story" that became the indelible stereotype at home and abroad, to last through generations and style-changes, good years and bad.

Descended from old Yankee stock, Horatio was the first son of a Unitarian minister and a pious mother. Known to his comrades as "Holy Horatio," he changed his Harvard College lodgings when his landlady appeared in her negligee. "I might have seen her bare, but I didn't look," he wrote home.

Confused and unhappy, he was sent for a visit to Paris, where many surprises awaited him. To quote his Paris diary: "I was a fool to have waited so long. It is not nearly so vile as I had thought."

Returning and reforming, he, too, became a Unitarian minister, but the situation got worse and worse. So he moved to New York to make his fortune as a writer. Since political biographies were in demand, and he knew the idiom of the times, Alger wrote three: *Webster: From Farm Boy to Senator; Lincoln: the Backwoods Boy;* and *Garfield: From Canal Boy to President.* The last of these he finished in 13 days, to reach the publisher before Garfield died. Before he finished, he had turned out 135 novels which sold over twenty million copies. "I should have let go," he wrote. "How many times I wanted to. Writing in the same vein becomes a habit, like sleeping on the right side. Try to sleep on the left side and the main purpose is defeated—one stays awake." [2]

[2] Herbert L. Mayers, *Alger, A Biography Without a Hero* (Mendota, Ill.: Wayside Press, 1964), p. 343. A later and more comprehensive study is Ralph D. Gardner's *Horatio Alger, or The American Hero Era* (Mendota, Ill.: Wayside Press, 1964).

That "same vein" consisted of telling one story, with minor variations, again and again:

I am a sturdy but poor lad in the cruel city. Come what may, I am bound to get ahead, since I have both pluck and luck. You may know me as Tattered Tom, Ragged Dick, New Newton, Jasper Kent, Tom Tracey, Luke Larkin, Plucky Paul, or Mark, the Match Boy—never mind, I'll make it under any name. True, my father is dead and my mother takes in washing. But I am resourceful and there is a cheery gleam (not fostered by beer, you may be sure) in my blue eyes.

I stand up to bullies or bandits, but tremble before flirtatious and teasing little girls. That's because I Live Clean, and await a turn of the tide. The tide turns. I find a wallet which Rich Man lost. Instead of keeping the money, and buying mother much-needed medicine, I take the wallet to Rich Man's house. The door is opened by his lovely blue-eyed daughter, who sneers at my clean but ragged clothes. She is Good Beneath, so I love her from that moment forward—even though she is Far Above me.

As I back away from the manor (she must not see the patch on the seat of my pants) Papa comes in, grabs the wallet, and counts all the money. All there. "You must be rewarded," he says, taking a shiny new dime from his pocket. "Come by my office and start up the ladder of success."

"You are kind, sir, but I must stay with my sick mother." Tears well up in my eyes. But soon her gallant heart gives out over the scrubbing board, and she goes to her reward. "Take Rich Man's job," she gasps with her last breath. So I do errands, trim pencils, and move up the ladder.

My chief competitor is a flash, mustached young man who wants not only the junior partnership, but the white goddess daughter as well. I watch closely and discover, by pluck and luck, that he's a secret swindler. At the revelation he resists, but in vain. (I live clean—he smokes.) I get both the promotion and the girl. Our children really are brought by the stork. Naturally, we live happily ever after.

Americans of his day not only could, but did, take such oversimplified fairy stories seriously. To them an Alger novel was as much a part of the scheme of things as state fairs, Sunday, progress, and the Declaration of Independence. Alger never let them down. Even as he finished another potboiler, some real-life American was making it. Did you know that Thomas A. Edison had been a newsboy, Adolph S. Ochs a printer's devil, and Andrew Carnegie a messenger? Like many other Americans, John D. Rockefeller had roamed the countryside looking for a job. The appeal of their lives, and of Alger's novels, was not to wild western adventure, but to a kind of humdrum practical success that could come to anybody—with a little pluck and luck. Because the story was rooted in historical fact and living example, it qualified (in sentimentalized form) as the closing examples of folkstyle America. Just ahead lay the fakestyle saga that substituted fiction for fact, exaggeration for essence. The self-made man, and his prolific promoters, hover between these two major styles.

None of the success which Alger meted out so freely to his boy heroes spilled over into his own life. He ended up tipping the Astor House desk clerk to point out celebrities. A love affair with a married woman, antagonism with his family, and a haunting fear of failure lined the face of the plump balding author, who sought refuge in the Newsboys' Lodging House. To the end he wrote steadily, desperately, parodying his own earthy, folksy style, writing for boys because he couldn't write for men. Finally even Sunday School teachers found it hard to present him with a straight face. Once America was enveloped in fakestyle, old folk idiom and stories were simplistic. There remained only the cruel game of parodying his life in epitaphs like this one:

Six feet underground reposes Horatio Alger, Helping Himself to a part of the earth, not Digging for Gold or In Search of Treasure, but Struggling Upward and Bound to Rise at last In a New World—where it shall be said he is Risen from the Ranks.

By a bit of poetic justice, the Alger books which have been shoved aside in the turbulent cities can still be found tucked away in small towns and farm houses. "Rural America is Horatio Alger country!" Ralph Gardner writes. "It is virtually the last place his books will still be found." The reason is not hard to come by. Where remnants of the old folkstyle exist, the last gasp of its literature—telling of country boys who made it in the cities—still has a place.

Not that Alger sentimentalized the farm, or looked back to the rural society with nostalgia. Just the contrary. When (in *Ragged Dick*) the bootblack Johnny Nolan goes back to the farm to escape the brutality of his drunken father in New York, he soon finds that he prefers the hardships of the city streets:

I dunno as I'd like to live in the country. I couldn't go to Tony Pastor's or the Old Bowery. There wouldn't be no place to spend my evenings.

Long before World War I, thoughtful country people had begun to ask (as the war song put it) "How Ya Gonna Keep 'Em Down on the Farm, After They've Seen Paree?" The real sentimentalists have been the folklorists and writers who fail to see that folkstyle, like the folk themselves, came into the city and found a home there. Caste and class, high life, native and foreign groups, tourists, skyscrapers, subways, gangsters, hippies would all provide fertile ground for the folk imagination. The Long Island Railroad makes an excellent villain and "fall guy" in the new order. Characters like Willie the Horse and Gertie the Broad (reflected in the pages of Damon Runyan) have real solidity and validity. Even some of the folk pageantry from county fairs would carry over into Central Park, as this August 17, 1967, news item proved: "Balloons will be launched in Central Park amidst dancing, singing, entertainment, and games. According to the sponsoring group, the true existential poverty of man 'consists in his having lost the power to celebrate a festival festively.' They aim to reawaken this power."

Nor should the fakestyle which came into being be scorned or dismissed. Fakestyle is simply an imitation of the real folkstyle that was driven underground by vast new cultural and technological changes. In place of *authentic* we have *synthetic*. Authorship was no longer communal but individual; the motivation was economic rather than sociological. One does not despise a mass-produced spinning wheel sitting in a modern suburban living room; but one recognizes that it serves a very different function from the hand-hewn model which, a hundred years ago, made the family's clothing. One does not expect the "cowboys" one finds in sophisticated night clubs to spend their lives roping cattle. Who can say that roping tourists is a less respectable, or profitable, occupation?

To the purist a great art style, such as the baroque, can be said to have "fake" elements. Columns support no weight, scrolls are added for no purpose, deceptive ceiling paintings create the illusion of space. Still, the grandeur and the illusion have a function of their own. If the total impact of a building is considered, a baroque palace might be placed above a no-nonsense international skyscraper. As with buildings, so with heroes. Taste, not morality, is the final judge in matters of style.

When Horatio Alger's prose style went out of date, others

91

presented the self-made man with a newer, more sophisticated façade; underneath he was the same aggressive fellow. Drawing from an episode in the Spanish-American War, Elbert Hubbard published "A Message to Garcia" in 1889. George Daniels of the New York Central Railroad distributed over 1,500,000 copies. Translated into Russian, French, and German, the sermon on self-help carried the American idiom back to the Old World. Hubbard himself was fond of classical allusions. Hence this comment on railroader Jim Hill: "Clio will eventually write his name on her roster as a great modern prophet, a creator, a builder. Pericles built a city, but this man made an empire."

From a twentieth-century perspective, some historians have been suspicious not only of the pious tributes, but of the validity of the self-made man. Perhaps, they argue, the middle class tried to smother social unrest with rhetoric. Perhaps the function of this mythologizing was to turn class frustration into class guilt, thus reducing the danger of social upheaval by directing working-class discontent inward against the discontented themselves.[3] The answer, in my opinion, lies in the record of those who *did* "make it" and thus validated the myth. If few blue-collar workers followed the Horatio ladder, many of their sons did enjoy marked improvement. Working families did acquire property and homes; some mobility did exist.

Alger's first major publisher, A. K. Loring, understood that despite all his flaws, this author had found something central in American life. "The turmoil of the cities is in his stories," Loring said. "You can hear the cry of triumph of the oppressed over the oppressor. What Alger has done is to portray the soul—the ambitious soul—of the country."

[3] See Stephan Thernstrom, *Poverty and Progress: Social Mobility in a Nineteenth Century City* (Cambridge, Mass.: Harvard University Press, 1964), chaps.1–3.

In our own day, biographer Ralph Gardner predicts that the spirit of Alger will remain a part of our folklore. "In the humble boy he created an unforgettable hero; the determined young lad who—much like America—pulled himself up by his own bootstraps." [4]

Many turned the Alger words into flesh, but none with more lasting impact than Henry Ford. He stands at the spot where the farm and the factory meet. People who have never heard of Washington, Boone, or Bunyan know the name Ford well. It bounces over the world's highway daily. Under his guidance, the automobile became for us what the cross had been for the Emperor Constantine: *in hoc signo vinces.*

For all his mechanical genius, Ford was oriented toward the rural folkstyle America from which he came. He was a hopeless anachronism in the second half of his life; not even a billion dollars could cover up his inadequacies. He lived in the fakestyle years without knowing it.

Of Scotch-Irish lineage, Henry Ford was born in rural Michigan in 1863. Hating farm chores, he spent his spare hours fixing farm machinery and watches. When sixteen, he overrode his family's wishes and went to Detroit. After a second short try at farming, he married and took a job at the Edison Company, rising from night fireman to chief engineer. Then he quit to market his gasoline quadricycle. He moved into the infant automobile industry, and in 1903 he set up the Ford Motor Company with a capital investment of $28,000. Five years later the first Model T came from his factory, and five years after that he built his assembly line. In 1914 Ford established a minimum wage of $5 a day in his plant. His rugged Model T's became America's leading car, the subject of a new mechanical folklore. Before the Great Depression he sold 15,000,000 cars, creating volumi-

[4] Ralph Gardner, *op. cit.*, p. 351.

nous Lizzie Lore—one of the fascinating chapters in folk-style America.[5]

What these pug-nosed, functional cars symbolized was Ford's role in creating a new culture on wheels. Ugly but useful, Lizzie came just in time to create a suitable basis for a machine-age folklore. No mechanical object has ever been the butt of so many jokes, or the source of so many wise-cracks as the Model T, alias Leaping Lizzie, Little Bo-Creep, Rolls Rough, Wanderer of the Waistland, the Answer to a Walking Maiden's Prayer, Bouncing Betty, Graf Zep's Uncle, Lizzie of the Valley, Passion Pot, and variations beyond number. Folklorist B. A. Botkin collected over a thousand for a single article in *American Speech*. Some, such as "Flapper," "No Charleston," and "Wanted—A Bootlegger to Share Our Home," were dated by the 1920s. Some, like "Henrietta Elizabeth Van Flivver" or "September Morn," affected a grand style; others moved over into Freudian realms—like the label, "I'm a second son of a last year's Lizzie," accompanied by a pair of coconuts hung from the differential.

Nicknames stressed Lizzie's all-round cussedness, and capitalized on America's fondness for slogans and wisecracks. They were mechanical adaptations of the mule and burro stories of European folklore, redone in the American idiom. When you saw a car bumping along labeled, "I'm From Texas, You Can't Steer Me," "Columbus Took a Chance— Why Can't You?" or "Sugar, Here's Your Daddy," you knew what country you were in. And you knew the old frontier optimism wasn't dead when others read, "We Ain't

[5] The most comprehensive biography is Allan Nevins's *Ford: The Times, the Man, the Company* (New York: Scribner, 1954). Also helpful are Keith Sward's *Legend of Henry Ford* (New York: Russell and Russell, 1948) and Garet Garrett's *The Wild Wheel* (New York: Pantheon Books, 1952).

Climbed Pike's Peak Yet," or "Lazy Loping Lizzie on her Last Lenthy Leap." Lizzie's maker also figured in the buffoonery. His staff called him Mr. Ford, but customers preferred Henry. Flivvers were inscribed "Turn over, Sis, Henry's Here," or "Don't worry, Lizzie, Henry will Fix You Up." Behind the razzing was pride in Ford's achievements. "When better Buicks are built, Ford's will pass them," went a popular slogan. Even Lizzie's obvious failings, such as a tendency to drop vitals en route, came in for spoofing. "Follow me for Ford Parts!" was a favorite.

Ford jokes flourished like Ford labels, both orally and in printed joke books. The usual theme was confidence in the man and the cars which were transforming America. They stressed inventiveness, productivity, or some ingenious triumph at the Ford plant. After-dinner speakers told about the old lady who sent her tomato cans, or the farmer his tin roof, to Detroit, and got a Ford car back by return mail. Rural humorists poked fun at the rich eastern banker who paid $15,000 for a fancy limousine, but kept a Model T in the trunk to pull it out of mud holes. They told the sad tale of the Ford worker who dropped his wrench on the assembly line and was twenty cars behind when he bent over and picked it up. Few of the jokesters knew it, but their tales echoed others which had been used for centuries. The Ford joke was the trademark of the gasoline age. Neither Jove, Caesar, nor Charlemagne had done anything more remarkable than Henry Ford, who turned bits of tin into automobiles.[6]

Had you heard that next year's Lizzies were going to be yellow so they could be sold in bunches like bananas? That

---

[6] In the 1960s another functional automobile, the German Volkswagen, was creating some of the same stories—indeed, borrowing some of the old ones from Model T days. At least one book of Volkswagen stories had appeared by 1967.

Ford planned to paper the sky with flivver planes? That Model T's were being shipped in asbestos crates, since they came off the assembly line so fast they were still hot and smoking? That a man got rich following Ford cars and picking up the parts that fell on the road? That Uncle Jeb got shaken up in Lizzie until the fillings came out of his teeth? That the next Ford would come with a can opener, so you could put doors anywhere you wanted them? That Henry would pay $100 for any flivver joke which made him laugh? Though not as frequent as they once were, Ford stories still thrive on the American scene. In May, 1953, Art Thomas, owner of a 1908 Model T, was fined for speeding. His courtroom comment was in keeping with the Lizzie tradition: "It was only hitting on three. If it had been hitting on all four I doubt if they would have caught me." On and on the jokes go, enhancing the stature of a man few Americans saw or heard. They keep Ford in the realm of heroic immortality.

Lizzie brought golden days to Ford. Introduced at the 1907 Chicago Auto Show, the Model T went immediately into production. Henry offered a stripped car; everything was standard and interchangeable, which made for simplicity of operation and repair. The end product was the first workable solution to the problem of putting a democracy on wheels. As the 1920s rolled on sturdy Ford axles, politicians began to talk of two cars in every garage. Henry never endorsed such extravagant notions; one would do, if it were a Ford. In two decades he produced 15,456,868 Model T cars in thirty assembly plants, selling them for as little as $265. When he started making Model T's his surplus balance was $2,000,-000. Before he changed to a new engine it was $673,000,-000. Although by 1923 he had not spent a penny on advertising for five years, he was making 7000 cars a day and still not filling all orders. Ford seemed to have answered the criticism about capitalistic production methods and the vitality of laissez faire. Instead of condemning what Ford did, the Russians tried desperately to imitate it. Europeans poked fun at Ford's methods and products, but envied Americans with their Ford cars. A British writer predicted that Americans would give up their homes to live and die on the road. As the lines of house trailers lumber around the new interstate highways, we suspect that he may have been right.

Ford's workaday and respectable rise lacks the color and drama which went with urbane Phineus Barnum, Diamond Jim Brady, and Jubilee Jim Fiske. He reflected the strength of the rural America which sustained his legend. Whimsical and retiring, he was at his worst in public appearances. Few admired him. Even fewer could claim to be his friend. Most workmen thought of him as a slave driver. Ford's legend did not spring, like the Lizzies, from the assembly line. The Mechanical Wizard was more esteemed by those who drove Fords than those who made them.

During New Deal days Ford's reputation went down. When his pro-Nazi tendencies became known, it hit rock bottom. After his death Ford underwent the hysteria of depreciation. In 1953, during the highly publicized 50th anniversary of the Ford Motor Company, this trend was reversed. His heirs opened Ford's private papers to the public. Although he had said history was bunk, he had collected enough personalia to cover 5000 feet of shelves in the Ford Library.

Life magazine took "A New Look at Ford," and devoted sixteen pages to him.[7] Other magazines and media followed suit. Company advertisements stressed technological growth since World War II; Henry Ford II worked hard to improve public relations.

[7] *Life,* Vol. 34 (May 25, 1953), pp. 134–150.

Throughout his life Ford suspected social innovation, criticism, and expert opinion. A dissenting voice infuriated Ford. So many employes were fired that a special name was coined for the unfortunates—the Ford Alumni Association. Ford replaced all doctors at the Henry Ford Hospital with chiropractors and cut off milk deliveries at Greenfield Village because medical men would not say that his son Edsel had contracted undulant fever. "Never trust earpiddlers or lawyers," he said. His personal world was as superstitious as his factory world was scientific. Fear of Jews, John Barleycorn, the duPonts, and international bankers gave him no rest. Black cats, broken mirrors, omens, and coincidences terrified him. Never would he change a sock that had been put on inside out. Not impressed with church theology, he nevertheless believed in reincarnation:

When the automobile was new and one of them came down the road, a chicken would run straight for home, and usually get killed. But today when a car comes along, a chicken will run for the nearest side of the road. That chicken has been hit in the ass in a previous life.[8]

Such bizarre stories tend to obscure Ford's real achievement and mechanical competence. He combined Eli Whitney's system of interchangeable parts and Oliver Evans's system of mechanical conveyors to create the modern system of power-driven assembly-line manufacture.[9] As early as 1915, French engineers Arnold and Faurote published their book on *Ford Methods and Ford Shops,* crediting the Michigan country boy with "the very first example of chain-driving an assembly in progress of assembling."

Such statements by Europeans emphasize the role of ver-

[8] Harry Bennett, *We Never Called Him Henry* (New York: Dell, 1961), p. 47.

[9] For full details see John Kouwenhoven, *The Arts in Modern American Civilization* (New York: Norton, 1967), chap. 2.

nacular style in America, and raise questions of its relationship to folkstyle and fakestyle. If vernacular is defined as "unself-conscious efforts of common people to create satisfying patterns," [10] we seem to be close to the heart of folkstyle. If at the same time vernacular is not folk art, but the art of sovereign if uncultivated people rather than groups cut off from the main currents of life, the necessary stability and isolation on which folkstyle is based has been removed. If "vernacular patterns" are not inspired by oldstyle traditions and folk wisdom, but instead by the Darwinian demands of an expanding machine economy, we are confronted by a new category. We are seeing folk arts transformed by progressive technology and new life-patterns. Some of those patterns did not and do not achieve a new integrity or beauty. Instead, they have a kitsch quality which can only point to phony values and vulgarity. Now we are in the area of fakelore, in which vernacular has gone to seed.

Vernacular is a link between folkstyle and fakestyle. We are proud to proclaim the integrity and beauty of our early sailing ships, Corliss engines, Colt revolvers, Model T cars—but shudder at claptrap that clutters up shelves of "souvenir shops" and "ten-cent stores." This same ambivalence exists in the life and thought of Henry Ford. How could he have had such good sense and bad judgment? Why did he never learn where his area of competence started and stopped? Why was he in sociology what Edgar Allan Poe was said by Lowell to be in poetry—three-fifths genius and two-fifths fudge? The mind of the automobile king roared down the night highway without headlights. When he crashed through the barricades, no one chastised him. So seldom did he listen that he learned little from other drivers. On he rolled, a hit-and-run driver whose victim might be the Jewish race,

[10] *Ibid.*, p. 13.

the Catholic religion, labor unions, leisure, the New Deal, or Wall Street. Ford's prejudices were those of rural Midwestern America. William Jennings Bryan, that crusading enemy of city slickers and religious modernists, supplied his political credo. Like Bryan, whom Ford befriended, he was a pacifist and isolationist. When newspapermen came to the docks to cover the departure of the Ford peace ship for Europe, Bryan posed with Ford on the deck.

"Any customer can have a car of any color he wants—provided it's black," Ford told his advertising staff. Only after a public rebellion reduced sales would he admit that he was not the final arbiter on such matters. His dogmatism increased with his assets, as did his bitter opposition to unions. The Ford Motor Company was run like a feudal dukedom, governed by a mutually distrustful group of executives, most of them without titles. No clear lines of authority or responsibility were anywhere delineated. If he trusted few men, he idolized one who encouraged him to build automobiles—Thomas A. Edison, whose relics Ford collected in a special museum and whose front yard Ford had dug up and carried reverently to Dearborn. He even kept Edison's dying breath in a bottle. Ford was cut from the same pattern. They were the Rover Boys on the Trail of New Trinkets.

An episode from Ford's early career accents his Edison idolatry. In 1914 he hired a special train to make the Detroit to Port Huron run on which Edison had worked as a boy. Ford purchased a vendor's box, and had Edison sell once more his nickel treats. Then, at the end of the run, Ford arranged to have his guest send a telegram from the station where he had served his apprenticeship. The aging Edison ticked out a halting message to his son in New Jersey. Delayed by Ford's historical pageantry, a distant operator broke in with, "Tell that kid to get off the line." He was right. There was a kid on the line. Another one had arranged

100

for his being there. Ford remained, in all but mechanical matters, a child. Like his own Model T's he was a triumph of functionalism, made to go but not to ponder.

Once he got going, Ford was hard to stop. Under him burned the fires of John Calvin's hell; because of him the Reformation invaded the River Rouge. His strict Scotch-Irish rearing left a deep mark on Ford, which wealth and leisure never concealed. Engraved over his fireplace was Franklin's line, "Chop your own wood and it will warm you twice." Laziness was at the bottom of America's troubles. The Bible verses he memorized dealt with hard work, frugality, justification by works. Rich Henry is, among American heroes, the mechanized version of Poor Richard.

If God gave John D. Rockefeller his dimes, he must also have given Ford his dyes. If men would only listen to him and do his bidding, Ford would run them as effectively as his factories. "When I think about the thousands of families dependent upon my enterprise," he said, "there seems to me to be something sacred about the Ford Motor Company."

The money he made neither spoiled nor satisfied him. In the best Calvinistic tradition, he considered himself his brother's keeper—whether his brother liked it or not. Not to remove the strain from his workmen's fingers, but from their souls, did he outlaw smoking in his plants. When he announced a minimum wage of $5 a day, he assumed that only moral people deserved such a rate; he could manage men as well as machines. That he never fully understood the social effects of his action should not make us forget that he never lost his social concern.

In many ways he was a real-life Horatio Alger hero; a farm boy whose pluck and luck never ran out. He always faced twentieth-century problems with nineteenth-century attitudes and solutions. This simplistic quality is one of his chief traits and his strongest tie to folkstyle America.

His mechanical interests became a kind of monomania. He loved the sight of driving pistons and the sound of whirring wheels. Recall another self-made man, Captain Ahab, pursuing the white whale. Henry followed the black Lizzie. Like Ahab, he could not turn back. Ahab knew the species of the whale by the way it spouted; Ford knew the make of a machine by the way it purred. They shared the same styles, the same dreams.

Ford's life stretched from Gettysburg to Hiroshima, from horses to jet planes. For all his mechanical genius, he died at eighty-three in the dark, since his electric power plant failed. In many ways, his was a sad life. His only son died an early death. Most of his friends deserted him. Machines whirred at his bidding, but human actions baffled him. Yet never once did he admit this to himself or his friends. The closest he came was when, after seeing order all about him, he remarked, "It isn't fun any more." The statement stands as the final assessment of Henry Ford's mentality. One of his last projects was to rebuild the schoolhouse of Mary and her lamb. There was ironical truth here, for from the little red school house the mind of Ford never graduated.

Ford was a world hero, especially admired in Russia and Germany. Many Russians placed his picture beside Lenin's to show their esteem. Germans lined up all night to buy securities when he built a plant in the Reich. Books about Ford in a dozen languages show his great influence outside America; what Ford's philosophy will come to mean to the Orient, no one can say. Japan and India have added such terms as "Fordize" and "Fordism" to their vocabularies. Who knows where they might lead millions of machine-starved Asiatics?

After his death Henry Ford entered the realm of legend. To the psychologist he is a mechanical Peter Pan, whose human understanding never increased. To the economist he is Sorcerer's Apprentice, who discovered how to make the broom carry water, but not how to make it stop. Philosophers think of him as Frankenstein, inventor of a robot that became master and conqueror of its maker. For the citizen who dotes on his mass-produced objects, Ford is a Prometheus who brought the secret of a new mechanized fire from heaven. To Europeans he symbolizes our industrial, mass-produced civilization—the full showcase and the empty mind. More than any man of his age he put us on wheels.

In politics, as well as in business, the self-made man continued to have a strong appeal well into the Roosevelt era. One of the most colorful examples was "The Kingfish," Huey P. Long. In Louisiana's bleak, Bible-fearing Winn Parish, he grew up like many a self-made man before him on his father's farm. By pluck, luck, and a lot of hard work he got to law school, where he finished a three-year course in eight months. "I came out of the courtroom running for office," he wrote, after having been elected governor and (in 1932) United States Senator. Showing a profound understanding of the yearnings of rural people, he adopted as his slogan "Every Man a King." Like the original Horatio Alger, who loved to stand around hotel lobbies, Long went there to read dispatches and awe the people. Eventually he personally dictated the appointment of every state official in Louisiana. In Washington he shouted out the secrets of the Senate cloakroom and shook his fist at the President of the United States. While working to prevent Roosevelt's re-election in 1936, he was assassinated in Baton Rouge by a young dentist, Carl Weiss. He would reappear in novels like Adrian Langley's *A Lion Is in the Streets* and Robert Penn Warren's *All the King's Men,* and in Statuary Hall of the National Capitol—perhaps as high an honor as a poor country boy could hope for. A few years later Harry Truman entered the White House. This hickory-hard haberdasher was another self-made man—in his way as remarkable as the Mechanical Messiah. Born in Lamar, Missouri, in 1884, this son of strict Baptist parents had generations of dirt farmers as ancestors. Turned down when he applied for West Point, he served as timekeeper for the Santa Fe railroad and wrapped papers for the *Kansas City Star*. After serving in World War I, he opened a men's clothing store in Kansas City, but it failed. "Big Tom" Pendergast, Democratic machine boss, made him overseer of highways for Jackson County in 1921. From there he rose to the U.S. Senate, Vice Presidency, and Presidency.

Soon all the world knew of the sign on his White House desk: "The buck stops here." The pithy, unadorned motto summed up not only his strengths, but his weaknesses as well. Without a college education, Truman was serving as Chief Executive of the world's most powerful nation. He had the inner strength, confidence, and intuition not only to lead, but to do it well. At the same time he had a strong streak of anti-intellectualism and a lack of flexibility which might, under certain circumstances, have been disastrous. He was, in short, a bona-fide self-made man, with strong folklore overtones. This hardy breed has accomplished incredible things in the past two centuries. But has American lifestyle so altered that they are now one with hand-cranked ice cream freezers and buggy whips? Pluck and luck may go well with the open market place, but with closed-circuit computers . . .

8

Jolly Giants

"Maybe the scholars have been following a false lead.
Maybe popular literature isn't a folk art at all."

BERNARD DEVOTO

"JERUSALEM, Nichols, it's a big Injun!" Gideon Emmons
whispered to Henry Nichols, as their shovels moved more
of the dirt from the body buried in "Stub" Newell's back
yard. And wouldn't *you* say the same thing if, while digging for a well, you uncovered a petrified figure over ten
feet tall, weighing 2990 pounds?

As was customary in rural America, 1869, the local minister was rushed to the scene. "This is not a thing contrived
of man," he quickly concluded, "but the face of one who
lived on the earth, the very image and child of God!" [1]

Next came James Hall, Director of the New York State
Museum, the most distinguished paleontologist in the area.
The creature was, in his words, "the most remarkable object
yet brought to light in this country." (He may have been
right about that.) Crowds thronged to "Giantsville," the
little village of Cardiff, just south of Syracuse, New York.

[1] James Taylor Dunn, *The True, Moral, and Diverting Tale of the
Cardiff Giant* (New York: Macmillan, 1948), p. 5. See also Curtis D.
MacDougal, *Hoaxes* (New York: Dover, 1940), A. C. Drummond and
R. E. Gard, *The Cardiff Giant* (Ithaca, N.Y.: Cornell University Press,
1949), and Louis J. Wolner, "David Hannum and the Cardiff Giant,"
Cortland Country Chronicles, II (Cortland, N.Y.: 1958).

105

A man from New York City offered $100 for a flake of stone from the body. "Stub" Newell's cow shed was turned into a restaurant. A new sign went up—"Warm Meals— Oysters and Oats." Chicago promoters came down to book the Giant; various "only authentic and reliable" guides appeared. David Hannum of Homer (the original David Harum) was soon "as busy as a hummin-bird with two tails" looking after the publicity, which included such poetic outbursts as this:

> And hast Thou walked about (how strange a story)
> In Syracuse more'n 40 years ago
> Before Salt Point had seen one half her glory
> Or Cardiff had a single hut to show?

Phineas T. Barnum offered $60,000 for three months' lease of the Cardiff Giant. Oliver Wendell Holmes bored a hole just behind the left ear (which can still be seen) and declared the Giant "of wonderful anatomical development." Ralph Waldo Emerson was reported to have pronounced it "beyond his depth, very wonderful and undoubtedly ancient." [2]

The Gilded Age was upon us; the era of the jolly giants had begun. Thanks to the efforts of Cornell University's Andrew D. White and Yale's Benjamin Silliman, the truth about the Cardiff hoax was uncovered. George Hull, a tobacco farmer from Binghamton, dreamed up the whole scheme, had the giant carved from a stone quarry in Iowa, and buried in "Stub" Newell's yard to be "discovered" later. Despite all this, the will to believe persisted. A generation later the Syracuse *Post-Standard* could report:

In spite of the admissions of Hull himself that the thing was a gigantic fake, there remained for years those who believed in it.

[2] *Ibid.,* p. 9.

Even today throngs gather round the Cardiff Giant, displayed on the grounds of the New York Historical Association in Cooperstown, New York, to do him homage.

Not from the barnyards of New York, but from the forests of New England did the prototype jolly giant come. Standing amidst the native corn, Carl Sandburg declared, "The people, the bookless people, they made Paul and had him alive long before he got into books." Dust jackets on a dozen Bunyan sagas repeated Sandburg's claim that "Paul is as old as the hills, young as the alphabet." The truth of the matter is that the Bunyan known to the American reading public is younger than Sandburg's *Chicago Poems*.

Undoubtedly there was an oral tradition about king-sized lumberjacks—Mike Blowitz, John Ross, and Paul Bunyan among them—in primitive American lumber camps. Over a century ago C. Lanman observed in *Adventures in the Wilds of the United States and British Provinces* (Philadelphia, 1856) that lumberjacks "possessed a fine eye for the comic and fantastic." The *Northwestern Lumberman* for November 15, 1890, carried an account of Blowitz breaking a 4′ by 4′ oak timber across his arm. Professor Herbert Halpert recorded snatches of Bunyan lore when he interviewed six ex-lumbermen who were in the camps between 1895 and 1907. But this giant—call him Paul Bunyan I— was a localized occupational hero, whose lore never spread far from the bunkhouses. Stories about him were raw, profane, and specialized. To a man who didn't know about a bubble cuffer, conk inspector, farmer splice, gunnysack show, kalispell hop, or ukulele choker, they were incomprehensible. No one far outside a lumber camp had heard of Paul Bunyan before 1910.

Moreover, when the need for brute strength in the forest passed, the feeble flicker that had kept Paul I alive began to die. "By 1910 Paul Bunyan was already moribund," notes

Professor Daniel G. Hoffman. "A generation later he was no longer an important part of living lumberjack folklore."

As old jacks disappeared from the American scene, a fresh crop of antiquarians, admen, and professional writers entered. A new, and very different kind of fake giant—Paul Bunyan II—was born.

We know his birth date—on July 24, 1910, James MacGillivray's "Round River Drive" appeared in the Detroit *News-Tribune*. Paul Bunyan had come into town. A night reporter, MacGillivray later claimed to have written the piece after 3 A.M. at an editor's request. In it he used logging terms like swath line, whiplash, "fellin' out" and "crosscuts brazed together" which were not generally known to urban readers. But at least it was a start.[3]

Four years later Douglas Malloch rewrote MacGillivray's story in doggerel couplets for the *American Lumberman*. Later still, a roving newspaperman, Lee J. Smits, attempted in the Seattle *Star* a 1920 series of Bunyan pieces, which lasted less than two weeks. That same year Constance Rourke examined thoroughly the Bunyan material for the *New Republic*, and asserted that there was no historical prototype for Bunyan.

Paul Bunyan II was alive, but in danger of dying of neglect. Thanks to two remarkable men, Paul not only held his own, but expanded until he became the embodiment of the new fakestyle—a national figure pushy enough to threaten the symbolic position of that old regular, Uncle Sam.

---

[3] MacGillivray claims he heard about Paul while scaling logs on the north branch of the Au Sable River. Another 1910 reference to Paul may be found in the diary of a young schoolteacher, Edward O. Tabor, who was a summer lumberjack at Palmer Junction, Oregon. The only recent claim of authentic Bunyan lore from an "old timer" which I have encountered is Dave Walton's "Lou Sesher Stories: III," in *Keystone Folklore Quarterly*, XII:3 (Fall 1967).

William B. Laughead, the first, left his native Ohio in 1900 to work in Minnesota logging camps when he was still a boy. Fourteen years later the Red River Lumber Company asked him to write a pamphlet "sandwiching in advertisement between stories about Paul Bunyan." Laughead was unsuccessful because "The men to whom our advertising was directed didn't know what we were talking about. And of course Bunyan was completely unknown to the public."

Trying again, he invented an *ersatz* Paul, designed to please the public, not the boys in the bunkhouse. Over 10,000 copies of the "popularized" 1922 edition were distributed, and new additions appeared annually for the next twenty years. The preface included this paragraph:

Everything we tell you about Red River lumber and its manufacture is the Gospel Truth. Everything we tell you about Paul Bunyan is lumberjack mythology. Paul is the legendary hero whose exploits have been related to generations of tenderfeet from time immemorial. We have gathered a few of them up, and pass them on to you with a few trimmings of our own.

Those "few trimmings" included Babe the Blue Ox, Brimstone Bill, and Big Joe the Cook. Laughead was responsible for devising the first pictorial representation of the giant (Paul has a round face, black hair, and a cat's whiskers moustache) which was copyrighted as the Red River Lumber Company trademark. Accompanying the original portrayal is a reminder that "he stands for the quality and service you have the right to expect from Paul Bunyan." Under the picture is the warning that the picture is "registered." How else could one protect so profitable a phony giant?

Eventually journalists, promoters, Chambers of Commerce, and merchants joined the swelling Bunyan crusade.

109

Aided by chauvinism and capitalism, the stories grew. "No one who ever retold a Bunyan story," Laughead complained, "was ever willing to let well enough alone."

Paul's second major manipulator, James F. Stevens, was an acknowledged disciple of Laughead. His education was meager; he was expelled from the eighth grade for chewing tobacco. Determined to become a writer, he contacted H. L. Mencken, who published his first essay in the March 1924 *American Mercury*. When Mencken asked for another article, Stevens did "The Black Duck Dinner," his first Bunyan story. Mencken took it and told him that Alfred Knopf would be interested in publishing his first book. Stevens was elated:

This was suddenly a lighting on the peaks of glory itself. It was the whole thing! Here was my chance to work up from laboring man to literary man. I had succeeded in taking all this rough stuff of Paul Bunyan and working it over and getting it into a form of literary art.[4]

Using Laughead's principal characters he added some of his own (Creampuff Fatty, Hot Biscuit Slim, Hels Helson, Shanty Boy, Mark Beaucoup). His 1925 Paul Bunyan book sold 252,000 copies. Stevens's Paul Bunyan is akin to earlier figures like Davy Crockett, Mike Fink, and Mark Twain's half-man and half-alligator: "powerful as Hercules, indomitable as Spartacus, bellowing like a furious Titan." The lumberjacks are "toiling demigods and sweating heroes." The bunkhouse resounds with the "history of Olympian feats." Stevens has always insisted that there *was* a real Paul Bunyan and that he is carrying on in the literary tradition that goes back to Homer: "I would say he is rooted in the forest

[4] "Oral History Interview with James Stevens, Nov. 12–13, 1957," by Elwood R. Maunder, p. 27. Permission to quote has been obtained from the Forest History Foundation, Inc., of St. Paul, Minn.

earth and that's what the critics evade. They are immune to the poetry of Paul Bunyan."

Stevens has been anxious to trace back those roots and refute the skeptical professors who have plagued him over the years—"fugitives from the lace-curtain class and academic grove who are too greatly troubled about trifles." These fugitives include J. Frank Dobie, who wrote that Stevens "assumes the liberties of a judicial novelist, frequently putting his own dull ideas into the mouths of characters," concocting stories "utterly foreign to the bunkhouse yarn." Another, Carleton C. Ames, toured Minnesota and the drainage basins of the Marinette, Wisconsin, Chippewa, and St. Croix rivers, seeking Bunyan informants. He found none. "It seems incredible that if the Paul Bunyan yarns had any kind of circulation during the heyday of the loggers, they should not have come to the attention of at least some people here," he wrote. B. A. Botkin combed the Library of Congress, but found no early Bunyan material. Mrs. Grace S. McClure, State Librarian of Michigan and a native of the Saginaw region, had hundreds of interviews with lumbermen, but never turned up a single authentic Bunyan story; she knows of no literary accounts in Michigan predating the items we have mentioned. Stevens has no sympathy with those who "sweated their pale blood to prove the legend a hoax, only to expose themselves as futile dabblers in nonsense." But he and his wife both sweated to confound their confounders. They spent months searching for Bunyan references in old journals and papers. In Stevens's words:

My wife would say a little prayer every evening as she'd go over to the library that this time she would at least come on a name of someone connected with the lumber industry or logging who had a name that would sound or seem like "Paul Bunyan." But this prayer remained unanswered. We just found nothing of the kind.

111

In short, Stevens (unlike Laughead) confused folklore and fakelore. He was so close to his own fabrications that he could not distinguish them from an earlier style, idiom, and origin. Paul Bunyan II is a pseudo-folk hero of twentieth-century mass culture, contrived and used by writers, journalists and promoters.

So are many other jolly giants, modeled on Paul, but less convincing and captivating. Prominent among these is Joe Magarac, "folk" hero of the steel mills and Slavic workers in them. The word Magarac, existing only in the Croatian and Serbian, has strong vulgar connotations, somewhat like the word "bloody" for the English. The fakestyle author, in this case, was Owen Francis, who published six Magarac articles in *Scribner's* between 1930 and 1935. In them he refers to the "child-like delight" of the Slavs, in the condescending manner that Rudyard Kipling described the Africans in the days of the White Man's Burden. Frequently Francis uses the word "Hunkie," considered degrading and insulting by the Hungarians. He never got inside the minds of the people with whom he talked. He came to exploit their material, not to understand them. A man with such a purpose might well accept seriously, and put into print, what he did not recognize as a joke at his own expense.

Owen Francis's accounts did not create much of a stir when they were published. Later writers promoted Joe Magarac as part of their advertising program. One would hardly expect them to recognize Francis's mistakes. Poets and folklorists gradually heard of Magarac. In the 1940s, with the tremendous rise of folklore interest and publication, Joe came into his own. In a story called "This Side of the Iron Curtain and Glad of It," published in the July 1948 *U.S. Steel News,* Joe was the answer to another powerful Joe (Stalin) in the U.S.S.R. Once Joe made the prominent anthologies, his position as a folk hero, in a major American industry that ought to have one, was taken for granted. Demand had created a hero where one actually didn't exist, but seldom in all our history has one been manufactured by such a back-handed process.

The Magarac tales have not yet entered the workers' oral tradition, even two decades after Francis released Magarac to the country. There are enough folklore elements in the Magarac tale—some in the older Bunyan tradition, some akin to the actual oral tales that do exist among steel men— to keep the general reading public unaware of the hoax worked first on Francis, then on the anthologists, and finally on them.

There was an actual Swede, Henny Palm, who could make horseshoes and pretzels out of bar stock with his bare hands. Another, Mike Lesnovich, made neckties out of thick bars. Stories of men who could go unprotected into furnaces, who could break world sprint records when a hot bar ran wild, and who could lift huge weights, naturally circulate in an industry where physical strength and endurance are required and admired.

To think there was an authentic steel folk hero named Joe might not make one a Magarac, but it certainly would indicate he was unaware of the process by which twentieth-century American fakelore has been created.

Open almost any book of American "folklore," and a whole parade of fakestyle giants will strut before your eyes. Despite editors' claims, Pecos Bill didn't come from the Wild West, but the typewriter of Edward ("Tex") O'Reilly. Annie Christmas's spicy saga does not stem from the New Orleans brothels, but the imagination of Lyle Saxon. Margaret Montague dreamed up two-ton Tony Beaver. Daddy Joe was contrived by Stewart Holbrook, Big Mose by Herbert Asbury, Whiskey Jack by Charles Brown, Strap Buckner by Florence Barns—jolly giants all. "Maybe the scholars have been following a false lead," Bernard DeVoto rightly concluded in 1955. "Maybe popular literature isn't a folk art at all."

Certainly that is the conclusion one reaches when he sees how industries have "created" folk literature as publicity stunts. Beware of books that promise, for example, "a good sloshing barrelful of oil folklore, complete with 'creekology' and doodlebuggers." [5] There may have been (and apparently there was) a real Gib Morgan, who drilled for oil after the Civil War and served as a sort of Muenchhausen in wildcatting days. But by the time one sees his picture in high-priced magazine ads by major oil companies, he is apt to be dealing with a very different Gib Morgan.

One instinctively prefers the company of the cape and mask jolly giants who came to light in the 1930s and 1940s in the graphic art of comic books. The first of these two-dimensional super-heroes was Superman, who first appeared in *Action Comics,* June 1938. "The advent of the super-hero was a bizarre comeuppance for the American dream," writes Jules Feiffer. "Horatio Alger could no longer make it on his own. He needed 'Shazam'!" [6]

There had been previous comic heroes like the Green Hornet, Speed Saunders, and Flash Gordon; but they were dwarfed by Joe Shuster's paragon who ran up the side of dams, stopped two-ton trucks, and hurdled skyscrapers in a fashion that even Paul Bunyan would have envied. To provide adequate tension the story was peopled with super-

[5] Mody C. Boatright, *Gib Morgan, Minstrel of the Oil Fields* (Dallas, Texas: Southern Methodist University Press, 1945); and *Folklore of the Oil Industry* (Dallas, Texas: Southern Methodist University Press, 1963).

[6] Jules Feiffer, *The Great Comic Book Heroes* (New York: Dial, 1965), p. 18. For a more philosophic analysis, see N. W. Yates, *The American Humorists: Conscience of the Twentieth Century* (Ames, Iowa: Iowa State University Press, 1964). See also David M. White and Robert H. Abel, *The Funnies: An American Idiom* (New York: Macmillan, 1963) and Coulter Waugh, *The Comics* (New York: Macmillan, 1947).

villains, super-mad scientists, and super-Orientals. Like the other giants we have mentioned, Superman wasn't much on such a sissy pursuit as girl-chasing. In fact, the story's heroine, Lois Lane, chased *him*. "The ideal of masculine strength," Feiffer observes, "whether Gary Cooper's, Li'l Abner's, or Superman's, is for one to be so virile and handsome, to be in such a position of strength that he need never go near girls. Except to help them. And then get the hell out." [7]

The immediate and enormous success of Superman encouraged a rash of successors, first in the comics, then in the movies, then (for hour after hour) on the television screen. Any red-blooded American can rattle off some of the names—Captain Marvel, Batman, Human Torch, The Flash, The Spectre, Hawkman, Wonder Woman, Sub Mariner, Captain America, Plastic Man, The Spirit. Our jolly giants have, in the main, left the forests, steel mills, and oil-fields for scientific laboratories and outer space—for the strange bubbly world of glass tubing, flashing lights, and gobbledygook. Comic book titles ransacked the English language for graphic adjectives—*startling, whiz, astounding, star-spangled, mystic, all-flash, crash,* and *smash,* for example. Suddenly our jolly giants were coming in all shapes, sizes, and disguises—robots, webbed men, ghost men, super dwarfs, flexible-sized men, doll men, white streaks, plastic men. Not only size and shape, but ideology was brought to bear on the confused scene. Superman was described as the "Lenin of super-heroes," with Captain Marvel acting as his Trotsky. Others complained that Superman was far too puritanical; if you didn't come from his planet, you couldn't even be super. Once again we see the American tendency toward exaggeration and gigantism

[7] *Ibid.,* p. 21.

exerting itself. There was another common denominator—moral purity. This edict from the *Code of the Comic Magazine Association of America* sums it up nicely: "In every instance good shall triumph over evil and the criminal punished for his misdeeds."

World War II gave the jolly giants more than enough new assignments and a whole new stable of Nazi and Oriental villains. Suddenly every superman had a war assignment and a flag which he waved incessantly. Real people got into the act. In a typical last-panel one sees F.D.R. or J. Edgar Hoover looking up into the giant's clear-blue eyes and saying:

My son, you are a true courageous American. You have saved America from the slimy clutches of master spies and saboteurs. The youth of our country can well look upon you as a model American!

Wars change, fads come, and the jolly giants adjust accordingly. But there will always be a space for them, whatever their guise, on the American Olympus. Just as myth is a charter of society, heroes are the personification of its ethos. The jolly giant is you, and he is me—writ large.

9

Smooth Roughnecks

Caesar and Cicero shall bow
And ancient warriors famous
Before the myrtle-wreathed brow
Of Buffalo Williamus.

WESTERN BALLAD

THERE he was, taking a snort in the theater wing before going on stage. (Snorts seemed to help the play.) By 1876, Buffalo Bill had tamed the West sufficiently to come East and reenact his role in the process. But during an evening performance in Baltimore someone rushed up with a telegram from Phil Sheridan. The Sioux were on the war path. Would Cody return immediately to scout for the U.S. Army? No time for a cue now. Cody dashed on the stage, read the message, and announced he was going. The crowd roared approval as he dashed off for the station. Several days later he disembarked in Cheyenne, Wyoming, still wearing his theatrical costume with the gold lace and silver buttons. "Let's go!" he shouted. They went.

Soon he "took the first scalp for Custer," or so the American public was told. Did Cody actually kill Chief Tall Bull, or was the tall bull in the story? *The New York World* credited Lieutenant Hayes with the Chief's death, but in Cody's autobiography, he was the hero, disposing of the Chief by firing the fatal shot at 400 yards. In subsequent accounts Cody sneaked ever closer. By the time he had put

117

True Tales in his publisher's hands, the distance was down to thirty yards. When Cody decided to reenact "with historical accuracy" the killing in his show, he disposed of the unfortunate Tall Bull with a knife. He wasn't disturbed when his fellow campaigner Lute North swore under oath that his brother Frank North had killed the Indian. "I asked Frank why he didn't correct Cody, but he just laughed and said he wasn't in show business." Lute added, nor the legend-making business, either.

For years Cody carried the newspaper account of the Tall Bull adventure which read: "Among those killed was the noted chief Tall Bull, killed by Cody, Chief of Scouts." Such a story had appeared in *The New York Herald*, but not the "killed by Cody, Chief of Scouts." A press agent had added it to the version Cody not only displayed, but believed.

Whether or not Buffalo Bill took the first scalp for Custer he carried one around with him for years afterwards. Finally an army officer offered him $50 if he would get rid of it. Never a man to treat cold cash lightly, Cody agreed, and mailed the trophy back to his wife. "Will Cody, don't you ever send me another Indian scalp as long as you live," she said. "I'll do better than that," he replied. "I'll never scalp another Injun!" He never did—except in dozens of dime novels and in the imaginations of thousands of Americans in the Gilded Age.

The scalp story is not only typical of Bill Cody, but the fakestyle of which he was a past master. Daniel Boone walked; Buffalo Bill rode a white horse. The tame roughneck was the *ersatz* Prince of the Plains. With him glass balls supplanted eyeballs as scout's targets. He insisted to the end that he stood most of his life between savagery and civilization. By paying your admission and going to the arena, you could see History ride by.

The sham that was his act was mirrored in the irony

118

that was his life. He knew what it was to be alone on the bone-haunted plains; in a creaking railroad car clicking off endless miles; in a foreign land. Women doted on him, but his own wife sought divorce. Admirers promised to devote their lives to him, but stayed only long enough to fleece him. Sick children improved at his touch; his only son died in his arms. Galloping forward on his white horse, he looked as free as the air; but he was putty in the hands of others. Despite his large income, Cody finally petitioned the Federal government for the $10-monthly Congressional medal-holders dole. In his twilight years he had to appear daily to avoid bankruptcy, and go through every performance with the fear of death in the arena. Here was poverty in opulence, chagrin in victory, despair in hollow triumph.[1]

Born in Scott County, Iowa, in 1846, William Frederick Cody was the son of a farmer who died of pneumonia. The young boy became the head of the family, and went to work for Russell and Majors of overland freighting fame. In the Civil War he was a jay-hawker who stole horses from slave owners, and private in the 7th Kansas Cavalry. After marrying Louisa Frederici in 1866, Cody was employed to hunt buffaloes and feed construction crews on the Kansas Pacific Railroad. Several months at this saw Cody bag (by his own tabulation) 4280 buffaloes and earn the nickname "Buffalo Bill." The Cody legend began to grow. Vivacious and popular, Cody was greeted as he rode through camp by such ditties as this:

> Buffalo Bill, Buffalo Bill,
> Never missed and never will;
> Always aims and shoots to kill,
> And the company pays his buffalo bill.

[1] See Richard J. Walsh, *The Making of Buffalo Bill: A Study in Heroics* (Indianapolis, Ind.: Bobbs-Merrill, 1928); and the Cody files at the Denver Public Library.

While he sent many a buffalo to the happy hunting ground, Cody didn't outdistance his rival. "Buffalo Jones" surpassed Cody without half trying. Born Charles Jesse Jones, this Plains adventurer went into the Arctic after musk-oxen, where he hunted in temperatures of 50° F. below zero, was attacked by wolves, encountered hydrophobia among his animals, and beat off carnivorous insects. Yet who knew of "Buffalo Jones"? No one but the buffaloes.

When construction work stopped and the buffalo market collapsed, Cody was out of work. He turned to army scouting and served under Generals Sheridan and Carr. By 1873 there was no further need of his services. Bill Cody was once more unemployed. Thus, the full-time Plains career of America's best-known plainsman ended when he was in his early twenties. Bill Cody reversed Horace Greeley's famous dictum. He thought his future rested with such a job as coachman or fire-engine driver. Eastward he went, but the buffalo legend went with him. By 1900 he had become more of a scout than he ever dreamed of in the West—the best example of the fakelife hero that his generation produced.

He was the prototype smooth roughneck—the well-oiled, highly dramatic performer of fantasies which the audience easily associated with reality. With Cody there was enough reality, to begin with, so that even he fell heir to the deception. That was part of his charm and his strength. With the help of three shrewd image-makers he created the most successful Wild West Show ever seen in America. The first, Edward Zen Judson, spent his life writing incredible stories. Yet none of the tales he told was more extraordinary than the life he actually lived.[2]

---

[2] See James Monaghan, *The Great Rascal* (Boston: Little, Brown and Co., 1952) for a full biographical study.

Born in Harpersfield, New York, young Edward grew up in a home full of hero stories—his father wrote biographies of George Washington and Patrick Henry, as well as a lengthy volume on *Sages and Heroes of the American Revolution*. Appointed a midshipman at seventeen, Edward came out of his corner fighting. In a single day he challenged thirteen midshipmen to duels, fought seven, marked four for life, and emerged without a scratch.

But instead of going to sea, Judson went to the Seminole Indian War, where he had to kill a large jaguar (or so he insisted) with his bare hands. Back in Paducah, he adopted a pen name and began to publish *Ned Buntline's Own*. Thus was opened a literary career that would include at least 400 novels, one of which (a 60,000-word thriller) he wrote in a single week.

Let no one think he did nothing but turn out manuscripts. For example, he captured two murderers single-handed and unarmed. Then Judson found it necessary to kill William Porterfield, who was foolish enough to complain because Buntline committed adultery with his wife. For this the local citizens put a rope around Ned's neck, and strung him up on a tree. The rope broke. The Sheriff took Buntline back to jail, presumably to die. Instead he escaped. "I hasten to tell you I am worth ten men yet!" he wrote to a friend. "I expect to leave here for New York in three or four days." His tasks as image-maker had not yet begun.

Escaping to New York City he married, re-issued *Ned Buntline's Own,* and led the mob in the 1849 Astor Place riot in which 21 people were killed. Convicted and imprisoned on Blackwell's Island, Judson wrote a series of novels there. When released he was carried home on admirers' shoulders and honored with a torchlight parade. So questionable was his role in directing the "Know Nothing" Party that he had to flee to the Adirondacks in

1856, where before long he acquired a new home and wife.

Soon the drums of the Civil War were beating; Buntline could never resist such a sound. He became a sergeant in the First New York Mounted Rifles, but for some reason he was dismissed from the service after a furlough in New York which entailed, among other things, marrying Mrs. Lavance Swart. A month's confinement at Fort Hamilton allowed him to write two thrillers. To recuperate from his war experiences and get new copy for his stories, he traveled westward in the late 1860s. While at Fort McPherson in 1869 he encountered an obscure scout who was to become a western hero—"Buffalo Bill" Cody.

Cody has recorded his first impression of Buntline in his *Autobiography*. "He was rather stoutly built, and wore a blue military coat. On the left breast were pinned about 20 gold medals and badges of secret societies. He walked a little lame as he approached us. I told Major Brown he looked like a soldier—but what a good mark to shoot at on the left breast!"

Cody must have coveted the medals, especially the head of George Washington on a gold shield with two American flags crossed. How he must have jumped into the saddle when Buntline suggested it! Cody was no more impressed than Buntline, who announced in the *Weekly* that he was at work on "Buffalo Bill, the King of Border Men." The Cody that appeared in the early dime novels was modeled on Boone, trailblazer in the Appalachians; he had Leather-stocking's humility and skills, and seemed more designed for Kentucky than Kansas. Buntline knew more about what the public wanted than he did about what Cody had actually done. On this basis he made Buffalo Bill a literary hero.

Buntline only began his services by making Cody a popular dime-novel hero. Impressed with his discovery, he persuaded Buffalo Bill to come to Chicago and try the drama.

Buntline would write the play, and Cody would be the hero. With "Texas Jack" Omohundro (who hailed from Virginia) Cody came east in December, 1876. In his enthusiasm Buntline had forgotten to hire a cast, rent a theater, or write a play. While Cody and Omohundro rounded up extras on the Chicago streets, Buntline rented a theater and sat down to compose a suitable piece. Four hours later *The Scouts of the Plains* was completed and hotel bell hops were busy copying the parts. In reporting the play and the conditions under which it was written, one vitriolic reviewer speculated as to why he had taken so long. Another one thought that "on the whole it is not probable that Chicago will ever look upon the like again. Such a combination of incongruous drama, execrable acting, renowned performers, mixed audience, intolerable stench, scalping, blood and thunder, is not likely to be vouchsafed to a city a second time, even Chicago."

The audience was more tolerant than the reviewer. They saw that the play was *not* the thing—only the vehicle for the ritual reenactment of the triumph of an admirable roughneck. To this very day, no one can accuse most Westerns of contributing much to the realm of immortal drama. Given enough blood and thunder, most Americans feel quite well satisfied.

Buffalo Bill—the scout for whom the Wild West held no cause for fear—broke into a cold sweat when confronted with the footlights of a theater. Not so with bumptious Buntline. He preferred benches to buffalo any day. So confident he could carry off his own part in the performance that he hadn't bothered to write out lines, Ned hastened to assure Cody that the plot was simple and sure-fire. The Indians were to capture Cody and prepare to kill him. In the nick of time "Texas Jack" and Buntline would save him from the burning stake and shout, "Now come on, you

Redskins!" The trio would proceed to avenge themselves on the newly hired extras until each had died an excruciating death, and the audience was choking with smoke. They would love it, the amateur author predicted.

They did. From the moment Buntline rescued the utterly speechless Cody by asking "Where have you been lately, Bill?" until the last Indian died, they cheered and applauded the West-brought-indoors. From Buntline's facile pen more articles and books came—*Buffalo Bill, Buffalo Bill's Best Shot,* and *Buffalo Bill's Last Victory.* With a man like Judson to dream up adventures, what chance had Cody to remain mortal? More than any other publicist, Buntline saw the time had come to exploit the plainsman. So he grafted the type on to the earlier pattern of the woodsman and hunter. He gave a continuity to the hero worship of a nation committed to Manifest Destiny. For him Cody was the exemplar of the type, worthy of following the path of Daniel Boone, Davy Crockett, and Kit Carson. A grateful Cody wanted to name his son after Buntline, but was convinced that he was historically obligated to name him Kit Carson. Eventually the restless Buntline tired of Cody and moved on to other ventures. But he had laid the foundation of an American legend, and with his inherent sense of popular taste made of it a formidable thing.

Buntline introduced Cody to the man who continued the cultivation of the Buffalo Bill legend—"Arizona John" Burke, who came from the District of Columbia. His early life was spent on the road, as stock-company actor, acrobatic troupe manager, and freelance journalist. Meeting Cody had a profound effect on him. "I have met a god," said Burke, and went on saying all the rest of his life. Motivated by this belief, he devoted years to making the rounds of newspaper offices, turning out stories and interviews, defending Cody against slander, inventing new fictions to supplement those that succumbed to reality. Fair-weather friends dropped the aging and decrepit Cody, but Burke stood by to the end. It was for "Arizona John" that Cody called on his deathbed.

Putting aside his Prince Albert and cultivated whiskers (which he had worn flying-buttress style), John Burke went "Western." Gentleman Johnny became Arizona John. When Buntline and Cody separated, Burke assumed command of the already thriving Buffalo Bill story and expanded its basis and appeal. Henry Nash Smith has summed up Burke's accomplishments in *Virgin Land:*

> To Burke belongs the credit for carrying through the major revision of the character of Buffalo Bill as Buntline had originally conceived it . . . He was to become an epic hero laden with the enormous weight of universal history. He was to be placed beside Boone and Fremont and Carson in the roster of American heroes.

Burke so infused myth into history that no completely reliable biography of Cody has been or ever will be written. As troupe manager, press agent, and personal adviser, Burke developed a thesis: "Buffalo Bill stands unchallenged as the Chevalier Bayard of American bordermen; he was the guide to the New World of the mighty West, and his name ranks with those few immortals who were not born to die." Flamboyant, rhetorical, ridiculous? Cody's generation did not think so, at home or abroad. At this distance, our Victorian grandfathers might have been gullible. But since we are at this distance, how can we say—we who never saw Buffalo Bill on his white horse?

While working on Cody's reputation, Burke found a female counterpart. Little Annie Oakley, girl sharpshooter who ranks with Calamity Jane as one of the two female hero symbols of the West. Star of Irving Berlin's *Annie*

Get Your Gun, she was, in part, the invention of John Burke's press agentry. "Little Missy," as Cody called her, brought a feminine touch to the show in the days when it became an American institution. Annie was impressed with Burke's Cody. "Our outfit was more like a clan than a show business," she wrote. "We remained just one big family with Buffalo Bill at its head." And with Arizona John Burke as its brain.

Everybody liked rotund "Arizona John." All doors were open to him as he described the immortal buffalo hunter. He was welcome in newspaper, railway, and theatrical offices. Even when editors doubted his tales, they printed them. Burke could secure railroad cars when none were to be had, rent theaters already under contract, strike a chord so delicately balanced between sentimentality and savagery that skeptics found themselves standing at the box office. When scandal plagued Cody, Burke had some plausible explanation to divert attention. He had a facility with Indians, and controlled them when firewater jeopardized the company. Kipling could have had Burke in mind when he spoke of the man who could talk with kings and yet not lose the common touch. Burke's power and enthusiasm came from unquestioning devotion. He believed in Cody as much, and probably more, than Cody believed in himself.

Burke tried to adjust his idol to the town they were playing. In Boston Cody was nine-tenths Irish, descended from an ancient line of Irish kings. Down the line at New Haven, Cody would become a spiritual brother of Garibaldi and Italian patriots who died in the Risorgimento. When the troupe pulled into a Germanic town in Wisconsin or Minnesota, the original spelling of Cody was "Koditz." Those who realized that Burke was merely making Cody all things to all men did not object. The English poet Coleridge called it the willing suspension of disbelief.

126

When toward the end, Cody became a tool in bankers' hands, facing bankruptcy and disgrace, Burke stayed on. He sacrificed his career, salary, almost the necessities of life for Cody. The more hard-pressed he became, the more Burke's essential character grew. The plump promoter became a man in those last nightmare years. Courtney Ryler Cooper has given us this account:

One wintry morning in Denver, I watched Burke, whiskers flying, threadbare coat pulled tight around his rotund form, set forth to what I knew by experience would be a meager breakfast. But in ten minutes he was back at the circus offices, a copy of *The New York Times* tucked under his arm.

"You didn't take long for breakfast, Major," I said. He grew red-faced.

"Well, I—I just decided I didn't want any," came at last. "I noticed this *New York Times,* and I just thought I'd see whether it had anything to say about the Colonel. He's in New York now, you know."

I bought the Major's breakfast that day. The ten cents with which he had started for his coffee and rolls—had gone upon the altar of his adoration.[3]

That a person so different from John Burke in background, temperament, and interest as Prentiss Ingraham could have been a Cody hero-maker shows more things were wrought by Bill than buffaloes dream of. "The only request I have to make, Ingraham," Cody said to the most prolific pulp writer in American history, "is that you will not depict me with an axe in one hand and a war club in the other, knocking out brains." If Ingraham honored the request, it was the only known method of killing Indians his dime-novel hero didn't employ. Under his *nom de guerre* of Buffalo Bill he performed such prodigious feats that even

---

[3] Quoted by Richard Walsh, *op. cit.,* p. 355.

Cody finally gasped and exclaimed, "Gosh, the things they write!"

Prentiss Ingraham lived a full life before he became Cody's staff writer. Born in Natchez, Mississippi, he became a Confederate officer at eighteen, fighting with Withers's Mississippi Regiment of light artillery. At twenty he was a Commander of Scouts—a title he applied effectively to Cody in the years ahead. Craving action after the Confederacy surrendered, this young firebrand moved to Mexico to fight with Juarez against the French. As a soldier of fortune he fought in South America, Austria, Crete, and Egypt. In Cuba, where he was both an army colonel and naval captain, the Spanish condemned him to death. Ingraham escaped and returned to the United States. Afterwards he worked for Beadle and Adams, the publishing house that from 1856 to 1898 sold tens of thousands of dime novels and penny dreadfuls to the American public.[4] The Southern colonel with the slouch hat and walrus mustache was their most successful writer. Composing in longhand, Ingraham completed nearly a thousand novels.

Buffalo Bill, whom he met on a trip west, was his favorite heroic model. Over two hundred Buffalo Bill titles were signed or ghost written by Ingraham—a Cody library turned out by one man in two decades. The feat has not been equaled. Ingraham also wrote *The Cowboy Clan or the Tigress of Texas* (1887) which started a new genre. Three of his episodes (throwing a steer by the horns, busting bronchos, picking up a neckerchief from the ground on a galloping horse) became stock items for the cowboy hero. In a vain effort to keep them for his own, Ingraham tried to discredit imitators: "Beware of Wild West imitations of the Buffalo

---

[4] For an account of the firm see Albert Johannsen's *The House of Beadle and Adams* (Norman, Oklahoma: University of Oklahoma Press, 1950), 2 vols.

128

Bill Stories. This is the only authentic account of Colonel William F. Cody, known all over the world as King of Scouts."

Ingraham, Burke, and Buntline crowned him, then made millions of Americans his courtiers. The foundation on which they built was historical, but the superstructure was fictional. The resulting fakestyle would later put Disneyland in the West that Buffalo Bill always claimed he had helped to conquer.

Compared with the more sophisticated methods of film producers, disc jockeys, and public relations firms, the architects of the Cody legend look like simple fellows. Yet they had a sure touch, and did a remarkable job. Historians point to the vulgarity and shoddiness of the Cody saga. They contrast his flamboyant accounts of the frontier with the well-documented and sober accounts of Professor Frederick Jackson Turner and his followers. In terms of cultural impact, we should not let the fact-finders claim too much for their side. While historians are applauding Frederick Jackson Turner, television and the popular imagination are following Buffalo Bill.[5]

In the years when Turner was compiling data and Cody was dramatizing the Wild West, America was becoming a major urban industrial power. No longer could a hero gallop up on horseback to save the fair maiden. Another kind of daredevil must appear; another model of the smooth roughneck which Cody had implanted on the American mind. Soon he would dominate the same newsstands that grew rich off Buffalo Bill—first as the private eye and then as the secret agent. The center of gravity moved and the pace quickened as the nineteenth century ended; the hero

[5] Archie H. Jones, "Cops, Robbers, Heroes and Anti-Heroines," *Journal of Popular Culture*, I, No. 2 (Fall 1967), p. 117.

moved with it. He would give up his faithful horse for a flashy convertible. The background changed from mountains to martinis; but the heroic show went on.

This was demonstrated by the *New Nick Carter Weekly,* one of the most influential pulp publications of the early 1900s. Nick had a clear formula for survival, expressed in a dime novel entitled *The Compact of Death or Nick Carter's Singed Hair Clew:* "A man of evil instincts is . . . no match for the cool, shrewd, self-contained man of integrity and intelligence." (Notice the adjective *cool.* Half a century later it would become the key to a new heroic type.) Not even the Mafia was a match for Nick. In an age mesmerized by the powers of science, this rough-and-tumble private eye explained his "method" to a police chief in *A Princess of the Underworld or the Mysterious Burglary at Lakeview:*

Let us, for want of a better word, call it induction. When I came here to see you and you told me about that series of burglaries, you gave me that which represents the simple figure two. I take that figure two, put it in my pocket, so to speak, and I set out at once to find enough to add to that figure . . . in order to make the total four. I don't deduct, I add.[6]

Instead of inventing his "method," the dime novelists learned it from Edgar Allan Poe (who has the best claim to having anticipated this heroic style) and England's Conan Doyle. One can also make a case for James Fenimore Cooper's influence through his obsession with tracking skills and violent Indian encounters.[7] The tendency to identify manhood with a capacity for physical violence has a long history in America.

[6] Chickering Carter, editor, *New Nick Carter Weekly* (New York: June 25, 1904), p. 2.
[7] This point is developed by Agatha Christie in her Introduction to *Omnibus of Crime* (New York: Dodd, Mead and Co., 1929).

130

During the 1920s and '30s variations of the earlier rough-and-tumble hero appeared in American fiction: the private detective, the proletarian, and the tough guy.[8] Critic Edmund Wilson called their creators "The Boys in the Back Room": James M. Cain, John O'Hara, John Steinbeck, William Saroyan, and Nathanael West. Despite variations of style and character development, there emerges from this group a tough vision of life which can be summarized with specific traits. The tone is hard-boiled, dispassionate, unglamorous. Syntax and grammar reflect those of the characters; the first-person point of view is used continuously. Characters are solid, elemental, two-dimensional. We are almost always in a large, impersonal city. The action is fast and furious.[9] This is the natural habitat of the heroic roughneck. Saul Bellow calls it in *The Dangling Man* (1944), "hardboiled-dom":

Do you have an inner life? It is nobody's business but your own. Do you have emotions? Strangle them. To a degree, everybody obeys this code.

Heroes cut from this pattern managed to invade the bucolic world of the Western disguised as the television paragon Paladin, with his engraved calling card reading "Have Gun—Will Travel." Unlike earlier range roughnecks, Paladin specializes in food, wine, and literature, as well as riding and shooting. On occasion he ends a speech with lines from Keats or Omar Khayyam; in the latter case he identifies the

---

8 See Philip Durham, *Down These Mean Streets a Man Must Go: Raymond Chandler's Knight* (Durham, N.C.: University of North Carolina Press, 1963); David Madden, ed., *Tough Guys Writers of the Thirties* (Carbondale, Ill.: University of Southern Illinois Press, 1968); and David Madden, ed., *Proletarian Writers of the Thirties* (Carbondale, Ill.: University of Southern Illinois Press, 1968).

9 David Madden, "James M. Cain: Twenty-Minute Egg of the Hard-Boiled School," *Journal of Popular Culture* (Winter 1967).

translator. On the other pole from this suave avenger is bully-boy Mike Hammer, brutal protagonist in Mickey Spillane's hard-boiled novels. The key work is *quick*. "You have to be quick, and you have to be able, or you become one of the devoured, and if you kill first, no matter how and no matter who, you can live. But you have to be quick. And able, or you'll be dead." [10]

The action has moved from the open plains to the city streets, but our hero is still the wanderer, without possessions, family, or a permanent home. Fate thrusts him into a life of violence which he cannot escape.

As he moves into the urban jungle Hammer reaffirms the Puritan strain in the American hero myth. The world is corrupted and unredeemed; our hero has to do it all himself. Society is helpless and the justice toward which he points is that of Jahweh, not Jesus—strictly an eye for an eye all the way.

Equally erotic and violent, if not so sternly moralistic, is the world of Dashiell Hammett's smooth roughneck, Sam Spade. In the average book one finds Sam making love to three or four sexually magnetic women, consuming bottles of liquor, bashing in assorted heads, and losing a few teeth of his own. It is like the enmity between animals. There is nothing personal in it.[11]

Whatever else he was, the roughneck of Buffalo Bill's generation was never impersonal. The age which he epitomized had a tender, sentimental streak right underneath its stylized exterior; Cody himself was hopelessly romantic. Changes in the roughneck mirror vast alterations in every aspect of American life. The frontier scout was soon obsolete. In his place stood the city detective. By the mid-

[10] Mickey Spillane, *My Gun Is Quick* (New York: Signet, 1960), p. 1.
[11] Leo Gurko, *Heroes, Highbrows, and the Popular Mind* (Indianapolis, Ind.: Bobbs-Merrill, 1953), p. 188.

twentieth century crime has replaced detection, bully boys the old detectives. Summarizing adventure stories of the 1950s, full of sadism, homosexuality, and flagellation, Ben Ray Redman found them improbable, incredible, absurd.[12] By then the Absurd Hero dominated the scene, as we shall see in Chapter 13. Still, as with the earlier, smoother roughnecks, the emphasis was on fantasy and pseudosignificance. In his own way, the roughneck is still "taking a scalp for Custer," just as Cody allegedly did. Thus comes the illusion of being released from guilt, and of restoring justice to a Darwinian universe. No hero can hope to do more than this.

[12] Ben Ray Redman, "Decline and Fall of the Whodunit," *Saturday Review*, XXXV (May 31, 1952), p. 8.

10

Poor Whites

"Mah land!"

JETER LESTER, in *Tobacco Road* (1932).

GOD knows the Clarks didn't start out to be heroes. They barely escaped the sheriff's clutches when they sailed for seventeenth-century Virginia. The head of the clan chose the wrong (at least, the losing) side of Bacon's Rebellion. His descendants hid out during the Revolution, but the next generation got all fouled up in the War of 1812. Begun in confusion and ended without victory, the war was hard on heroes in general. How can an army produce heroes when it turns tail and runs from the Redcoats?

At least Dolley Madison carried off the Declaration of Independence from burning Washington, Old Hickory held out against the British at New Orleans, and Joe Clark laid hold of a strip of land up Irish Creek. A genuine hillbilly, he earned a spot in American folklore—and paved the way for fakestyle hillbillies who created a style of their own in the twentieth century.

Joe enlisted in 1812, as a patriot from Henrico County, Virginia. Though his military career was not distinguished, at least he did not desert. For this Virginia was grateful— not enough to pay his back wages, but to offer Joe and his brother Nelson free land on the frontier. Being of a mind

134

to move out where there was elbow room, the Clark boys were elated. Then they saw the land. It was mostly straight up.

The Irish Creek district of Rockbridge County, covering the western slope of the Blue Ridge Mountains, was and is remote, rocky, and rugged. Inaccessible even by mountain standards, this corner of the county had been avoided by early Scotch-Irish settlers, then selected as the place to exile migrant Indians with smallpox. The Indians that survived intermarried with fugitive Negroes and Revolutionary War deserters who fled to this sheriffless haven. By the time the Clarks reached Irish Creek in 1815, it was a bona-fide example of the American melting pot.

This didn't faze the Clarks. Having left Tidewater, they intended to make a life here. So they married Indian girls, built log cabins, and cleared trees for a patch of corn. Joe's great energy and good sense won for him a place of leadership in the area. Here Darwin's law prevailed, and Joe Clark was the fittest.

The winters were cold and the nights were long; Joe Clark had two dozen children. Before long, his progeny outnumbered everyone else from Wigwam Mountain to Norvells Flats. They still do.

The Clark Kingdom has had no chroniclers. Historians have ignored them completely. No Ph.D. has studied their close-knit exclusive world; there are no scholarly documents to lure the literate up-creek. But there *is* something there, for anyone who bothers to look—a lively body of folklore, indigenous, dewy-fresh. The distilled experience of two centuries of birthing, living, and dying is passed on orally, in tales, proverbs, and songs. They tell of the mystery and wonder of the earth; they are history transmuted into poetry.

For generations the Clarks have sung about their tribal

135

patriarch who came to the Unpromising Land—Joe, a genuine king-sized cockalorum demigod:

> Old Joe Clark had a mule
> His name was Morgan Brown;
> Every tooth in that mule's head
> Was sixteen inches around.
>
> Old Joe Clark had a cow
> She was muley born;
> It took a jaybird a week'n half
> To fly from horn to horn.
>
> I went down to old Joe's house
> He was sick in bed;
> Rammed my finger down his throat
> And pulled out a wagon bed.

Although not many of the movements of the period penetrated Irish Creek, the Great Awakening did. The gospel got back into the hills, and Joe himself became a preacher of sorts:

> Old Joe Clark set out to preach
> He preached all over the plain.
> The highest text he ever took
> Was high low Jack and game.
>
> Old Joe Clark had a yaller cat
> She'd neither sing nor pray
> She stuck her head in the buttermilk jar
> And washed her sins away.

With Joe the law of love did not prevail. Nor were all those who followed him distressed by it:

> Old Joe Clark killed a man
> Killed him with a knife.
> I'm damned glad he killed that man
> Now I'll have his wife.

Eventually book learning came up-creek, and a school-teacher appeared on the local scene. If this verse of "Old Joe Clark" is any indication, she was not treated in a way befitting Virginia Cavaliers:

> I wouldn't marry a school teacher
> I'll tell you the reason why;
> She blows her nose in yaller corn bread
> And calls it pumpkin pie.

In get-rich-quick America, the Clarks were poor, and destined to grow poorer. Unsophisticated, uneducated, and unrepentant, they were prototype poor whites—the mudsill of the Anglo-Saxon heroic tradition in America.

In the twentieth century the term "poor white" as a noun rates a specific dictionary definition—"a member of an inferior or underprivileged white social group; often taken to be offensive." Instead of climbing up the ladder of success, they took to the hills, which effectively blocked them off from the main stream of American life. They became our first anti-heroes.

Other derogative words were coined for them—lubber, cracker, peckerwood, tarhill, woolhat, cajun, redneck, sandhiller, apple knocker, ridge-runner, swamp rat, clay eater, turd kicker.[1] Long before the term "poor white" was widespread, the stereotype was widespread not only in America, but Europe as well.[2]

Here, according to the stereotype, was a subculture where feuding, hunting, and commanding were a hero's preroga-

[1] Archie Green, "Hillbilly Music: Source and Symbol," *Journal of American Folklore,* Vol. 78 (September 1965).
[2] See Shields McIlwaine, *The Southern Poor-White: From Lubberland to Tobacco Road* (Norman, Okla.: University of Oklahoma Press, 1939); and Cratis Deal Williams, *The Southern Mountaineer in Fact and Fiction* (New York University dissertation, 1961). Fanny Kemble is the most famous visitor to describe backcountry Americans in detail.

tives. There was an Old Testament flavor to this land beyond the law. The operating word was *patriarchal*. A raw, Darwinian environment favored those who were strong of limb and will. Spinning wheels, banjos, weaving looms, and dulcimers were in daily use. So was the long rifle, when the occasion demanded. Women, bears, and snoopy neighbors, take note. This image of mountain country persisted well into the twentieth century. "We fight among ourselves. We kill one another," wrote James Taylor Adams in the January 1932 number of *The Cumberland Empire*. "But one thing is certain; we don't relish the idea of outside investigators coming into these hills to investigate *our* affairs." This same antique flavor was echoed in crude local diaries and record books, like this one collected by Donald Peattie:

Soonzy Ollis. age 84. dide June 10 1871. Grate bar honter. Kilt turkies and ratel snake by 100. Kilt deer by thosand. I knewed him well.[3]

Not only bear and rattlesnakes got killed, as the well-known legend of the Hatfields and McCoys proved. Turn to this saga, with its strong factual basis, to see what the "old-time" hillbilly hero was like and how he operated in the Old Testament world of vengeance.

The tale is set on the rugged banks of the Tug River, which winds through the Appalachian Mountains. On one side lived the Hatfields, led by Anse, six foot of devil and two hundred pounds of hell. Opposing him was Randolph McCoy, clan patriarch, who saw three of his sons slaughtered in one day. Geography, history, and hysteria blended to make the story of their feuding a bloody chapter in our history.

During the Civil War the Tug River was not only the

[3] See Marshall W. Fishwick, *The Virginia Tradition* (Washington, D.C.: Public Affairs Press, 1956), p. 68.

boundary between Virginia and Kentucky, but also between the Union and the Confederacy. Virginia's Hatfields had some scrapes with Kentucky's McCoys. As in all civil wars, the animosity was deep and enduring.

It took a lowly pig to set off all the pyrotechnics. Finding an extra pig with his brood, Floyd Hatfield took it to town to sell. Randolph McCoy stopped him, claiming it was his pig. A trial ensued. The jury, loaded with Hatfields, gave Floyd the pig. The McCoys swore vengeance. Then, when Johnse Hatfield took Rose Anne McCoy home to cook for him, they got it. In the words of the ballad-makers:

> Come and listen to my story
> Of fair Rosanna McCoy.
> She loved young Johnse Hatfield,
> Old Devil Anse's boy.
> But the McCoys and Hatfields
> Had long engaged in strife;
> And swore no damned fool Hatfield
> Would take a McCoy to wife.

So Talbot McCoy crossed the river with two younger brothers, found a Hatfield, and stabbed him 27 times. The sheriff took the three McCoys into custody, but "Devil Anse" recaptured them. The captives were tied to paw-paw bushes and riddled with bullets. Then the real shooting began. Not until the 1888 Battle of Grapevine Creek did it abate. No one knows for sure how many people were killed. Certainly a hundred; others claim twice that many.[4]

Sometimes the mountaineer's penchant for mass killing coincided with patriotic fervor—as with Alvin C. York. Born on a mountain ridge in Tennessee, when the Hatfields and McCoys were banging away at Grapevine Creek, York

[4] See Virgil C. Jones, *The Hatfields and the McCoys* (Durham, N.C.: University of North Carolina Press, 1949).

139

enlisted in the U.S. Army in 1917 and went to France with the 82nd Infantry. This provided a chance for target practice on Germans. On a single day in October, 1918, he killed 20 singlehanded, and forced 132 others to surrender. Marshal Ferdinand Foch called it "the greatest thing accomplished by any private soldier in all the armies of Europe." Here was a hillbilly hero in which all America could and did take pride.

By the time Sergeant York came back to his Tennessee hills, to start the York Foundation to educate mountain children, the phonograph and radio were in vogue. A "revival" of plantation and mountain music swept across America. One new idol was Vernon Dalhart, born Marion Try Slaughter in the late nineteenth century. Coming to New York, he began his recording career in 1916 with a "downhome folk style." In 1924 the Victor Record company released "two Southern mountaineer songs by Vernon Dalhart with fiddle accompaniment." "The Wreck of the Old 97" and "Prisoner's Song" sold over seven million copies. Such singers as "Pop" Stoneman, Charlie Bowman, "Blind George" Reneau, and "Blind Andy" Jenkins all profited by recording songs that found a ready market in America. Their music borrowed freely from other styles, but repaid the debt to folk music by creating songs that subsequently became "folk" music. We need to know more about this reentry process. Not only does "folk" become "commercial"; the reverse occurs. Just how, why, and when is not clear.

Certainly the "American style" is neither simplistic nor unilinear, but a hybrid springing from unique circumstances and soil. Styles, like ethnic groups, go through hyphenated stages before they emerge full-blown. Back-country culture remains partly hyphenated—the country-western style. Other word tags include mountain, Dixie, old time, familiar, sacred, gospel, cowboy, western, hillbilly, hill and range,

140

Nashville, rockabilly, and bluegrass. Just as the medium is the message, the song is the hero. Its basic shape and theme remain, though singers come and go. Only a few attain the fame of Vernon Dalhart, who in the 1920s was as much of the public domain as Babe Ruth or Will Rogers. If recordings flourished the poor white withered as a new industrialized America emerged on the postwar scene. History left him standing on his mountain peak, an outmoded rifle and ideology his only possessions. Unable to adapt, he became unheroic, finally ridiculous. Once feared and respected, he became the pathetic patriarch.

The change was heralded by the development of a popular stereotype in the American theater. He has disappeared now, but "Toby" was the darling of tent repertory companies and small-town theaters for three decades. Though scholars find proto-Tobies in characters like Sample Switchess and Tom Twinkes, no one doubts that Tobe Haxton, created in W. C. Herman's 1909 melodrama *Clouds and Sunshine,* set the style for a whole generation.[5]

Audiences in the 1920s couldn't see enough of the "darn fool Toby." Fred Wilson's success in the part was accidental. "I came into this world with a shock of unruly red hair and a flock of freckles," he wrote. "Toby was myself plus a hickory shirt, patched jeans, boots with run-down heels, and a battered hat." He was the hillbilly as buffoon. Uncouth and uncultivated, he was a cruel parody of the frontier that was suddenly as out of date as the horse and buggy.

As Albert F. McLean points out in *American Vaudeville as Ritual,* Toby emerged during a period of crisis in Ameri-

[5] Robert Downing spent four years researching the "Toby problem." His results are summarized in the November 1964 issue of *Theatre Arts.* See also Larry Dale Clark's *Toby Shows: A Form of American Popular Theatre* (University of Illinois dissertation, 1963) and Jere C. Mickel's "The Genesis of Toby, a Folk Hero of the American Theater," in *Journal of American Folklore,* Vol. 80 (October-December 1967).

can social life. Modernism was changing everything. City life was becoming the norm. Progressive people were determined to leave the hearth and the hills behind. Seeing what a silly bumpkin Toby was merely reaffirmed this determination; if the big city seemed wicked to the small-town citizens, all the more reason to yearn for it. Fred Wilson played Toby as a believable character; those who followed played him essentially for the low comedy element, even as a grotesque clown. The hero had been turned upside down.

In the novels of Erskine Caldwell, he would, in fact, crawl around on all fours. *The Bastard* and *Poor Fool* were followed by *Tobacco Road* (1932), with a portrayal of the American hillbilly that set a world stereotype. The "hero" is Jeter Lester, a deceitful, lascivious fellow who tends to reduce everything around him to animality. One still meets Jeter in bookstores and literary conferences around the world.

As a Broadway play, *Tobacco Road* broke all records for endurance. In the 1940s people went to see it for the same reason that our children flock to super-spy stories—sex and violence never go out of style. The post-World War II rural world, in cartoons, films, and plays, is a world of Gothic horror, in which latrines, insects, and fornication dominate. People are gunned down for amusement, as slightly clad mountain children slither around the stage, ready to sell body and soul for a turnip.

Unfortunately, as anyone who has bothered to go up the ridges and into the lonesome valleys knows, such a caricature is built on a stratum of truth. Over the years a relentless cycle of hard scrabbling and deterioration set in. In order to find land and game, families had to go to the very heads of the hollows and up the sides of the mountains. All the game was soon killed. Razorback hogs provided the only chance for meat. If they went any further, they would cross the ridge and meet other families coming up the other side. Names on the land told the unheroic story—Poverty Hollow, Scuffle Ridge, Hungry Hill, Scrabbletown, Jump Mountain, Purgatory Creek.

Here is a real American tragedy. The "poor whites" ancestors were the bravest of our pioneers. They carved homes out of the wilderness, and set the style for American freedom. They were heroes of a special sort. Then their heroic moment passed, and they had nothing to do but hold on or move out:

> Then I'd live in Nashville,
> Where all the lawin' goes.
> I'd walk on all them asphalt streets
> And wear them furrin' clothes.

Pathetically, those who held on perpetuated a special way of living—and dying. In an age of scientific medicine, they passed on their remedies by word of mouth:

> Pole cat oil applied to the neck prevents croup.
> Smoke life-everlasting to cure catarrh.
> Smoke crushed coffee beans for a sore throat.
> For bloody flux swallow an Indian penny.[6]

Tucked away in the Blue Ridge, Cumberlands, and Ozarks, people are such deep fundamentalists that cocks are roosters and bulls "gentlemen cows" in mixed company. Yet they send maidens to dance nude and couples to fornicate in newly planted fields, to assure good crops. Gathering data on such matters, folklorist Vance Randolph observed a farmer and his wife in the field at sunup, both naked. They sang a rhyme with the line "Up to my ass and higher too."

[6] These Ozark remedies are recorded by Mary and Kenneth Clarke in *Introducing Folklore* (New York: Holt, Rinehart and Winston, 1965), p. 141.

Every few steps the man threw seeds against the woman's buttocks. "When the planting was done," the scholar noted, "they just laid down on the ground and had a good time."

Professor Randolph also found out something about growing turnips. An informant told how a mixed group of nude mountain people started planting at sunrise. "The boys throwed all the seed and the gals kept a-hollering 'Pecker deep! Pecker deep!' When they got done the whole bunch rolled in the dust like some kind of wild animals. There ain't no sense to it, but them folks always raised the best turnips on the creek."

How easy to parody and ridicule *this* America; we are not many steps away from the Beverly Hillbillies. Yet even this television spoof has its roots in sociological reality. Elmore M. Matthews's *Neighbor and Kin: Life in a Tennessee Ridge Community* (1966), documents the native distrust of education and special skills, and the need for scapegoats. In the Atomic Age moonshiners still protect stills by telling stories of haunted stumps, creaking rocking chairs, phantoms, and ghosts that devour all who walk after dark. How can a hero emerge from such a *Weltanschauung* and enter into the main stream of American style?

Some of these dilemmas and contradictions crop up in the life and work of Woody Guthrie (1912–1967), one of the most influential recent folk singers. Left alone with his young brother Roy in a two-room Oklahoma shanty, Woody was an orphan of living parents. Most of his life was spent in compulsive, aimless rambling. Yet he was able to compose over a thousand songs, telling mountaineers and workers about their deeds and dreams in their own language. Americans found in the man authenticity and originality which put Guthrie far above *ersatz* folk singers who invaded every night club, bar, and studio in the land. "Some of my songs are purty dern left-handed," Guthrie admitted in

144

1939. "They are so left wing I had to write 'em with my left hand and sing 'em with my left tonsil." Pete Seeger, Joan Baez, Bob Dylan, and many others followed in his wake. From them we begin to discern the *gestalt* of folk consciousness in the 1960s—Folk + Rock + Protest = Hits.[7]

But there are few "hits" in the real lives of America's poor. When the Poor People's March placed thousands of the dispossessed in the middle of Washington in the spring of 1968—inhabitants of instantly created Resurrection City —the paradox of their lives was televised and photographed for the whole world. Not in theory, but in fact, one could now visualize the duality which is central to the American tradition. He could confront the virgin land—and the raped landscape, full table—the empty stomach, American dream —and American nightmare.

Such duality reflects built-in and mounting tensions between country and city—between corncob and computer. To be a truly national hero, one would have to resolve or reconcile that tension. As violence and latent revolution spread throughout the most affluent nation in history, it became apparent that some resolution of that tension was necessary if the American democratic tradition were to survive.

[7] See David A. DeTurk and A. Poulin, Jr., *The American Folk Scene: Dimensions of the Folksong Revival* (New York: Dell, 1967).

11

Cool Ones

"There is just one simple rule:
Never lose your cool."

POPULAR BALLAD

"James Bond is halfway between fantasy and realism. This
indicates his role as a contemporary hero."

KINGSLEY AMIS

ANYONE would have been hot and bothered—captured, condemned, hearing your own death sentence. "You will be hanged by the neck until you are dead dead dead!" the Judge thundered. "And you can go to hell hell hell!" the young prisoner replied. By any standard, that was cool.

Billy the Kid was a rebel, a maverick, an under-emotional detached loner who killed 21 men before he was 21 (not counting Indians and Mexicans). To put it bluntly, he didn't give a damn. Billy is dead, but his heroic style goes marching on. Computers click, circuits close, and we grow cooler every day.

Our prototype hero, whose real name was William H. Bonney, was born in New York City in 1859. With the Civil War the family moved to Bleeding Kansas, where the father bled and died. Mrs. Bonney moved on to Colorado and married a man named Antrim. They drifted on to New Mexico, where her teen-age son killed his first victim—a blacksmith who reputedly insulted his mother. There was more shooting; young Billy fled to the Pecos Valley. The climate was hot, but a drifter could play it cool on that part of the frontier. Everyone knew there was no law west of the Mississippi and no God west of the Pecos.

Billy was not the kind of person you'd expect to raise much hell. He was slight, about 140 pounds and five feet eight inches tall. Unassuming and quiet, he moved like a panther, peering out of gray, lusterless eyes. His face was long, his feet and hands small, his hair light brown. The most conspicuous thing about him was protruding front teeth. Studying the one authenticated photograph of Bonney, Dr. Chesmore Eastlake has diagnosed him as "an adenoidal moron who may have been given to fits of cowardice." But then, Eastlake never met Billy when the chips were down.[1]

Quickly sucked into the Lincoln County cattle war, Billy saw his employer J. H. Tunstall killed by a posse of the Murphy faction, and Tunstall's partner shot with his Bible in his hands. Young Bonney (who practiced shooting by picking snowbirds off fence posts at a gallop) reacted quickly and savagely. He brought retribution to the range, killing Sheriff James A. Brady and a deputy, and refusing to surrender when ordered to do so by Governor Lew Wallace. Suddenly an obscure and trigger-happy cowpuncher became King of the Cools. His reign was short. On July 14, 1881, Sheriff Pat Garrett ambushed Bonney in a dark room and shot him dead. He had lived exactly 21 years, 7 months, and 21 days.

Townspeople dragged Billy's body across the street to a carpenter's shop, where they stretched it out on a bench.

[1] See Alfred Alder, "Billy the Kid: A Case Study in Epic Origins," *Western Folklore*, X, No. 2 (1950); and Marshall Fishwick, "Billy the Kid: Faust in America," *Saturday Review* (Oct. 11, 1952).

The next day he was dressed in a borrowed shirt too large for his slim neck and placed in a plain wooden coffin. Admirers (there were many) collected $208 for a gravestone, which was later splintered and carried away by relic hunters.

No need to trace here the phenomenal growth of the Bonney legend.[2] Within a year Ash Upson's *Authenic Life of Billy the Kid, The Noted Desperado of the Southwest* had appeared, the first of scores of books that would soon follow. Heroic reputations make good companions. By 1906 the firm of Street and Smith was issuing titles like *Buffalo Bill and Billy the Kid: or, The Desperadoes of Apache Land*. By then Billy had become as colorful a rogue as Robin Hood, Dick Turpin, or Fra Diavolo. Frozen egotism plus recklessness and minus mercy, Billy had "painted his name in flaming colors with a six-shooter across the sky of the Southwest."

What kind of person was the real Bonney? If he is the prototype of the "cool" heroes that are so prominent today, the question is important. We wish we had more exact information, and that the information we had was more reliable. Still, we get a vivid picture, from available material, of an easy, unstudied, devil-may-care man who watched like a hawk for an advantage and seized it instantly. He killed a man as nonchalantly as he smoked a cigarette. As long as he killed a man who offended him, it made no difference to him how he did it. Incapable of remorse or regrets, he put a bullet through a man's heart as coolly as he plugged a tin can on a fence post.

His best biographer, Walter Burns, speaks of the "subzero vacuum" which was a hiatus in his character and the

[2] For a detailed account see James C. Dykes's *Billy the Kid; the Bibliography of a Legend* (Albuquerque, New Mexico: University of New Mexico Press, 1953).

"cool unruffled poise" with which he met every crisis.[3] On the surface Billy was quiet, unassuming, courteous—even courtly to the women, who found him irresistible (just as they did the three B's of the 1950s—Bogart, Brando, and Bond). "One chance in a million" was one of his favorite phrases. He depended on a sort of subconscious mail armor to protect him, no matter what the odds. With Billy, and the cool ones who followed, it was not fire but ice that showed to the world. Thus he was the very opposite of the gushing, sentimental hero of Victorian times, who externalized all his emotions. To be cool is to keep it to yourself.

Because he lived and died in lush Victorian times, Billy was a desperado to his contemporaries. His fame came when the heroic climate cooled in the 1920s. Today tourist agencies refer to "Billy the Kid" country. As a source of revenue Billy rivals the Grand Canyon or the Carlsbad Caverns; he is being advertised and exploited accordingly.

The source of this fascination is not hard to discover. Billy did in fact what many Americans yearn to do in fancy —especially in a culture in which wide-open spaces and free-for-all individuality are more and more mirages. Few people know the rightness or wrongness of his fight. Such things are confused in the type of grass-roots gunplay in which he specialized. What everyone knows is that Billy had *guts;* he was cool.

So, for that matter, were Wild Bill Hickok, Cherokee Bill, Geronimo, Cochise, and Jesse James. The second son of a Baptist minister, James was raised on a Missouri farm. During the Civil War he rode with Quantrill's guerrillas and launched his colorful career. By holding up a Rock Island Railroad train in 1873, Jesse added a new crime to the American story. Once he rode with a posse in his own pur-

[3] Walter N. Burns, *The Saga of Billy the Kid* (New York: Doubleday, 1926), chap. V.

suit. Finally he was hit in the back, by a "dirty little coward," who "laid poor Jesse in his grave." James was widely admired—especially by Southerners, since it was Yankee money he stole. Songs that folklorists have collected point up the sentimental attachment:

> Jesse was a man, a friend of the poor,
> He never would see a man suffer pain;
> And with his brother Frank he robbed many a bank
> And stopped the Glendale train.

Another lament, recorded by Bascom Lamar Lunsford, hints at a kind of deification for the fallen hero:

> Goodby Jesse, so long Jesse
> Farewell Jesse James;
> Robert Ford caught his eye
> And shot him on the sly
> And laid poor Jesse in the grave.

Soon after the slaying a "James Boys Series" appeared and has been continuing, in one form or another, ever since. The publishing house of Street and Smith published 6,000,000 copies of 121 James novels between 1901 and 1903—the all-time record for bandit publicity. Jesse has subsequently been a bang-up success in movies and television.

Like Robin Hood, Jesse was bad to be good, so was Pennsylvania's Lewis the Robber and many local hell-raisers. Another popular variation is the man who is bad, but admits he's bad and finally assigns his wicked soul to the hands of God. Having given all the juicy details of "the deed which brought him nigh," during which he keeps his cool, he then warns others not to follow his example. A good example is James Bird, a Marine in the War of 1812 who turned tail and ran after having fought bravely. Willis Mayberry is another "po' boy" who done wrong. Tom Dooley is willing to "bow down his head and cry," because he knows where he'll be tomorrow—"a-hangin' from a white-oak tree." Full of *sangfroid,* such characters must be distinguished from the trickster—the weak, cunning, sneaky fellow who wins by secret means. Anglo Jack is a good example. Indians and Negroes have their tricksters, too—the coyote and the rabbit, about whom whole series of tales are woven. There are many variations, but a common denominator—a ruthless realism, a Darwinian capacity for accepting the consequences of the survival of the fittest.

This same icy-cool quality kept cropping up in nineteenth-century America. It characterized Civil War nurse Clara Barton, for example, who never hesitated to move into the line of fire to help the wounded.[4] After the battle of Antietam she was reduced to using corn leaves for bandages, while doctors operated by the light of a two-inch stub of candle. Slim Clara worked until her face turned "the color of gunpowder, a deep blue." Later on she crossed the Rappahannock under fire at the Battle of Fredericksburg, working until the Northern forces were compelled to retreat in terrible confusion. Red blood covered the white snow. The wounded soldiers' bloody clothing was frozen so tight to the ground that it had to be chopped free with axes. Eventually 1200 wounded men were crammed into the twelve rooms of an old Virginia mansion. "When I rose to leave I wrung the blood from the bottom of my clothing before I could step," Miss Barton wrote. She was a cool one.

Many foreign observers have commented (especially in 1968), on the streak of violence in American life, and in the landscape as well. We have always been plagued by the

[4] Marshall Fishwick, *Illustrious Americans: Clara Barton* (New York: Silver, Burdette, 1966); and Rose Ishbel, *Angel of the Battlefield* (New York: Harper, 1956).

continental waywardness of rampaging nature, by violence and paradox, by the cold blue wind in the day and the hot human blues in the night. Nature rumbles, roars, and gurgles. Hurricanes are so dreadful that we try to appease them with names like Doris, Ethel, or Bertha. All told, it is a wild, bone-breaking landscape fit for uncouth exiled gods. In the heroic style there is a tendency to match the manner of the landscape.

That is as true of cities as it is of the country. The bad sections of Chicago produced gangsters just as the Bad Lands of South Dakota produced lead-slinging lawmen. The proper word is "transformed," rather than produced, since the best-known gangsters were Italian and Sicilian immigrants. Most notorious of the new Tommy-gun barons was Al Capone, alias Scarface, Boxcar Tony, and the Big Fellow. Born in Naples in 1899 and brought to America as a child, he worked his way up to be vice king in Chicago. His syndicate's business was so profitable that others began to horn in. The result was a decade of gang warfare and over five hundred violent deaths.

Capone's cool brutality fascinated America, just as Billy the Kid's had done. Yale seniors voted him the "most interesting personality of the age," newspapers talked of "Capone's Odyssey," and F. D. Palsey published *Al Capone: Biography of a Self-Made Man.* Paul Muni portrayed the Capone legend in *Scarface,* and pulp magazines magnified it. When Al was jailed for income tax evasion, his place as "Public Enemy Number One" was taken by John Dillinger, an Indiana desperado who specialized in bank robberies. Some of his exploits, transferred to a minor historical hoodlum named Clyde Barrow, blossomed into a 1968 camp-style movie called *Bonnie and Clyde.* Looking at the 1930s in retrospect, the gangster was a kind of ballet dancer, his career a sort of art-form. Here is the nightmare inversion of

152

the earlier success story. The gangster is doomed to be punished because he succeeds by his own unsocial Darwinian standards. When "Scarface" is killed in the film, we see across from his apartment a big neon sign reading, "The World Is Yours." The world is *not* his, any more than it is ours. By living so cool a life, and dying so violent a death, he pays for our fantasies and releases us momentarily from the concept of success. He "has to do" what he does, just like the heroes of Greek tragedy.

The gangster represents grass-roots provincial America. With the Second World War, the American mentality went overseas, and heroes became internationalists. In place of the man with the Tommy-gun, we got the man who is only a silhouette—the secret agent. The most popular and influential of the new breed had both a name and a number—James Bond, 007. Created by Ian Fleming, Bond has been characterized by Richard C. Carpenter as "just about the most 'in' and 'cool' character in modern fiction." [5]

Despite all the contemporary details about places, machines, techniques, and customs, Bond is closely and specifically related to past legendary heroes. In novel after novel he repeats the deeds and thoughts of past paragons. The story of 007 is a modern myth, played in the special muted tones of our time. There were ten versions of it between Fleming's *Casino Royale* (1953) and *The Man with the Golden Gun* (1965). Womanizing with such gorgeous sex-machines as Kissy Suzuki, Tiffany Case, Honeychile Rider, and Pussy Galore, the clean-cut cool agent with the longish straight nose is Billy the Kid on wheels. He doubles Billy's record, killing twoscore men by shooting, throttling,

[5] Richard C. Carpenter, "007 and the Myth of the Hero," *Journal of Popular Culture*, I, No. 2 (Fall 1967), p. 79; and George Grella, "James Bond: Culture Hero," in Harold Lubin, editor, *Heroes and Anti-Heroes* (San Francisco: Chandler Press, 1968).

stabbing, and burying. Without his direct intervention others are eaten by piranhas, chopped up in snow-fans, burned in wrecked cars, and shoved down bobsled runs without a bobsled. There is enough Bond lore, in fact, to enable Kingsley Amis to compile and publish *The James Bond Dossier* (1965).

The man who never blows his cool, 007, is no ruffian of the James-Capone-Dillinger sort. He knows the right drink, the right food, the right car. You can be sure that his wristwatch is a Rolex Perpetual, and that his Bentley car has the Amherst-Villiers supercharger added by the Rolls people. Yet he is closely linked to Achilles, Dionysus, and Perseus. He, too, embarks on difficult voyages, encounters monsters and dragons, goes to the underworld, and returns victorious, bearing the marks of his journey. No hero in history has faced more terrifying villains than Goldfinger, Dr. No, Ernest Blofeld, and Sir Hugo Drax. Bond risks all and saves all. He is not too fussy about how he does it, provided it can be done. With all cool ones, means are less important than ends. Fire must be fought with fire; Bond has his "license to kill." In modern mythology there is no place for decency or chivalry. When the helpless victim is clinging to the edge of the trapdoor over the shark-infested pool, you don't hesitate to step on his fingers. *Lex talionis.*

Still, Bond is plainly on the side of the hero; he proves that the possibility of heroism still exists in the Age of the Double Cross. We can still find the razor's edge of danger, if only we dare to look. And who knows who among us is not a drab little clerk or teacher, but a fiendish killer and irresistible lover? Suppose *I* am a low-number secret agent? [6]

With the imaginary secret agents came the real-life beats

[6] See Kingsley Amis's *The James Bond Dossier* (paperback ed., New York: New American Library, 1965) for the full Bond story and style.

154

and hippies—a small but dedicated army of *enfants terribles* turned inside out. The beat was Everyman's existentialist, reduced to guts and grunts and gonads. His program was to divorce oneself from society, exist without roots, accept the terms of death, take the unchartered journey into the rebellious imperatives of the self. Here was the tradition of the Bohemian and the juvenile delinquent coming face to face with the disillusioned Negro (a ménage à trois) producing a new phenomenon in American life.

The walking embodiment of the credo was Norman Mailer, who had written a powerful war novel called *The Naked and the Dead* (1948) and played it cool in the years following. *Advertisements for Myself* (1959), an extraordinary combination of pathos and bathos, serves as a position paper for the beats:

> The decision is to encourage the psychopath in oneself: to explore that domain of experience where security is boredom and therefore sickness; to exist in that enormous present which is without past or future, memory or planned intention ... The life where a man must go until he is beat, where he must be with it or doomed not to swing ...[7]

The younger beats have been even more outspoken against the middle-class Establishment which is the enemy. "Life's too wild today, sonny, to worry about the fate of the race or private morality or nun-like delicacies of should-I or should-I-not," wrote Seymour Krim in 1959. "Anyone with brains or even imagination is a self-driven marauder." [8] Better known are Jack Kerouac, author of the novel *On the Road,* and Allen Ginsberg, whose slim volume of poetry

[7] Norman Mailer, *Advertisements for Myself* (New York: New American Library, 1959), p. 339.
[8] Elias Wilentz, editor, *The Beat Scene* (New York: Citadel, 1960), p. 83.

called *Howl* had a widespread vogue. A typical Ginsberg poem goes like this:

I'll grow a beard and carry lovely bombs,
I will destroy the world, slip in between the cracks of death
  And change the Universe—Ha!
I have the secret, I carry
  Subversive salami in my ragged briefcase. . . .

The beat is a barbarian in reverse. He insists that he, the outsider as outsider, is the real Greek who has the integrity that the insiders (that is, the middle-class squares) have sacrificed for phony security. His main interests are not with the universals and the duplicable, but with the individual and the unique. To this extent he is the direct descendant of the cool ones examined earlier. All of them are caught in the toils that ensnare anyone who sets up a program which at its heart is negative.[9]

The notoriety and influence of beats and hippies after World War II confirmed the blossoming of American teen culture. "Beat" is a way of life that consecrates the pose and gestures of adolescence. The tragicomic predicament of the beats is that, having forsworn maturity, they tend to truncate their own creative lives. Some critics suspect that such adolescent attitudes and beliefs threaten to become normative for much of the adult population. If this be true, then all of American culture is "cooling off" or "copping out" at a rapid rate.[10]

Enter a whole new cool pose, with special vocabulary and paraphernalia—pot (marijuana), coke (cocaine),

[9] This idea is explored by Walter J. Ong in *The Barbarian Within* (New York: Macmillan, 1962).
[10] See James Scott, "Beat Literature and the American Teen Cult," in *American Quarterly* (Summer 1962); and Dwight Macdonald, "Profiles: A Caste, A Culture, A Market," in *New Yorker* (November 22, 1958).

smack (heroin), acid (LSD), and speed (Methedrine). Enter a new lifestyle, which has yet to create its own enduring heroes and values. Some, like James Dean, seemed on the way to Olympus—only to disappear en route.[11]

We agree with George Bernard Shaw: it *is* a shame to waste so wonderful a thing as youth on children. But once we *have* wasted it on them—showered them with all the richest nation in history can produce—why do they still feel alienated and trapped?

Searching for identity (the new psychological cliché, popularized by the work of Eric Erickson in the 1960s), they examine both past and present idols. Hence the rediscovery of Henry David Thoreau and his *Essay on Civil Disobedience,* and of the "tough guy" films of Humphrey Bogart, who died in 1957 only to be revived as a major cool guy a decade later. In a single year, five new books on "Bogey" appeared, and his 75 films were in demand everywhere.[12]

Born in 1899, Bogart played on Broadway and in minor movies until he became famous as Duke Mantee in the 1936 film called *The Petrified Forest.* Here was Everyman's gangster, with a special cool-yet-caring flavor. His melancholy was imitated, and hats began to be worn in "the Bogart manner." His style was caught and put into a poem called "Nobody Dies like Humphrey Bogart," written by Norman Rosten. It began:

[11] James Dean died in a 1955 auto crash when he was twenty-four. For several years the cult took over. Several teen-agers actually committed suicide to join him. Then the whole thing stopped as quickly as it had begun.

[12] These were the books, all published in 1965: Richard Gehman, *Bogart: An Intimate Biography* (New York: Fawcett World); Johah Ruddy and Jonathan Hill, *Bogey: The man, the Actor, the Legend* (New York: Tower); Clifford McCarty, *Bogey: The Films of Humphrey Bogart* (New York: Bonanza Press); Paul Michael, *Humphrey Bogart: The Man and his Films* (Indianapolis, Ind.: Bobbs-Merrill); and Ezra Goodman, *Bogey, The Good-Bad Guy* (New York: Lyle Stuart).

Casual at the wheel, blinding rainstorm.
The usual blonde doll alongside—only
This time our man knows she's talked,
The double-c, and by his cold eyes
We can tell it's the end of the line for her.

But not, certainly, for Bogey, whose films bore such titles as *Bullets or Ballots, Isle of Fury, Kid Galahad, Dead End, Crime School, Racket Busters, King of the Underworld,* and *High Sierra.* One of his finest films, the 1941 version of *The Maltese Falcon,* found him playing the part of Sam Spade, "private investigator with ice water in his veins." It would serve as a model for hard-boiled private eyes for years to come. After 42 films Bogart had become King of the Cools.

On film he was invincible; in real life he was felled by a cancer of the throat. When a premature newspaper story announced on January 3, 1957, that he was about to die, Bogart, determined to be as tough in real life as he had been in scores of films, released a statement denying his imminent end, concluding with this typically sardonic passage:

All that I am lacking is about thirty-three pounds, and I am sure that a good number of you would be ready to grant them to me. And I will not be hard on the parts of your bodies from which they could come.[13]

Two weeks later he was dead. But the cool guys he had brought to life on film—Duke Mantee, Turkey Morgan, Baby Face Martin, Sam Spade, Rick, Charlie Allnut, Captain Queeg, and Eddie Willis—would not die with him. Nor would the last verse of Norman Rosten's poem:

Any way we go, baby, one or the other,
You'll look a lot prettier than me

[13] Paul Michael, *op. cit.,* p. 12.

When we're laid out in the last scene
You in pink or blue with the angels,
Me in the same scar I was born with.

Only after his death did serious literary critics try to relate the Bogart style to earlier American precedents and characters. One of these, John Seelye, asked a key question —is there not a Leatherstocking lurking inside the wry, ironic detective created by Humphrey Bogart? [14]

The bond holding together the cool heroes from Billy to Bogey is alienation. They scorn our pious bourgeois values; they are turned off. The outsider theme, stretching back to Job, Ulysses, and Beowulf has special relevance in the Darwinian history of the United States. Being "way out" has become, for many, better than being "in." Over the years externalism has become an established orthodoxy.

The transcendentalist George P. Marsh put his finger on a pivotal factor in American history. Here was the most notable example of the struggle between civilized man and barbarous uncultivated nature. Generally the culture hero is the savage, the theatre a wilderness, the drama one of slow progress against nature. But in America the full energies of advanced European civilization were "brought to bear at once on a desert continent."

One certain tag for such a landscape and history is pluralism. With two powerful weapons—dynamism and the will to experiment—the continent was conquered. In the national motto and destiny *unum* was always counterbalanced by *pluribus*. *Unum* has been hot, *pluribus* insists on being cool. This *pluribus* is the real starting point for our excursions into unreality.

As Bogart's films reveal, the cool hero is no longer

[14] John Seelye, in *Journal of Popular Culture*, I, No. 1 (Fall 1967), p. 57.

unilinear, as he was for generations; he no longer knows what he "has to do" to register protest and establish heroic identity. Surrounded by brutal delinquencies, structureless jazz, anti-patriotic demonstrations, and emotive, grunt words, he is confused, distorted, bruised. Sometimes he becomes a purile fellow whose style consecrates narcissism and gestures of adolescence. Violence intermingles with sentimental clichés; he believes none of it or all of it, with equal coolness.

To many teen-agers the motorcycle is a symbol of escape. Some cycling groups, such as Hell's Angels, have received considerable fame by performing such normally unheroic acts as punishing a woman by nailing her to a tree. Marlon Brando portrayed this cool mentality in *The Wild Ones*. The tendency is always to push a pose until it becomes a *reductio ad absurdum*. "My name is John Filler and I represent the latest rage in American Freaklore, the hip-beat author who doesn't write," an article in the July 1963 issue of *Esquire* began. "I don't write because it is the tradition of my school to stop, once enough insight is gained to graduate from student to mastery. You only put on paper what you hope somebody will buy. This school is a sort of fraternity, but none of us pledged it."

Why, asks the student of heroic style, do cool ones warm our blood and excite us? Characters like Billy the Kid, Jesse James, Al Capone, James Bond, Norman Mailer, and Humphrey Bogart are not only lacking in the usual heroic virtues (compassion, forbearance, sacrifice); they are visceral, ruthless, and virile. Dixon Wecter is right in calling Billy an adenoidal farm boy with a rifle; the type summed up in the Western cliché "dirty little killer." And are not such James Bond episodes as the blown-up bulgars in *Casino Royale,* the dismemberment of Mr. Big by barracudas, the attack on a naked woman by an army of voracious

160

land crabs, and the murder of Milton Krest by stuffing the Hildebrand Rarity into his mouth while he sleeps simply sadism?

Frontier wolves and savage Redskins have gone, but America is still a wilderness shared. Heroes must still face incredible cruelty and meaningless evil. The further we go into the thickets, the more desperate we become.

12

Celebrities

"He's the greatest!"

ANONYMOUS (BECOMING UNANIMOUS)

SHE was incredibly beautiful. On the screen she exuded a tender warmth that made her unique and irresistible. When Jean Baker became a celebrity, ogled and admired by millions, she changed her name to Marilyn Monroe. In a few years she was an embodiment, an institution, a doctrine, a fashion idol, a sex goddess. There wasn't anything or anyone she couldn't have. Then, at the peak of her career in her mid-thirties, she committed suicide.

Could it have been something else? Did Marilyn Monroe murder Norma Jean Baker?

Her tragedy was that she wanted to be recognized and understood as herself, not idolized as a celebrity—a thing to twang the male erotic nerve. She was so profoundly disturbed by the idea of not being accepted as a real person that she felt herself being destroyed and did nothing to resist that destruction. She was one of the tragic figures of our times.[1]

After her death she lives on to haunt us in the work of pop artists—symbol of the gorgeous, erotic, glossy embrace

---

[1] So argues J. P. Priestly, "Marilyn Monroe," *Saturday Evening Post* (April 27, 1963), p. 12.

of cornflake materialism. This lost illegitimate child who killed herself with barbiturates became a myth and died of it. She is a kind of monument to heroic obsolescence. What she stood for was summed up in terms like "hot stuff," "some dish," and "a gorgeous piece." The key adjective for celebrities is *hot*—emotional, tactile, torrid. To end up with a girl like this is to be "hot stuff," and to "make the sparks fly." An earlier generation had praised the "Red Hot Mamas," who had "it." Mae West was a sex-celebrity for years, with her purring tag-line, "Come up and see me some time." During World War II the life jacket that inflated when a sailor was in the water was known to the Navy as a "Mae West."

Her male counterpart was the incredibly hot (by now he seems camp) hero, Rudolph Valentino. Dark and well-groomed, he fairly breathed passion as he galloped over the hot desert playing such roles as *The Sheik*. Otherwise respectable ladies collected his cigarette butts and hid them in their bosoms. When he died suddenly, mass hysteria swept over many females. A cordon of policemen had to stop admirers from plucking off his buttons as his body lay in state.

But one who was hotter, and more celebrated, than Valentino was already on the scene. Clark Gable was often "leading man" to Mae West and Marilyn Monroe, and also to Mary Astor, Claudette Colbert, Greta Garbo, Ava Gardner, Greer Garson, Grace Kelly, Norma Shearer, Barbara Stanwyck, Lana Turner, and Loretta Young. Born in small-town Ohio in 1901, the big-eared youth quit school at seventeen to become a day-laborer, then a bit actor known as Billy Gable. Married to a woman thirteen years his senior, who had been on Broadway and knew its ways, the dashing over-confident stage Clark Gable was "invented by his first wife." In 1924 he went to Hollywood, then to Broadway, then back to Hollywood. The special alchemy of the silver screen started to work. While Fairbanks was creating a celluloid swashbuckler, Gable became the lover-adventurer, certain to get the girl and to come out way ahead. He was irresistible. Instead of asking for love, he demanded it. This wholly authentic All-American Guy was, by the mid-nineteen thirties, a household image. "Who do you think you are?" a wisecrack of the times went, "Clark Gable?"

Blessed with rare strength and great endurance, he reached his pinnacle as Rhett Butler in *Gone With the Wind*. (Thirty years later the revamped film is still breaking box-office records throughout the world.) At fifty-nine Gable went to the Nevada desert to film his ninetieth picture, "The Misfits"; Marilyn Monroe was his leading lady. He was her fantasy-father as he went through the strenuous part. Shortly afterwards he died of a heart attack; four months after his death, Gable's only son was born to his fifth wife.

In the first half of the twentieth century the silver screen was plainly the best place for a "sex-queen" and a "he-man" to prosper. The movie camera seems to confer celebrity, not just on people, but on objects and places. The camera brings stardom to everything it records—and thus breeds celebrities. That is why innovating film makers like Ingmar Bergman, Michelangelo Antonioni, François Truffaut, Michael Cacoyannis, and Peter Watkins may be the Parson Weems's of tomorrow.[2]

Meanwhile the old print-oriented celebrity makes a last stand as Playboy. Like Mickey Mouse, he stands before the world in all his two dimensions—the creation of a living promotion story named Hugh M. Hefner.

Started in the mid-1950s on only $7000, the first issue

[2] See Penelope Houston, *The Contemporary Cinema* (New York: Penguin, 1968) and Andre Bazin, *What Is Cinema?* (Berkeley, Calif.: University of California Press, 1968).

of *Playboy* Magazine wasn't dated, with the expectation that there might not be another. A decade later, with a circulation of 2.2 million, it was one of the nation's leading magazines. In its pages the Playboy model or stereotype is pounded into the reader—a sophisticated, urbane, affluent, promiscuous, mature bachelor. This goal, scholars have suggested, is "what most Americans have long desired as a perfect style of life." [3]

The Lenin of the fast-spreading sex revolution, Hugh Hefner tuned into the new hedonism and shrewdly turned it to his advantage. In addition to publishing he is involved with night clubs, concerts, a modeling agency, a television show, and assorted other ventures. From his half-million-dollar home in Chicago he directs his elaborate popstyle world, absolute master of over seven hundred "bunnies." His is the world of now, pop, hot. In his round bed, which revolves electronically, Hefner outstrips and updates all the boyhood dreams of an older generation—Tom Swift and his Sextronic Keyboard.

The real celebrity is not Hefner, but the *Playboy* rabbit he has invented. (Similarly, Mickey Mouse, and not Mickey's creator, is the Message.) The rabbit, ever-present symbol for Hefner, is always dressed in expensive, fashionable clothes, off to enjoy such "in" activities as yachting, skin diving, night clubbing, or racing foreign sports cars. Sexy girls, scantily clad, are always near by, but they don't seem to unnerve him. His eyes remain half-closed in a bored fashion; his mouth turns up slightly at the corners, reflecting a smug self-satisfaction. Here, at last, is a rabbit who is a man of the world. *Playboy* is more than mere diversion and dream-fulfillment. Every issue teaches readers the symbols,

[3] Walter M. Gerson and Sander H. Lunc, "*Playboy* Magazine: Sophisticated Smut or Social Revolution," *Journal of Popular Culture*, 1:3 (Winter 1967), p. 220.

styles, and rituals of a real Playboy, the attitudes, beliefs, and gestures that are required. The key is "cool but active sophistication." A typical cartoon shows a husband dutifully serving his wife and her lover cocktails in bed. Ours is not (as T. S. Eliot said) "a culture of a thousand lost golf balls," but a culture of a thousand lost chances for coitus.

To give substance to their reveries men buy keys for Playboy Clubs in various American cities. While the magazine appeals largely to a college-age audience, the Clubs serve an older clientèle—men who don't mind paying well to ogle "bunnies" who serve as waitresses and hostesses. A lucky few can go right to Hefner's Chicago home and watch bunnies swim in the nude in the great glass pool. In this world clock and calendar are redundant. Night can be day, Tuesday can be Saturday, if one has the cool and the courage to control his environment.

To be a celebrity, in Playboyland, one has to be multi-dimensional; up on the latest authors and theories; equally at home at diplomatic receptions and hippie beer bashes. The whole process is full of wish-fulfillment and reinforcement. Here is a way to make the scene—to be the talk of the town.

Celebrities are known for their well-knownness, notorious for their notoriety. Such new-model "heroes" are nothing but ourselves seen in a magnifying mirror. They are the perfect embodiment of tautology—the most familiar is the most familiar.

Our generation has not only produced celebrities, but has recast heroes in the new mold. Jesus becomes "no snob, but a regular swinger," while God is (in James Thurber's satiric phase) "my pal Jehovah." Washington becomes an "everyday guy," and Lincoln "just one of the boys." This tendency helps to explain the success of a series of banal juvenile books called "The Childhood of Famous Americans" and the familiarity and vulgarity of current political campaigning.

In the spirit of the times, Earl Blackwell and Cleveland Amory compiled in 1959 a *Celebrity Register,* containing 2200 biographies. "It is impossible to list accurately the success or value of man; but you *can* judge a man as a celebrity—all you have to do is weigh his press clippings." Thus do Bertrand Russell and Jane Russell move dos à dos down the pages of heroic history.

National culture is being replaced like the horse and buggy when the automobile came by a synthetic substance that exists in the media. "Entertainment" is never just entertaining, being chock-full of attitude-forming information. Ads not only sell—they shape. Just as the nineteenth century took its toll on the worker's body, so does the twentieth century on his mind. Not the illusion of progress, but the illusion of technique, ensnares us. Not our jobs, but the texture of our personalities is endangered by the new lifestyle. The new American *imago* is couched not in terms of causes or events, but of images picked up by our constant involvement in vicarious activities of the human race all over the world.

Elitist critics view this *imago* with alarm and despair. *What Happened to the American Dream?* Daniel Boorstin asks as the subtitle to his volume on *The Image.* A generation earlier Gilbert Seldes and Edmund Wilson wrote about what was then called (with Leftist overtones) mass society; but it was Dwight Macdonald who wrote most influentially about the difference between "serious" (high, sophisticated, authentic) and "popular" (low, unsophisticated, synthetic) art. Occasionally, as with jazz, the blues, and silent movies, "pop" could be "authentic." In the main, however, it was *kitsch,* designed to exploit an increasingly apathetic and alienated mass audience. Younger writers like Richard

Hoggart, Raymond Williams, and Denys Thompson continued the argument and applied it to Europe. The collection of essays that Thompson edited under the title *Discrimination and Popular Culture,* struck the typical elitist cords. Entertainment has become a form of propaganda excluding all forms of civilized diversions. We exist off a well-packaged, superficially attractive, but fake, culture. "Our rich national culture is replaced by a synthetic affair which glamourizes a consumption-for-its-own-sake civilization." [4]

Such critics fail to see the revolutionary changes not only in the arts, but in our modes of sensibility. The new-style involvement with popular culture has altered the whole picture, and our heroes. In this sense our celebrities are exported, on film and paper, all over the world. They in turn are affected by, and are sensitive to, their global audience.[5] The world is wired for sound; Olympus teems with celebrities.

New mass media (especially television) have greatly increased the visibility of the entertainer, and inflated his general importance. No movie star who has not been on TV rates as high with most Americans as even moderately successful TV stars. Publicists know that the best way to solve problems is to put entertainers on a pedestal that casts rational objects of respect and affection in the shade. The line between hero, artist, and salesman has merged.[6]

Nineteenth-century Robber Barons grabbed natural resources and staged "The Great Barbecue." Now, in the twentieth century, we have show-business Robber Barons who go beyond the old saw that business is business. Now

[4] Denys Thompson, *Discrimination and Popular Culture* (London: Penguin, 1964), p. 21.

[5] This new involvement of man with man is the central concern of Walter Ong in *The Barbarian Within* (New York: Macmillan, 1962).

[6] For a detailed analysis see Patrick D. Hazard, "The Entertainer as Hero," *Journalism Quarterly,* Minneapolis, Minnesota (Spring 1962).

show business is show business. By their celebrities ye shall know them.

These techniques affect politics, art, journalism, criticism, and education. Image-making is revealed in almost everything we do, say, or see. Television is chewing gum for the eyes. The question is no longer "Do you like me?" but "Do you like my shadow?" Like the people in Plato's allegorical cave, we mix illusion and reality, mistaking the shadows for ourselves. We have turned from the three-dimensional emancipator to the two-dimensional entertainer.

The problem now confronting America is not unlike that of the hero of Anton Chekhov's play, "The Hollow": "You remember, before the wedding, Anisim brought me some new rubles and half rubles? I hid one packet, the rest I mixed with my own. Now I can't make out which is real money and which is counterfeit, it seems to me they are all false coins."

With such ephemeral heroes, we develop extravagant expectations.[7] We expect anything and everything—the contradictory and the impossible—a TV spectacular every week, a best-selling masterpiece every month, a new hero every season. Gresham's law operates as bad plaques, medals, trophies, and awards drive good ones out. Celebrities push out heroes. "At some point general rebellion will set in," Eric Sevareid predicts. "Community bonfires in public parks will celebrate the end of the awards. But— if Yankee prudence sets in—all medals and plaques will be shipped to a central place and melted down. Then one monument, half a mile high, will be erected—the Award to all Americans for Existing." [8]

[7] This idea, and others used here, are more fully developed by Daniel Boorstin, *The Image; or What Happened to the American Dream* (New York: Atheneum, 1962).

[8] Syndicated column in *Philadelphia Bulletin* (June 9, 1963).

Celebrities are part of the American lifestyle which is suspended between the figures of Rousseau and Darwin. We are eternally drained by our unresolved allegiances to both the romantic natural man and the naturalistic man in nature. Pioneer-believers as well as pioneer-brutes, we see every log cabin as a potential Shangri-la. We want both at the same time. The double craving turns out to be a lasting crucifixion. The nails that bite the flesh from the outside turn out to be inside.

The celebrity triumphed early in spectator sports. Playland is a carrousel world where tinkling music, colored lights, and hysterical cheers hypnotize. Sport is a separate culture—the physical culture—of our time.[9]

It is something the common man can observe, talk about authoritatively, cast in old heroic patterns. He can immerse himself emotionally and viscerally in sports, finding there a sense of identity and destiny. Sports engage the time, energy, and monies of the general population to a far greater degree than science or humanities. For better or for worse, sport gives form and substance to much in American life.

The peculiarly American sport of baseball produced Babe Ruth. His monument is Yankee Stadium, "the House that Ruth Built." George "Babe" Ruth's rise from a Baltimore charity school augmented the Horatio Alger mythology. After his "first Homeric swat" of May 6, 1915, he continued to break records in a game which is better designed for statisticians than spectators. In 1919 Ruth hit the longest home run; in the 1926 World Series he pointed to a distant spot and yelled at the hooting fans, "I'll knock it out there for you!" He did. Out of such episodes celebrities are created.

[9] See Robert H. Boyle, *Sport: Mirror of American Life* (Boston: Little, Brown, 1964).

Folklore and legend took over. Cultivating a Bunyan-like stance and appetite, he ate eleven hot dogs in one afternoon. Ruth also liked stiff drinks. Referring to Ruth's weakness for alcohol, teammate "Lefty" Gomez said, "He's the only man in the United States that if you took a pint of blood, it would need a revenue stamp."

Paul Gallico, the sports writer for whom Babe Ruth was "His Majesty the King" (an odd title for use in a democratic society), called him "the most accessible of all our heroes." He then repeated one of the standard Ruth legends, about the kid who, after an operation, "needed something tremendous to bring him back." A baseball autographed by Ruth might do the trick. A newspaperman told him the story and asked Ruth to autograph a ball for the boy.

The next morning the nurse said, "Johnny! Johnny! You must open your eyes and sit up for a moment. Someone is here to see you." Then, in Gallico's words "the door opened and it was God himself who walked into the room, straight from His glittering throne, God dressed in a camel's hair polo coat and a flat, camel's hair cap, God with a flat nose and little piggy eyes, a big grin, and a fat black cigar." [10] God even spoke, "Ya know what I'm going to do this afternoon? I'm gonna hit a home run just for you. You watch. It's gonna be your home run. Now you hurry up and get well so you can come out and see me play." He performed the "miracle." He hit that home run that afternoon. Celebrities always produce—or else they stop being celebrities.

"His home runs brought forth pandemonium," Gallico continues, "a curious double rejoicing in which the spectator celebrated not only Babe's feat, but also his excellent luck in being present to behold the great happening." Scientists

[10] Paul Gallico, "His Majesty the King," from *Farewell to Sport* (New York: Knopf, 1938), chap. 4.

171

added to the aura by taking "psycho-technical test" and proving that his eyes functioned 12 times faster than most men's and that he outdid 499 out of 500 men in the responsiveness of his nerves. Call him the Sultan of Swat; Beowulf at Bat. Call him a celebrity.

So was Ruth's contemporary, Charles Lindbergh—the "Lone Eagle." By flying the Atlantic solo in May 1927, he captured not only a $25,000 prize, but the heart of the world. Only twenty-five at the time, unmarried and unpretentious, this "tousle-haired boy" who lived off sandwiches and chocolate bars arrived in France to say simply, "I did it." (Or had he said, "Somebody cable Mother" or "So this is Paris"?) Some called him Mercury, shod with wings—others, the New World Galahad. From that day forth he was a celebrity, and his life would be tinged with unreality.[11] His return called forth the greatest national ovation ever given an American.

In a single month (June 1927) Lindy received 3,500,000 letters, 14,000 parcels, and 100,000 telegrams. *The New York World* got two bushels of Lindbergh poems. While he was eating in New York, a woman defied guards to peer into his mouth and find out whether he liked green beans or peas. (There was no such adulation for the first space heroes of the 1950s and 1960s.) "Five centuries have been required to make a saint of Joan of Arc," Marquis Childs noted, "but in two years Colonel Charles A. Lindbergh has become a demigod."

He would not remain so. By accepting medals from Nazi Germany and vigorously opposing America's entry into World War II, the "Lone Eagle" was widely discredited, and called a "Copperhead" by President Roosevelt. The effort

[11] See Dixon Wecter, "Charles Lindbergh," in *The Hero in America* (Ann Arbor, Mich.: University of Michigan Press, 1963).

to revive his reputation with a major film production starring James Stewart was a failure; in 1968 Lindbergh was reported giving speeches in Alaska to help preserve the vanishing polar bear. His rise and fall is a fully documented history of the celebrity in twentieth-century America.[12]

As Lucky Lindy faded on the horizon, an unbroken line of celebrities took over, with new signs, images, and responses. Articles and books have been written about them, many by baffled and angry authors. England's Anthony Burgess, for example, wants nothing to do with this "teen-age God, finger-clicking to pop mass, worshipped in pop lyrics." America's Dwight Macdonald conjures up the image of a production line grinding out a uniform product which aims not at entertainment but distraction. Out go old barriers of class, tradition, taste, cultural distinctions. In comes a homogenized culture, from which the cream has disappeared. Trot out a gloomy quatrain by an earlier cultural arbiter, Alexander Pope:

> Lo, the dread empire, Chaos, is restored;
> Light dies before thy uncreating word;
> Thy hand, great march, lets the curtain fall
> And universal darkness buries all.

Shall we label the odd, defiant, and structureless world of celebrities springing up like mushrooms "universal darkness"? Or is it so illuminated that the light dazzles our eyes, and leaves us incapable of seeing?

The last time I walked down Broadway they were tearing down the Astor Hotel. Many of us found its lobby and bar one of the consolations for World War II. Watching the 1968 dismantling, the action seemed symbolic. A new generation is engaged in a house-wrecking task. Down come

[12] See Kenneth S. Davis, *The Hero: Charles A. Lindbergh and the American Dream* (New York: Doubleday, 1959).

173

forms, styles, assumptions that sent us off to "Sink the Rising Sun." Japan is still rising, our chief ally in an Asia in which our former ally, China, is the enemy. German cities we bombed are rebuilt now, "bulwarks against the enemy." We wrecked houses, too. Our children have other battles to fight, other issues to solve, other houses to wreck. They will have their own heroes.

To the social historian none seem more significant in the 1960s than John, Paul, George, and Ringo—not the Four Apostles or the Four Horsemen, but the Four Beatles. These young British singers adapted the American idiom, then made the "British style" internationally famous. Electronics took the hyphen out of Anglo-American culture.

"The solid gold door to Beatleland," to quote the Authorized Version, "is open to anyone who is young of heart." The rulers are John Lennon (born 1940), Ringo Starr (born 1940), Paul McCartney (born 1942), and George Harrison (born 1943).[13]

Onstage they sing banal lyrics (sample: "I crossed the room and my heart went boom!") set to a personalized, Americanized music that whines and thumps. Offstage, they hold press conferences like heads of state, outsmarting reporters with off-the-tops-of-their-shaggy-heads answers to questions like "How do you find America?" (answer: "Go to Greenland and turn left.") "Which threatens you most, the atom bomb or dandruff?" (answer: "The bomb, we already have dandruff.")

Beatleland exports wigs, buttons, posters, clothes, songs, and the Beatles themselves. Beatle fans (called Beatle People by the Beatles) are all over the world. Like hero-worshippers throughout the ages, they will find and suffer

[13] See Hunter Davies, *The Beatles: The Authorized Biography* (New York: McGraw-Hill, 1968); and Julius Fast, *The Beatles: The Real Story* (New York: G. P. Putnam's Sons, 1968).

for their idols, paying any money asked for a ticket to a Beatle concert. Whenever they see a Beatle they scream. This golden rule no Beatle Person wants to be the first to break.

What do the Beatles think about Beatle People? "We think they're all a bit soft yelling after us like that," says John, "but we luv' them. We'd be nothing without them, now, wouldn't we?"

"They paid to get in," adds Ringo, "they can do whatever they want to." The tone is similar to that in his reply to the charge that celebrities like the Beatles are only fads: "Yeah, but when we fads go, we'll be taking all the money with us."

After a nondescript beginning, including several earlier group names (Moon Doggies, Silver Doggies, Silver Beatles) and jobs in German rathskellers, the Beatles recorded "She Loves You" and "I Want to Hold Your Hand" in 1963. The result (back to the Official Version) was "Beatlemania." Thousands of female fans loved them, adored them, chased them, threw things at them. The fact that they often threw jelly beans gave psychiatrists the chance to make Freudian comments. The Beatles "invaded" the United States in 1964, appearing on Ed Sullivan's TV show, in Washington, and in New York's Carnegie Hall. To accommodate a fraction of those who wanted to come, hysterical audiences were admitted to rehearsals as well as performances. While in New York the celebrated Four visited the Playboy Club. Paul commented: "The bunnies are even more adorable than we are."

American imitators of the British Beatles are legion; no group has had the same impact. The Beatles have insisted on moving ahead musically, experimenting with new sound, sequences, ideas. They also had the services, until his premature death in 1967, of Brian Epstein, "the man who made the four lads from Liverpool what they are today." Forced

175

to leave the Royal Academy of Dramatic Art to help out in his family's Liverpool store, Epstein handled his bumptious quartet well and became "the most talked-about manager in show business." His mastery of new techniques and media made him the era's chief hero-maker. Epstein had the Beatles announce that they were better-known than Jesus. The spring of 1968 found them in India for an extensive course in meditation with their special guru, Maharishi Mahesh Yogi. This process was interrupted by faithful fans. The unruffled Maharishi sent his aides out to sell prayer books to the visitors, while he personally bestowed blessings on the photographers.

There is nothing fake about the Beatles' musical innovations. Employing unorthodox key shifts, unequal phrase lengths, and basic triads, they have achieved a straining tenderness, primitive boldness, haunting beauty. In their wake have come new movements—bluebeat, ska, Oriental, raga. Current options are extremely diverse—electronic experimentation, crackling blues, soul, piercing psychedelia, love rock. "Rock," Nat Hentoff writes, "celebrates a vision, a world music. And within that open-ended gestalt, it offers a chance for those within it to do their thing." Significantly, the Beatles in particular, followed by the Rolling Stones and Eric Burdon and the Animals, have developed their own material and their own ways of shaping that material." [14] Is this not proof that there is more to ephemeral celebrities than meets the eye—or ear?

With the throb of a new beat is the burden of an old quest for heroic recognition, reality, comradeship. Some hero-hungry young people want to love the world into submission. "What matters," their singer-idols say, "is the feeling

[14] Nat Hentoff, *The New York Times* (November 26, 1967).

of the person inside." In this sense, the Rock Revolution is profoundly Christian. The Kingdom of God is within you.

Many churchmen have tried to produce jazz masses and anthems. One of the best was Duke Ellington's *Concert of Sacred Music*. When it was scheduled for a 1967 Washington performance, a Ministers' Conference refused to endorse the concert, since Ellington's life "is opposed to what the church stands for."

"Every man prays in his own language," the aging celebrated Duke replied, "and there's no language God does not understand. Of all man's fears, I think men are most afraid of being what they are—in direct communication with the world at large." The Duke's *Concert* goes on from church to church.

No young American is in such direct communication with his own generation as Bob Dylan. Born in Minnesota in 1941, a guitar player at ten, the slim youth drifted around the country, soaking up the sounds of blues, hillbilly tunes, and country music. Having taught himself the harmonica, piano, and autoharp, he began to write songs like "Blowin' in the Wind" and "The Times They Are a-Changin'," and suddenly became a celebrity. "All I'm doing is saying what's on my mind the best way I know how," he said. "Whatever else you say about me, everything I do and sing and write comes out of *me*."

Indeed Bob Dylan was and is his own person. His work has a sort of dark laughter and mockery:

> Get born keep warm
> Short pants romance learn to dance
> Get dressed get blessed try to be
> A success . . .
> Don't want to be a bum you better chew gum
> The pump don't work cause the vandals took the handle.

177

"Anything I can sing I call a song. Anything I can't sing, I call a poem. Anything I can't sing or that's too long to be a poem, I call a novel." This sense of structurelessness, of the accidental, likens him to such different contemporaries as Andy Warhol, John Cage, Marshall McLuhan, and Tom Wolfe. But more than any of them, Dylan stood for a rejection of prettiness, over-refinement, smoothness, even subtlety. To the older generation he symbolized the leather-booted, wild-animal-type young man who was going ape. At them the young idol hurled his famous taunt: "Something is happening, and you don't know what it is—do you, Mr. Jones?"

Style is never free from fad—that exaggerated zeal that clouds judgment and compounds errors. Celebrities are unquestionably faddish. What if the fad becomes a trend, then a style? That happened with the *enfants terribles* of the Kennedy Years, the Beatles. "This will surely pass," we said five years ago. But we were wrong. Even those who never expected to like or accept it can look back with a kind of nostalgia to the sweetness and simplicity of the early Beatles, drowned out today by the thumping cacophony of the Monkees, Jefferson Airplane, Fugs, and the Grateful Dead.

Changes in fads and styles are complicated. Caused by many unmeasurable factors, they affect all parts of the culture. Who can measure accurately the changing audience, the evolving aesthetic, the change in the heroic climate? Style is the essence of humanness.

Celebrities have appealed as never before to a generation with new signs, images, responses—many of them lodged in the subconscious. People under thirty usually accept the urban world forced upon them—not the world which Daniel Boone pioneered or Henry David Thoreau eulogized, but the world of neon lights, billboards, comic strips and strippers. The TV commercial is the new *lingua franca.* The unreality of the environment is what makes it seem so real.

Popstyle, from which celebrities emerge, makes of the phony an epiphany. Shallowness, repetition, frustration are all built into the model. "I find Andy Warhol's movies long and boring," playwright Edward Albee said recently. "But that's all right. I like long and boring things."

My teen-age daughter is right. "Give your ulcer a break, Dad," she advises. "Don't fight it."

13

Off Brands: Anti, Non, and Absurd

"The more subtle and close our psychological knowledge of the protagonist becomes, the less he appears to us heroic."

DAVID DAICHES

THE All-American hero died on Flanders Fields. He went into World War I wrapped in bunting, certain to make the world safe for democracy. He came out in gunny sack, having made the world safe for dictatorship. He went Over There chanting the heroic words of Virgil: "Arms and the man I sing." He came back to read a new best seller called *Farewell to Arms*.

Ernest Hemingway, literary father of anti-hero, wrote the book. In it Lieutenant Henry arrived at a bitter conclusion:

They threw you in and told you the rules and the first time they caught you off base they killed you. . . . I am always embarrassed by the words sacred, glorious, and sacrifice and by the expression in vain.

Other Hemingway heroes, like Jake Barnes and Nick Adams, made similar discoveries. Cut off from the traditional heroic meanings and attachment to community, they turned their backs on public values for personal ritual. They simply refused to play society's game, realizing that it was, like one of Hemingway's titles, *Winner Take Nothing.* So keep your medals, your statues, and your big brass bands; I will be true to myself, and die with honor and integrity.

To give Hemingway, or any American, credit for the anti-hero is, of course, an oversimplification. The Book of Job, and Greek dramas like *The Oresteia,* point out that all is vanity and chasing after winds. Certainly *Don Quixote* is anti-heroic, as is Shakespeare's Falstaff, who knew that honor is but a word. Thackeray's great novel *Vanity Fair* is subtitled *A Novel Without a Hero,* and Mario Praz has shown that this can be applied to most Victorian novels.[1]

We move from outside triumph to inner trauma, to man's swarming interior world, made up of disparate and contradictory things.

Critics also point to different types of unheroic or antiheroic characters, with roots deep in the past—fool, clown, scapegoat, freak, rebel without a cause, angry young man. Still, the heroic climate changed drastically after World War I. The works of Huxley, Waugh, and Orwell in England, and of Faulkner, Dos Passos, and Farrell in America give ample documentation; Hemingway seemed best able to describe the new hero, both in his books and in his own life. The trick was to face up to the tragic moment of crisis, to emerge defeated but not broken.

Hemingway himself suffered two plane crashes going across Africa in 1953 with his fourth wife, "Miss Mary." Miraculously he survived, emerging from the jungle clutching a bunch of bananas in one hand and a bottle of gin in the other. Later on he reported the damage that had been

[1] Mario Praz, *The Hero in Eclipse in Victorian Fiction* (New York: Oxford University Press, 1956). For more on this score, see also Sean O'Faolain's *The Vanishing Hero* (London: Eyre and Spottiswode, 1956) and Raymond Giraud's *The Unheroic Hero in the Novels of Stendahl, Balzac and Flaubert* (New Brunswick, N.J.: Rutgers University Press, 1957). Movie and television non-heroes are also popular.

done: "I jammed my spine, ruptured my right kidney and liver, collapsed my intestine, suffered a concussion which seriously affected my eyesight, and was burned severely on the scalp." And what did he do about all this, living out his own invention? He hurried on to Madrid, since it was the peak of the bullfighting season.

Confronted with the news that he had an incurable ailment, Hemingway made the ultimate gesture and committed suicide. "Hemingway's suicide was not a betrayal of his life," Morse Peckham notes, "but a fulfillment of it." [2]

Half a century after Hemingway's war, young writers were following faithfully in his anti-heroic footsteps. A typical example was John Weston's *Hail, Hero!* published in 1968, and described by a reviewer in the *Plain Dealer* in Hemingwayesque terms:

A warning ... to the dull-minded mass of professional patriots, unctuous politicians, aged non-combatants and the whole dismal spectrum of hard-headed and hard-bellied peddlers and purveyors who find it so easy to assume that only they are fashioned in God's image.

Sociologists document the dramatic shift in heroic interest in the early twentieth century. Before World War I, Leo Lowenthal reports, there was a high interest in political figures and an almost equal distribution of business and professional men on one hand, and of entertainers (largely serious artists) on the other. This picture changed completely after the war. Political figures were cut by 40 percent, business and professional men by 30 percent. But entertainers (largely popular artists) of the mass media have more than doubled. "We called the heroes of the past 'idols

[2] Morse Peckham, *Romanticism: The Culture of the 19th Century* (New York: Braziller, 1965), p. 235.

of production'; present-day magazine heroes can be called 'heroes of consumption.' " [3]

This consumption society—in which we crave an indefinite number of cars, cans, deodorants, and celebrities—produced a kind of pop pseudo-hero whom we shall examine later on; in serious literature and thinking, the anti-hero not only survived, but flourished. A new generation grew up to reject the phony prizes of its parents. In the 1920 statement of a young writer named John F. Carter, Jr.:

> We're not babes in the wood, hunting for big red strawberries and confidently expecting the Robin Red-Breasts to cover us up with pretty leaves if we don't find them. . . . All may yet crash to the ground, for aught that we can do about it. [4]

In his 1929 appraisal of *The Modern Temper,* Joseph Wood Krutch went further, and proclaimed that tragedy was dead. Tragedy must have a hero, but now anti-hero had taken over. "Our cosmos may be farcical or it may be pathetic, but it has not the dignity of tragedy and we cannot accept it as such." [5] Automation, computerization, nuclear fission, and rocketry should have made us free, but they have only tyrannized us to a degree unparalleled in history. Our ancestors thought we would, by now, have built the "Brave New World." Instead, we seem unable to figure out ways to prevent blowing it up.

The time for grand Utopian schemes and the old "blah blah words," has passed. The general human predicament must be confronted in every particular situation. Instead of

[3] Leo Lowenthal, "Biographies in Popular Magazines," in *American Social Patterns,* William Peterson, ed. (New York: Doubleday Anchor Books, 1956).

[4] Quoted by Malcolm and Robert Cowley, eds., *Fitzgerald and the Jazz Age* (New York: Scribner, 1966), p. 50.

[5] Joseph Wood Krutch, *The Modern Temper* (New York: Harcourt, Brace and World, 1929), p. 141.

being antireligious, existentialists represent an ultimate religious concern—far more telling than that of many who grind out Sunday School literature or dignify pulpits on Sunday morning. Man, they tell us, is a born phony, full of bad faith. He dodges responsibilities on all levels. Like the dishonest dentist, he is content to make his living by disguising decay.

Terrified by the threat of meaninglessness, we retreat into anonymity. Life becomes bearable, but routine—like getting second-class mail without a name. Another escape is nostalgia, with syrupy talk of the good old days. Rainer Maria Rilke spoke scornfully of this kind of deception in the *Valais Quatrains:*

> Everything here sings the life of yesterday
> But not in a way which would destroy tomorrow . . .
> It is the land which rests in its image
> And which consents to its first day.

A harsher view of the "return to the womb" emerges from Franz Kafka's *Die Verwanglung,* whose hero becomes a man-sized insect who eats anything rotten. Here is an unforgettable depiction of the sense of being cast out—*das Ausgestossensein*—which is echoed in other writers like Ernest Junger, Hermann Hesse, and Heinrich Boll. Anyone who finds modern painting or sculpture grotesque or exaggerated should read their works, and that of other young Europeans. There he will find the same themes, tensions, and situations that others have put on canvas or turned into tortured metal and clay.

Martin Buber, the century's leading Jewish philosopher, spoke on "life on the narrow ridge." Driven from Europe by Hitler, disinherited for his anti-Zionist opinions in Israel, Buber was a one-man Lost Tribe roaming the world. Yet he knew his life was more than a problem—it was a mys-

184

tery. (Problems can be solved, mysteries, never.) Real living is meeting. Authentic selfhood results only from the I-Thou encounter. To turn "thou" into "it" is to deny personhood, and cut the heart out of life. Life is more than objective versus subjective; it can be transjective as well.

"My role is not to transform the world, or man," wrote Albert Camus, the existentialist novelist. "For that I have not virtues enough, nor clearsightedness. It consists in serving, where I can, those few values without which a world, even transformed, is not worth living in; without which a man, even new, would not be worthy of respect." What sort of art, music, movies, and television might result from people who opted to "serve those few values" which captured Camus? Is some of the evidence in, or has *verbal* existentialism still to find an outlet in the *visual* world? The question deserves an answer.

By the mid-1960s there were signs that the influence of existentialists (especially in America) was waning. The failure to weld ethical meaning into their analyses caused many intellectuals to look elsewhere for new inspiration. The works of Jean Paul Sartre, in particular, show how existentialism, a good servant of the life of faith, makes a poor master. Its proponents are anthropocentric, often egocentric. Like medieval monks, they prefer to turn their backs on the world rather than to contend with it.

Though they do not give final answers, existentialists have raised critical questions. Tough-minded thinkers for turbulent times, they achieve ultimate importance by refusing to give final answers. They have completed the intellectual backdrop against which that lively drama of pop culture is being staged.

In the theater, too, the war against clichés, heroics, empty formulas, and sweet slogans has been vigorously waged. In Edward Albee's play *The Sandbox* we watch Grandmother

185

dying painfully beside the ocean, as Death approaches in a swimming suit. In *The Blacks,* by Jean Genet, three cloaked Negroes imitate whites. The butcher in Arnold Weinstein's *The Red Eye of Love* amuses himself by building a skyscraper out of used meat.

As in Hemingway's novels, the effort is not only to ignore but to ridicule old conceptions of the hero. Instead of being muted, the themes are played back off key. "The hero of our age," Michael Glenn writes, "is the psychopath. Free from responsibility, free from guilt, he pursues his interests without compunction, manipulating others to reach his goals." [6]

The subject of Eugene Ionesco's play *The Chairs* is "the absence of people, the absence of the emperor, the absence of God, the absence of matter. The theme is nothingness."

Digits, sounds, syntax, logic are jumbled in a totally unheroic situation. This passage from *The Chairs* is typical:

"Where's my mamma? I don't have a mamma anymore."
"That's not true. I'm an orphan, hi, hi."
"My pet, my orphan, dworfan, worfan, morphan, orphan."

The acknowledged master of the absurd, the most controversial British writer since James Joyce, is Samuel Beckett. Born in Dublin in 1906, veteran of wanderings in England, France, and Germany, he writes in a manner that is outrageously simple yet endlessly complex. Since publishing a poem called "Whoroscope" in 1930, Beckett has done stories, translations, novels, and plays. They center on amputees, battered clothes, the letter M, bicycles, and inane conversation. Molloy, the protagonist of one of Beckett's novels, resembles $\sqrt{2}$. His is a universe in which people

[6] Michael L. Glenn, "The Hero of Our Age," *Village Voice* (Sept. 14, 1967). See also William Barrett, *Irrational Man: A Study in Existential Philosophy* (New York: Doubleday, 1962).

endure hopeless misery. The normal signs of human solidarity seem not so much perverted as anesthetized.

In the existential world of Beckett, anything can and does happen. A man sits on nothing identifiable, which exists in a gray space, while a figment of his past invention rotates around him. The whole world crawls from left to right along an invisible track. Hats are exchanged in a meaningless ritual. Twenty-eight people yearn day and night for the day when their combined total ages will be exactly 1000 years. That facts are fiction is itself part of the fiction.

Beckett is imperious and fastidious in his private Bohemia, evading all the nets with which we like to catch dramatists. He is as elusive as the twelfth-century poet who, weeping, left the country of the laughing. This is the zero world of Samuel Beckett, in its all-pervasive void. Zero times anything equals *zero*. The protagonist, more accurately, the anti-hero, is shut off, stifled, dehumanized. The situation is exasperating, pointless, static. Beckett's summation is essentially gibberish. The theater (to say nothing of the audience) is in a state of shock.

Waiting for Godot is an apt example. When the play begins, our eyes fall upon a bare stage, with only a thin, lifeless tree on it. Then we see two tramps, Vladimir and Estragon. They have come here to wait for Godot.

"Let's go."
"We can't."
"Why?"
"We're waiting for Godot."

Over and over, the same words, the same futility. To pass the time they remove their boots, dust off their hats, contradict and carp. Purposeful action is paralyzed. All is futility.

A messenger comes to announce that Mr. Godot won't

come this evening "but surely tomorrow." He asks the tramps what he shall tell Mr. Godot. "Tell him you saw us," Vladimir says. Quickly he adds: "You *did* see us, didn't you?" In the zero world, nothing can be taken for granted.

"We'll hang ourselves tomorrow, unless Godot comes," they declare. With that, they decide to go. But they do not go. The play finally stops, rather than ends. *They do not move.*

Vladimir and Estragon—and most of the pitiful semi-human beings who lumber and drag themselves through absurd plays—are outsiders. They are *out* of the cultural norm, just as their creators are *off* Broadway playwrights. In this, at least, they have a goodly heritage. The outsider theme stretches back to the days of Job, Ulysses, and Beowulf. But it has flared up with special relevancy and poignancy in our generation. We are alone in our crowded cities, busy factories, ant-like apartment houses. By some ironic twist, being "way out" has replaced being "in" as the expression of social acceptance. The furthest out of all are the eggheads. In the world of intellect, externalism has become an established orthodoxy.

By 1965 even the off-Broadway theater had begun to seem orthodox to some, and the off off-Broadway theater sprang up. Lofts, barns, and studios were preferred to theaters. Instead of watching, the audience was engaged, insulted, and even on occasions molested. In one of the most successful "off off" plays, *Hair,* the first act ended with several cast members suddenly appearing stark nude. With arms outstretched they chanted, "Free at last."

More conventional playwrights—the kind whose work is *on* rather than off Broadway—reflect some of these same themes and doubts, though their structures and characterizations are more orthodox. Inner contradictions and ab-

188

surdities dominate Lillian Hellman's *My Mother, My Father, and Me,* as is the case with Irwin Shaw's *Children from Their Games.* Shaw's 56-year-old hero, Melvin Peabody, revels in pain and confusion. He records the noises that make a hell out of urban life. Starved for love, he rejects a woman who offers it. Desperately in need of money, he refuses $250,000 for his house. He even refuses a pill to relieve his physical pain.

"I am in pain," Peabody says. "I am in pain for myself today, in pain for myself for everything I did since I was born. I believe I would be better off dead." Not a single speck of the heroic has survived in him.

The "alienated man" has moved from company town to suburb; from factory to office. His children want neither to live in suburbia nor to work down town. They prefer to take to the road, or to "cop out" and join kindred spirits who take for themselves the title of beats, hippies, or yippies. Norman Mailer, whose World War II novel *The Naked and the Dead* brought him fame in the 1940s, continued to inspire off brand youth in the 1950s and 1960s. He helped to formulate their *credo,* in such passages as this one from *Advertisements for Myself:*

The decision is to encourage the psychopath in oneself; to explore that domain of experience where security is boredom and therefore sickness; to exist in that enormous present which is without past or future, memory or planned intention.

Youthful dropouts in the post-World War II period drew from the long hobo tradition in American. The word, thought to be derived from "Ho, boy," has been used for a century to describe homeless and penniless vagrants who first traveled the rails, then the roads of America. Strong backers of the Populist revolt of the 1890s, then of the

Wobblies labor movement, the hobos have long shed their fears and social shackles for the open road: [7]

> "Hallelujah, I'm a bum!
> Hallelujah, bum again,
> Hallelujah! Bum a handout,
> Revive me again." [8]

Like the angry young men, the beats turned to literature to vent their wrath and earn their daily bread. They earned so much that in a few years they were neither angry nor beat, but quite respectable. Allen Ginsberg and Lawrence Ferlinghetti were major off-brand writers of the 1950s. Their attacks on Wall Street, Madison Avenue, suburbia, and the Pentagon were able to outlive the beat fad and carry over into the era of the hippie. The hippies—city- and politics-oriented—were more anxious to do than to write. Translating liberty, equality, and fraternity into turn-on, tune-in, and drop-out, they made a groovy scene in their off-brand way.

The gloomy anti-utopian sentiments popularized a generation earlier by Aldous Huxley and George Orwell do not figure prominently in young people's thoughts today. Similarly, the "kitchen sink hero" popularized by British writers like Kingsley Amis, John Wain, and John Braine in the 1950s seem far away in time and space. The action has moved from Europe to Asia. Vietnam has become the leading symbol of the anti-heroic. For the first time in American history, thousands of young people greet the prospect of "serving in the armed services of our country" with the cry, "Hell, no! We won't go!"

[7] Kenneth Allsop, *Hard Travellin': The Hobo and His History* (New York: New American Library, 1968).

[8] From *The Hobo's Hornbook, A Repertory for a Gutter Jongleur,* George Milburn, editor (New York: Washburn, 1930; revised ed., New York: Ungar).

The hero, American style, confronts a crisis. The crisis isn't the disease, but the turning point, as Pitirim Sorokin points out in his influential book, *The Crisis of Our Age*. Our trouble is not reducible to economic, political, or social terms; it is far deeper than that. For five centuries Western thought has been basically rational, dedicated to scientific observation, classification, and tabulation. Now this culture is breaking down. Nothing we do will stop it. All we can hope to do is shorten the ensuing tragic period, and mitigate its ravages.

With this and other gloomy analyses before them, scholars try to pin the blame for the trouble on some group or person. Politicians can always blame their opponents; the U.S.A. and the U.S.S.R. can always exchange unpleasantries. The class-conscious can blame the unbending aristocrats, or the unwashed proletariat. Others have demonized the machine, feeling helpless in its presence. For the anti-technologists, the multimegaton bomb makes an obvious target. By an ironic twist, the place chosen to reopen the 1962 atomic tests was the Christmas Islands in the South Seas. To most people Christmas connotes a quiet manger, where the Prince of Peace was born. But in December 1962 different words seemed appropriate for old Christmas tunes:

> Yet in the dark streets shineth
> The radioactive light;
> The hopes and fears of all the years
> Are in the Bomb tonight.

The bomb-makers, the homemakers, the verse-makers all embark on a similar journey—to find themselves. If they fail in this, nothing else they discover or conquer matters. "Money, position, fame, many loves, revenge are all of little consequence," James Michener warns us in *The Fires of Spring*. "When the tickets are collected at the end of the

191

ride they are tossed into a bin marked *failure*. But if a man happens to find himself . . . he has a mansion which he can inhabit with dignity all the days of his life."

For thousands of young Americans in the 1960s "finding myself" involved "freaking out." A whole new vocabulary of drug addiction cropped up. This loose-knit confederation of disenchanted youth bothered the bourgeois considerably; at the 1968 Chicago Democratic Convention, hippies and yippies staged a protest heard round the world, and helped unseat the political party which had, only four years earlier, swept into office with the largest plurality in American history. The fact that many young people would accept neither candidate nor party indicated to thoughtful commentators that what they were witnessing was not riot but revolution.

Many writers, thinkers, and preachers don't want to probe this deep, or slug this hard. They retreat to situation comedies which can be counted on to draw forth the quick laugh and the easy dollar. The best minds seek no easy solutions. They know that evil cannot be defeated by being ignored. These children of Faust will at least give Mephistopheles a run for his money.

The wider connotations of absurdity are apparent. To say matters are ambiguous implies there may be some answer; to say they are absurd implies that rational answers are out of range. "Absurd is that which is devoid of purpose," Ionesco writes, "cut off from religion, metaphysics, and roots. Man is lost. His actions become senseless, useless, *absurd.*"

Edward Albee puts it this way: "Man attempts to make sense out of his senseless position in a world that makes no sense. The social structures man has erected to 'illusion' himself have collapsed." But the explanation with the most poignancy and poetry is that of Albert Camus. "In a universe that is suddenly deprived of illusions and light, man feels himself a stranger," he said. "He is an exile, deprived of memories of a lost homeland, with no hope of a promised land to come. This divorce between man and life, actor and setting, truly constitutes the feeling of absurdity."

Dozens of passages from recent plays serve as specific, dramatic illustrations. This is all that can be said of the hero at the end of John Osborne's *Epitaph for George Dillon:*

> Even his sentimental epitaph is probably a pastiche of some-one or other, but he doesn't quite know who. And in the end, it doesn't really matter.

The sacred and sentimental cult of Mother came under increasing attack half a century after Miss Anna M. Jarvis persuaded her Philadelphia church to set aside a "Mother's Day" in 1907. After World War II Mom took over—a heavy-handed insensitive creature who ruined everything she touched and squelched men like bugs. In a generation of vipers, she stung the hardest. We must not forget the anti-heroine when examining the changing climate of opinion.

Off-brand heroes (anti, non, and absurd) represent a strong reaction against sentimentality and rhetoric. They ask us to see through the outmoded and absurd illusions of ourselves and others. The modern hero must deny his heroic quality, as part of his essential integrity.

In so doing, does he negate heroism itself? I think not. Instead, he reveals a new potential for meeting the predicaments confronting us. In so doing he harks back to the oldest hero in literature, the trickster-rogue of primitive folklore. "When the society of many becomes as fearsome, as inhuman a thing as the world of nature was to primitive man," Raney Stanford points out, "then the trickster returns to literature as the minimal hero." [9]

Thus might the off-brand hero be a new brand, shaped in an ancient mold. We may return to truths known for centuries, but ignored for generations. In place of *cogito ergo sum* the new hero says *dubito ergo sum*. Whatever else it does, doubt assumes an order of truth. We pass through the agony of doubt to arrive at the courage to be.

[9] Raney Stanford, "The Return of Trickster: When a Not-a-Hero Is a Hero," *Journal of Popular Culture,* 1:3 (Winter 1967), p. 238.

14

Red and Black on White

"White Americans have, from the first, hopelessly confused
the real Negroes and Indians with certain projections of
their own deepest minds."

LESLIE FIEDLER

"People talk about Negroes as if they were objects."

BOB DYLAN

NOT until 1968—three and a half centuries after the first
Africans arrived in Jamestown—did a black man become
a national hero in America. Not until Martin Luther King
was assassinated did schools pause, bells toll, and the flag
fly officially at half-staff for a black man. The night before
his death, Dr. King said he had been up on the mountain
and seen the Promised Land. The next day he was in it.

The bullet that ripped still another hole in the fabric of
racial relations followed many earlier ones. The story of
black on white has been written in red—blood-red. In the
1960s it seemed that the Negro was not merely (as historian
U. B. Phillips declared) "the main theme in Southern history." He was becoming the main theme, or counter theme,
in American history.

Afro-American culture has run both parallel to and across
the grain of Anglo-American culture. The black subculture
is not rooted in native soil, like the American Indian's. Instead it was transplanted, under the most difficult imagi-

195

nable circumstances, from Africa. The pendulum swings back and forth between separatism and integration. Cultural uniqueness obsesses the minority Negro even more than the majority American. Robert Bone is only one of many recent writers who lists "distinctive Afro-American culture traits" such as diet (soul food), gesture, humor, speech, religious forms, art forms, survival stratagems, and emotional conditionings. "We do not choose our culture," he writes, "we inherit it." [1]

Though he has spread throughout the land, and related himself to the world scene (two-thirds of the human race is colored) the Afro-American retains special connections with the old Confederacy. Hence folkstyle has special relevance and reality in the American South, with its unique intertwining of Latin romance, Anglo-Saxon ritual, and African primitivism. The blending took place on extensive isolated plantations, free from the dourness of many New England farms and the boorishness of most frontier towns. Unlike Washington Irving or Herman Melville, Southerners didn't have to go to Spain or Tahiti for genuine folk material. There it was, outside their windows: a traditional society, rural, conservative, hierarchical.

No one mirrored its inner values better than Joel Chandler Harris, an archetypal folkstyle writer. Born in rural Georgia in 1848, Harris went to "Turnwold" plantation to work as a printer on a weekly paper, *The Countryman*. Surrounded by slaves, he soaked up their folk tales and mannerisms. After the bloody Civil War, Harris moved to Atlanta and got a job on the *Constitution*. Two years later, when Samuel Small gave up a Negro dialect column which he had been

[1] Robert Bone, "Clarity and the Culture Concept," *Negro American Literature Forum*, I, No. 2 (Winter 1967), p. 11.

writing, Harris continued it.[2] Through him the largely neglected field of Negro folklore and legend was made available to the literary world. Having spent days hunting 'coons, 'possums, rabbits, and foxes, Harris knew rural life and character intimately. His friends included Uncle Remus the gardener, Uncle Bob Capers the teamster, and Uncle George Terrell the recluse. "I just walloped them together into one person and called him Uncle Remus," Harris explained. "You must remember that sometimes the Negro is a genuine and an original philosopher." [3]

Tales of animals and "creeturs" were common in the Old South. James Audubon encountered them in the bayous, Opie Read in the mountains, Mark Twain along the rivers. Northern children with Southern antecedents heard them, too. In his *Autobiography,* Theodore Roosevelt writes: "Aunt Anna and my Mother used to entertain us by the hour with tales of life on the Georgia plantations; of hunting fox, deer, and wildcat; and of the queer goings on in the Negro quarters. She knew all the Br'er Rabbit stories, and I was brought up on them."

Folk tales of the Negroes and the Cherokee Indians intermingled. In *Myths of the Cherokees,* James Mooney shows that the Great White Rabbit is the hero-god, trickster, and wonder-worker of many tribes east of the Mississippi. The Indians regarded the rabbit as the fitting type of defenseless weakness, protected and made safe by constant

[2] The standard biography is Julia Collier Harris, *The Life and Letters of Joel Chandler Harris* (New York: Biography Press, 1918). This may be supplemented by consulting the sketch and bibliography in the Spiller-Thorp *Literary History of the United States* (New York: Macmillan, 1948); and Hennig Cohen's essay on "American Literature and American Folklore" in T. D. Coffin, editor, *Our Living Traditions: An Introduction to American Folklore* (New York: Basic Books, 1968), pp. 238–247.

[3] Quoted by Jay Hubbell in *The South in American Literature* (Durham, N.C.: Duke University Press, 1954), p. 789.

vigilance. Thus many Southern stories now cherished by the white man were cherished by the black and red men before him.

Ancient and amiable Uncle Remus is the Aesop of the plantation world. Though eighty, he is still able to load the wagon and drive home the corn. During the War he had protected the plantation and supervised the other slaves, had hid the stock from the Yankees, and had even shot a Federal soldier who attempted to enter the Big House. His old age is given over to whittling in the sun, talking to the little boy in the evenings, and keeping Old South memories fresh and green.

Stoicism is his secret weapon. Uncle Remus makes the best of the world around him. Humor and wisdom provide a lifetime of quiet contentment. Like Dilsey, his spiritual descendant in the pages of William Faulkner, he endures. So does the plantation cosmology which Harris understood and described so well.

Humility and acquiescence make the humans and the animals in Harris's stories eventual victors. The meek inherit the earth. Harris himself was extremely diffident—so shy that when embarrassed he stuttered. Once asked to lecture at Vanderbilt University, he replied, "I wouldn't deliver a lecture in public for one million dollars." Br'er Rabbit speaks for him.

His tales, like *Alice in Wonderland,* are only ostensibly for children.[4] Harris himself never read or told them to his own children and labeled them allegorical. "It takes no scientific investigation to show why the Negro selects as his

[4] See, for example, John Stafford's "Patterns of Meaning in Nights with Uncle Remus," *American Literature,* XVIII (May 1946); T. H. English's "The Twice-Told Tale and Uncle Remus," *Georgia Review*, II (Winter 1948); and Louise Dauner's "Myth and Humor in the Uncle Remus Tales," *American Literature,* XX (May 1948).

hero the weakest and most harmless of all animals, and brings him out victorious," he wrote. "It is not virtue that triumps, but helplessness; not malice, but mischievousness." His ten volumes of Uncle Remus stories are monuments to poetic justice and mystery. We watch Br'er Rabbit going to sunset prayer meeting to get himself freshened with the Lord; Br'er Fox providing Br'er Rabbit with firewood from sheer compassion; Br'er Hawk soaring up to say "Howdy" to the sun.

On such material the myth of the Old South, shining and golden, could be erected. In it the region is, first and foremost, a land of enchantment. Novels and folk tales are convincing ways of depicting it. While historians check each meticulous brush stroke, creative writers capture with a few bold and bright colors the feeling and motivation of past glory.

We err in considering myths untrue renditions of the past. If not built on at least a partial framework of historical truth, they will not survive. Most myths are closer to half-formulated beliefs than to facts. As any reader can see, Uncle Remus is an anti-heroic black man, a symbol of the acceptance of segregated status quo. Key virtues are humility and acquiescence. One is reminded of Saint Francis's motto about sparing the lowly and striking down the proud, and of his talking to the animals.

In the special world into which the genius of Harris leads us, the first are last, the last first. The cow outlives the lion, the rabbit outwits the wolf, and the mud turtle drowns his attackers by unloosing the foundations of the earth. Here were themes and stories which a people subjected to slavery and segregation could and did come to know and love.

Another black man sang a different song. John Henry refused to demur; he defied. He did not depend on cunning, but strength to win his battles. And he died with his hammer in his hand.

John Henry's origins were obscure but auspicious. He had a bass voice like a preacher, shoulders like a roustabout, and blue gums like a conjure man. He would have no part of servility:

"Did de dogs had they supper?" he asked.

"They did," said his mama.

"Well den," answered John Henry, "ain't I as good as de dogs?" So saying, he reared back and broke the slats out of his bed, cleaved his tongue and spat, and put out the fire.

"Don't make me mad!" he yelled. "Don't git me mad on de day I'm bawn, 'cause I'm skeered of my own-se'f when I'm mad." [5]

Men, women, and mountains could agree on one thing: John Henry was a powerhouse. Although scholars have been on his folk trail for over half a century (Louise Rand Bascom published a monograph on him in 1909), they have never pinned him down. Confusion over his career and that of John Hardy (a black murderer and outlaw) has increased the difficulty.

In 1916 W. A. McCorkle published a piece describing John Henry as "a man of kind heart, very strong, pleasant in his address, a gambler, roué, drunkard, and fierce fighter." This vignette has persisted ever since. Seven years later Howard Odum and Guy Johnson published eleven texts of "John Henry," and four versions of the song. Dr. Johnson later published a whole volume on his scholarly quest devoted to the single ballad, *John Henry: Tracking Down a Negro Legend*.

[5] Roark Bradford, *John Henry* (New York: Harper, 1931), p. 5. Quoted by John T. Flanagan and Arthur Palmer Hudson, *Folklore in American Literature* (Evanston, Ill.: Northwestern University Press, 1958), p. 355.

He finds the question of authenticity a side issue. For countless admirers, John Henry is real—hero, idol, spokesman for the "natural man." John Henry's superstrength, his endurance, and his martyrdom strike fundamental notes. "John Henry stands for something which the pick-and-shovel Negro idolizes—brute strength," Dr. Johnson concluded. "Mention John Henry to a group of working men and the chances are that you start an admiration contest." [6]

Dr. Louis Chappell continued the scholarly quest. In his opinion, the John Henry saga had its origin in actual construction on the Big Bend Tunnel in West Virginia during the 1870s.[7] Though the Negro was by then technically free, he was not psychologically free. He still had to do the bidding of the white man as laborer and inferior. When the engineers of the Chesapeake and Ohio Railroad needed men to tackle the Big Bend Mountain and build a mile-and-a-quarter tunnel, they turned to black men for the muscle power. From Big Sandy to White Sulphur the drill hammer clanged from morning to night.

Railroad camps were squalid, moral stands nonexistent. Laborers often worked in the nude. There were so many deaths from silicosis, cave-ins, suffocation, and falling rocks that the whole area was closed to the press. Casualties were thrown into fills at the far end of the tunnel.

Negroes worked as drivers and shakers. Drivers pounded steel bars into rocks to make holes for dynamite charges. Shakers held the bars between their legs to prevent slip-

[6] Guy B. Johnson, *John Henry: Tracking Down a Negro Legend* (Chapel Hill, N.C.: University of North Carolina Press, 1929), p. 143. See also Lowry Charles Wimberly's account of the book in B. A. Botkin's *Folk-say* (Norman, Okla.: University of Oklahoma Press, 1930), pp. 413 f.; and the essay on John Henry in Frank Shay's *Here's Audacity! American Legendary Heroes* (New York: Macaulay, 1930).

[7] Louis W. Chappell, *John Henry* (Jena, Germany: Walter Biederman, 1933); American edition (Chicago: Argonaut, 1967).

ping, and to rotate them between blows. It was dangerous business:

> John Henry told his shaker,
> "Shaker why don't you pray
> For if I miss this six feet steel
> Tomorrow be your buryin' day,
> Lawd, Lawd,
> Tomorrow be your buryin' day."

Eventually John Henry, man among men, was pitted against the newfangled steam engine. He accepted the challenge:

> John Henry told his Cap'n,
> "A man ain't nuthin' but a man,
> And befo' I let that steam-drill beat me down,
> I'll die with my hammer in my hand,
> Lawd, Lawd,
> Die with my hammer in my hand."

There, in the bowels of the earth, John Henry fought for his own integrity and that of his race. He swung straight and true and hard. He won, but paid a terrible price:

> John Henry was hammering on the mountain
> And his hammer was striking fire;
> He drove so hard till he broke his poor heart
> And he lied down his hammer and he died,
> Lawd, Lawd,
> Lied down his hammer and he died.

Turning away from Jim Crow, Uncle Tom, and Uncle Remus, twentieth-century black sympathizers have made much of John Henry. This song, Margaret Just Butcher declared in 1956, is "the parent of the Negro ballads." Ignoring Dr. Chappell's study, she located his saga in the lower seaboard South. F. O. Matthiessen saw the John Henry story as an allegory of "the tragedy of the black man subjected to the power of the white." Though touched with wit and laughter, it is written with sweat and blood.[8]

Most Americans, black and white, felt the echo of John Henry's spirit not in the words of Matthiessen but the sounds of black "soul" singers. "Say it loud, say it proud, I'm black!" shouted James Brown, king of "sock-it-to-me soul." In his strength and fervor he was almost a living embodiment of John Henry.

Both Uncle Remus and John Henry reappeared, as black leaders, in twentieth-century America—the former as Booker T. Washington, the latter as William E. B. DuBois.

Like those whose praise Uncle Remus sang, Booker T. Washington triumphed over incredible hardships. His autobiography, *Up From Slavery* (1901), documents his rise. Having worked in salt furnaces and coal mines to obtain money for schooling, he graduated from Hampton Institute in 1875. Taking over the newly formed Tuskegee Institute in 1881, he created a major educational institution and became an outstanding Negro spokesman of his generation.

He accepted separatism and urged his people to train themselves in agriculture and the trades. Unwilling to see an intellectual élite develop, as had been the case in Haiti, Washington preached "the gospel of the tooth brush," stressing cleanliness and adaptability. Some of his critics say that he accepted political and social bondage as the price of industrial progress; but he did believe that "in all things that are purely social we can be as separate as the fingers, yet one as the hand in all things essential to mutual progress." He urged Negroes to adopt a policy of severe and constant struggle rather than one of artificial forcing. "No race that

[8] See Margaret Just Butcher, *The Negro in American Culture* (New York: Knopf, 1956), p. 60; and F. O. Matthiessen, *American Renaissance* (New York: Oxford University Press, 1941), p. 641.

has anything to contribute to the markets of the world," he said, "is long to any degree ostracized." [9]

His best known speech was given at the Atlanta Exposition in 1895. It drew universal praise from the white press. Said the *Boston Transcript:*

> The speech of Booker T. Washington at the Atlanta Exposition seems to have dwarfed all the other proceedings and the Exposition itself. The sensation that it has caused in the press has never been equalled.

Here was a man saying in highly polished English what Uncle Remus had said a generation before in the folk idiom: Be patient. The way to win is not to fight.[10]

Not all black men agreed. William E. Burghardt DuBois, who studied at Harvard and the University of Berlin before taking up a professorship at Atlanta University in 1896, had an entirely different program. His solution was the National Association for the Advancement of Colored People, which he was instrumental in founding in 1909. His goal was to recover social and civil rights under the Constitution. The tone of his work was embodied in the title of the magazine he founded and edited: *The Crisis.*[11]

One of the major bastions which Dr. DuBois decided he must attack was the idolization of Booker T. Washington.

[9] Quoted by Francis Simkins, *The South Old and New* (New York: Knopf, 1962), p. 876. See also Emma L. Thornbrough, "More Light on Booker T. Washington and the New York Age," *Journal of Negro History,* XLIII (January 1958), pp. 34–49.

[10] Booker T. Washington was an ardent admirer of Harris's work and Uncle Remus's philosophy. He wrote Harris to express "appreciation of your enlightened attitude toward my race."

[11] See especially Mary Law Chaffe, "William E. B. DuBois's Concept of the Racial Problem in the United States," *Journal of Negro History,* XLI (July 1956); Elliott M. Rudwick, "The Niagara Movement," *Journal of Negro History,* XLII (July 1957); and Elliott M. Rudwick, "W. E. B. DuBois: in the Role of Crisis Editor," *Journal of Negro History,* XLIII (July 1958).

As early as 1903 he wrote: "The time is come when one may speak in all sincerity and utter courtesy of the mistakes and shortcomings of Mr. Washington's career."

These mistakes, in his opinion, had led Washington into tragic contradictions:

a) Booker T. Washington wanted to extend black men's rights; but they could never defend their rights and exist without the right of suffrage.

b) He insisted on thrift and self-respect, yet counseled a silent submission that sapped the Negro's manhood.

c) He advocated common schools and industrial training instead of higher learning; yet none of these schools (including Tuskegee) could remain open were it not for teachers trained in Negro colleges, or by their graduates.

Booker T. Washington's career to him seemed to have encouraged the disfranchisement of his own people, the legal creation of a distinct status of civil inferiority for the Negro, and the steady withdrawal of aid from black colleges. Nor would DuBois concede that the differences were only political. His struggle against the Uncle Remuses and the Uncle Toms was, he insisted, ideological; and he waged it unrelentingly all his long life.[12]

There are many historical and political ramifications of William DuBois's life. His own eighteen books and hundreds of pamphlets and articles speak for themselves. Both DuBois and his followers insisted on seeing him as a mythical figure; this image reflects (either consciously or unconsciously) aspects of the John Henry saga.

---

[12] Documents dealing with the Washington-DuBois controversy are reprinted in Herbert Aptheker's *A Documentary History of the Negro People in the United States* (New York: Citadel, 1964), pp. 876–886. A bibliography of DuBois's work is available at the Widener Library, Harvard University. The best biography is by Francis L. Broderick (1959). DuBois's *Autobiography* was published by International Publishers, New York, in 1968.

Looking first at DuBois's own work, we find (says his leading biographer) "one autobiographical essay after another reconstructing the heroic figure of a man of principle fighting a universal battle for the right against an ignorant or hostile world." [13] DuBois thinks of himself (in *Dusk of Dawn*) as "crucified on the vast wheel of time," and "flying round and round with the Zeitgeist." His program is "an absolutely correct scientific procedure, foolproof." He is strong enough to fight off the "regiment of influential Americans" who attack him. His battles are titanic struggles, his disagreements monstrous conspiracies, his successes epochal contributions. No friend of John Henry ever erected a more grandiose image than DuBois made of himself. On his seventieth birthday, says Francis Broderick, he "paid tribute to the clarity of his own thought," and of the clearness of reason, which, said DuBois, was partly the gift of the gods, "but also to no small degree due to scientific training and inner discipline."

What DuBois asserted his followers endorsed. Herbert Aptheker renamed the Age of the Depression the Age of DuBois; Shirley Graham called him "a voice crying in the wilderness"; Doxey Wilkerson declared him "the recognized 'Dean of American Letters.'"

Youra Qualls, a black scholar, declared in the *Southwestern Journal* that DuBois's *Dusk of Dawn* struck the same universal note as did *Pilgrim's Progress*.

Leading white writers vied with each other to honor the militant black writer. J. Saunders Redding thought only Carlyle could match his "combination of scholarship and emotional power woven into bolts of symbolism." To Henry Steele Commager, DuBois best represented the aspirations

---

[13] Francis L. Broderick, *W. E. B. DuBois, Negro Leader in a Time of Crisis* (Stanford, Calif.: Stanford University Press, 1959), p. 227. The other DuBois quotations in my paragraph are also quoted on this page.

of the American Negro. John Gunther compared his position to that of Albert Einstein and George Bernard Shaw. "There is no longer reason to doubt that Negro leadership bespeaks the heart of the Negro people," wrote the Little Rock editor, Harry Ashmore, in 1959. "The pathetic Uncle Toms who still occasionally dance their feeble jigs in the pages of white Southern publications are talking through their tattered wool hats when they proclaim that Negroes really prefer segregation." [14]

Simultaneously, criticisms of Harris and Uncle Remus increased. Arthur Fauset would deny the Uncle Remus tales folk status "because the narrator plays a too-important role." Sterling Brown saw the old Negro as a walking apologist for slavery. In *The Negro in American Culture,* Margaret Butcher goes so far as to accuse Joel Chandler Harris of "using Uncle Remus as a medium for projecting social propaganda." [15]

If Uncle Remus's and Booker T. Washington's reputations are at a low ebb, the historian hesitates to discount either the stories or the leaders who personified them. We have the contention of James Weldon Johnson that the Uncle Remus stories "constitute the greatest body of folklore America has produced." At the same time, we have the polar opposite of heroic meekness in the violence and bitterness of LeRoi Jones, Rapp Brown, and Ray McIver.

We also have a flood of studies and reassessments that make it almost impossible for historians to gain perspective in the midst of the Black Revolution. "Like flotsam from the current storm of race relations," Louis R. Harlan wrote in the October 1968 *American Historical Review,* "pub-

[14] Harry Ashmore, "Race in America: A Southern Moderate's View," in Houston Smith's *The Search for America* (Englewood, N.J.: Prentice-Hall, 1959), p. 47.
[15] Butcher, *op. cit.,* p. 159.

lishers are tossing up reprints of dubious pertinence, super-ficial surveys of Negro history, catchpenny notebooks, warmed-over rejected manuscripts, and pastepot documen-taries." Such a process creates fads, idols, and cults; but heroes are made by a different process.

White writers like de Crèvecoeur have asked "What is an American?" and have replied: "He is a European, or the descendant of a European—" without even considering the implications for those who are colored. Hence the Indians' heroic obscene coyote, and the Negroes' "bad for the sake of bad," blackhearted Stackerlee seem downright "un-American."

The hippies have rediscovered the Indian. Seeing him as the original dropout, student of drug "trips," white youth-rebels have imitated Indian costumes and customs. This has caused Shoshone Chief Rolling Thunder to declare that hippies are "the reincarnation of Indians who have fallen. They are the ghosts of warriors who have come back to re-claim their lands." [16]

A 1968 psychedelic movie called *Indian Givers* depicts cowboys as the Establishment, Indians as hippies. This may please the freak-outs, but most Americans still favor the oldstyle stereotypes, entrenched in mass media, in which goodies (whites) defeat baddies (reds) to preserve the true, the just, and the beautiful.

If there was little threat of a red reversal, there was much evidence for such a thing among black men. A powerful new ethnic weapon, Black Power, emerged in the 1960s. Not Malcolm X or Stokely Carmichael, who had expounded

[16] In *The New Indians* (New York: Harper and Row, 1968), Stan Steiner reports on the gathering "Red Power" movement—a revolt against the white man's culture and its debasement of the tribal way. There is little chance, however, that it will achieve anything like the in-fluence and stylistic importance of Black Power.

this doctrine, but Martin Luther King, who had preached nonviolence, emerged as the New Moses.

Born in 1929 in the Jim Crow South, educated in Atlanta and then in Boston, King was an ordained minister serving in a church with his minister father. But the focus of his interest and power was always on the world rather than narrow denominational boundaries. "From my Christian background I gained my ideals," Dr. King said, "and from Ghandi my operational technique." Coming into national prominence for his leadership of a Montgomery, Alabama, bus strike in 1956, King led the Southern Christian Leadership Conference, crisscrossing the country and evolving what he called militant nonviolence. Sit-ins, lie-ins, and pray-ins became powerful new weapons, the basis of a new heroic role in American life. "My creed of nonviolence is an extremely active force," King said. "History is replete with instances of men who by dying with courage and compassion on their lips converted the hearts of their violent opponents."

Still King had no romantic illusions about the lack of compassion, even decency, among those he sometimes called "our sick white brothers." This leader of black America was well aware of what had happened to red Americans. "Even before there were large numbers of Negroes on our shores," he wrote, "the scar of racial hatred had already disfigured colonial society. Our children are still taught to respect the violence which reduced a red-skinned people into a few fragmented groups herded into impoverished reservations. We have not permitted ourselves to feel remorse for this shameful episode. Our literature, films, drama and folklore all exalt it." [17]

[17] Martin Luther King, *Why We Can't Wait* (New York: Harper, 1964), p. 120.

Dr. King's "Letter from Birmingham Jail," dated April 16, 1963, has already become a key document not only in the civil rights movement, but in the making of a black hero. "I am in Birmingham," he wrote, "because injustice is here." The scope is global, as befits a hero of the twentieth century:

Caught up with his black brothers of Africa and his brown and yellow brothers of Asia, South America, and the Caribbean, the United States Negro is moving with a sense of great urgency toward the promised land of racial justice.[18]

Later in 1963 he led the March on Washington and spoke to thousands of people. In the shadow of the Lincoln Memorial he evoked the national anthem, the Constitution, and the Bible—three mainstays of the heroic style in America. In his full-blown theology of social action the true objective was the achievement of complete unprejudiced equality based on the natural laws of rights and privileges. Thus he stood squarely inside the American tradition.[19]

Accepting a Nobel Prize in 1964, King insisted again that nonviolence is the answer to crucial political and moral questions of our time. In the ensuing months he spoke out strongly against the war in Vietnam, serving again as a symbol of reconciliation and peace. While Black Power people derided him as "De Lawd," poor Negroes in both the North and the South saw him as their Moses, ready to lead them out of the wilderness. "King is the Man, Oh Lord."

King was always careful to identify himself with the main streams and motives of American life, rather than with special-interest or ethnic groups, and also careful to couch his main hopes in theological terms. "Before the Pilgrims landed at Plymouth, we were here," he wrote in 1963 from

[18] *Ibid.*, p. 87.
[19] See John W. Rathbun, "Martin Luther King: The Theology of Social Action," *American Quarterly,* XX (Spring 1968), pp. 38–53.

the Birmingham jail. "Before the pen of Jefferson etched across the pages of history the majestic words of the Declaration of Independence, we were here. We will win our freedom because the sacred heritage of our nation and the eternal will of God are embodied in our echoing demands." This is the rhetoric of the Founding Fathers. For King, Jefferson's "sublime words" lifted America to "cosmic proportions." Still Jefferson had to combine forces with conservative Washington, radical Paine, and autocratic Hamilton to win the American Revolution. The four could collaborate "because the urge of the colonials to be free had matured into a powerful mandate," King wrote. He also venerated Abraham Lincoln, comparing him (in his 1961 Lincoln University Commencement Address) with Amos and Jesus as three who worked "for the bright and glittering daybreak of freedom and justice."

Among his contemporaries, Dr. King thought John Kennedy had "a deep grasp of the dynamics and necessity of social change." The President's last speech on race relations was, the black leader said, "The most earnest, human, and profound appeal for understanding and justice that any President has uttered since the first days of the Republic." [20]

King's essential achievement, before his assassination, was formulating and implementing a philosophy of revolution. He avoided both the conservatives and the extremists, since "neither reach the people who have a crying need to be free." Only the "sweeping and majestic power of nonviolence" can bring real community and end racism. Black men should condemn violence "not only because they know they cannot win freedom through physical force but because through physical force they can lose their souls."

His life symbolized the duality of American life, and the

[20] Martin Luther King, *op. cit.*, p. 144.

persistence of an Old Testament flavor in an age when modernists said God was dead. Millions watched as his casket passed through Atlanta, drawn by ancient mules in an old wagon which Martin Luther King had intended to use in the Poor People's March. Alongside was his widow, frozen in pain, a black Madonna staring out at a guilty world.

"God's allowed me to go up on the mountain," this latter-day black Messiah said to his people on April 3, 1968, the night before he was killed. "I've looked over, and I've seen the Promised Land." The references were Biblical, the cadences and inflections completely Southern. In the Age of Interface, he may have been one of the last authentic regional heroes in American history.

But he did not speak only to or for Southerners, this first major civil rights leader to live below the Mason-Dixon line since Booker T. Washington. "I speak to the masses," King liked to say—and so he did. This genuine unselfish identification with the wretched of his race and all races was his greatest strength. "He did not," Michael Harrington has written, "like some of his militant critics, appoint himself tribune of the people. He was selected by the people themselves. It will be a long time before the poor ever again have the opportunity to choose such a leader."

Though he lived less than forty years, King's life had, in American terms, a sort of antique quality. As he talked we could see the Depression, the Dust Bowl, the scrawny cotton-field mules, and unpainted backcountry churches. He was light-years away from the evangelical hero Billy Graham ("God bless you real good!"). Significantly and symbolically, it was not horsepower but mulepower that pulled his coffin along the streets of Atlanta, as a stunned world watched on television and Telstar.

One thing, at least, was instant—his apotheosis. Only

John F. Kennedy went from mortality to immortality as quickly—and in his case, too, the method was electronic.

"I may not get there with you," King said the night before he died, "but I want you to know tonight that we as a people will get to the Promised Land. So I'm happy tonight."

Happy, but not free. For Martin Luther King, as with all men, freedom came only with death. That is why he had chosen earlier these words for his epitaph:

> Free at last, free at last,
> Thank God Almighty, I'm free at last.

15

The Mouse Is the Message

"What Walt Wrought: The Squeak Heard Round the World."

COVER OF *American Heritage,* APRIL 1968

FOLKSTYLE and fakestyle wed to produce a two-dimensional three-fingered mouse. Thriving not on cheese but film, Mickey inhabited a popstyle magic kingdom called Disneyland. All this was explained in *Understanding Media,* Marshall McLuhan's manifesto for the Age of Circuitry. Mickey magic media McLuhan: the mouse is the message.

Folklore is the country mouse talking. The little creature's weakness inspires stories of mice stronger than men, braver than lions. The Greeks told of a magic mouse skin. In Germany a mouse put his tail in a sleeping thief's mouth and made him cough up a magic ring. A Spanish mouse tormented the bull who couldn't catch him.[1] Mice cut capers on the American frontier.

But no rodent in our time can match the style and fame of Mickey Mouse, with his own emblem, fan clubs, oath, songs, handshake, and cult. He was invented by Walter Elias Disney, Chicago-born artist who drove an ambulance in World War I and returned to draw sketches for farm

---

[1] See Stith Thompson, *Motif-Index of Folk Literature* (Bloomington, Ind.: University of Indiana Press, 1936), Vol. VI.

magazines. Later on, with the help of one of the best-oiled publicity staffs anywhere, he released official versions of everything, including Mickey's conception. The date was set at 1927 (when Walt was 26), the place as the train moving from Chicago to Los Angeles. He and his wife were headed west to find work in Hollywood, after an unsuccessful encounter with animated cartoons in New York. This is how Disney put it in a 1934 story for *The Windsor Magazine:*

Out of the troubles and confusion stood a mocking merry little fellow . . . a romping, rollicking little mouse. The idea completely engulfed me. The wheels turned to the tune of it. "Chug, chug, mouse, chug chug mouse," they seemed to say. The whistle screeched it. "A m-m-mouaouse," it wailed.

"I've got it!" he told his wife Lilly. "I'll do a series about a mouse called Mortimer."

"Mortimer sounds too dignified for a mouse," she replied.

"All right. Let's call him Mickey." So they did. A mouse was born.[2] Aided by Roy Disney, an older brother who took over as business manager, Walt developed into one of the most spectacular successes in popstyle history. Whether or not it was as accidental as the Disneys claimed, they did hitch their wagon to a mouse. Mickey was not Disney's first animated hero; nor was he the first to use film as a means of projecting his paragon. Disney had tried Oswald the Rabbit before his 1927 inspiration. Years before, Georges Mélies had established an animated film studio in France. Mélies's *Trip to the Moon* (1902) was widely acclaimed. Russia's Ladislas Starevitch animated La Fontaine's fables and also a full-length version of *The Adventures of Reynard*

[2] To celebrate the Silver Anniversary of the Disney Studios, *The Saturday Evening Post* published "The Amazing Story of Walt Disney" on October 31, 1953. The article, which had Disney's full sanction, provided the birth details used here. See also Richard Schickel's article in *American Heritage,* XIX, No. 3 (April 1968).

before World War I. In America Winsor McCoy pioneered during the same decade with animated versions of Gertie the Dinosaur and Felix the Cat. Still, the rough sketch which Disney made on that 1927 train ride was destined to change the heroic style in ways which his predecessors never dreamed of. Within four years nationwide Mickey Mouse clubs had more than a million members. Mickey, dressed in his red velvet pants with two huge pearl buttons, won a place of honor in Madame Toussaud's waxworks. Mahomet Zahir Khan, potentate of Hyderabad, called Mickey "the leading American hero in India." Long before World War II, or the Roosevelt Era, Walt Disney electrified the American hero.

Early Mickey was a masterpiece of functionalism with black dots for eyes, legs like rubber hose, ears bigger than Clark Gable's, a string-bean body, and three fingers per hand. When he started to talk, his creator supplied the voice—this for "Steamboat Willie," a short which (said *The New York Times*) "growls, whines, squeaks, and makes various other sounds that add to the mirthful quality." No one could have guessed what would follow, once the psychedelic era opened.

Soon Mickey's image was everywhere. Though Russian art critics were quick to note that Disney "showed the capitalistic world under the mask of pigs, mice, and penguins," most of the world took Mickey Mouse (alias Michel Souris, Musse Pigg, Mikel Mus, Miguel Ratonocito, Michele Jopolino, Miki Kuchi, Mikki Hirri, and Mikkii Mausu) to its heart. Defying time, space, and gravity, he was a fantasy-parody of the Horatio Alger success myth. With mock seriousness, David Low dubbed Disney "the most significant figure in graphic art since Leonardo da Vinci."

The cartoons in which Mickey, and then other Disney-inspired characters, starred were in the full sense of the

216

word large-scale cooperative enterprises. It takes sixteen drawings to make Mickey move once on the screen. A ten-minute cartoon requires 14,400 pictures, carefully synchronized with sound tracks by a process called "Mickey Mousing." The technique worked well for Disney. Exacting and scientific, it nevertheless gives a new freedom of expression to the film maker and artist. Mickey Mouse is tons of drawings transferred onto miles of film—proof that science has become one of the chief factors and forces shaping the hero.

No man, myth, or system has affected American culture as much as science. Americans have never lived in a pre-scientific culture. The earliest settlers were already fully committed to the Scientific Revolution. The most theocratic elements of colonial society reflected this. Cotton Mather and William Byrd were proud to be members of England's Royal Society. Franklin performed valuable experiments with electricity; Jefferson dabbled with science all his life. Capitalism and science were wedded before Europeans arrived on our shores; it has been a long, fruitful, uninterrupted union. Without science, the whole frame of American technology, and hence power, would have been different. Except in a climate of innovation, the American experiment would have been impossible. American society has become the enormous laboratory.

In that society, some critics complain, science has become not only a crucial factor, but a sacred cow. Like oldstyle witch doctors and folkstyle "conjur men," scientists make up a priestcraft and hero-class. Their mumbo-jumbo impresses the uninitiated; their incantations awe the populace. We may not understand the scientist peering up from his multimillion-dollar equipment, but at least we will believe him.

Mickey Mouse, Donald Duck, and the rest of Disney's creations are the indirect results of science and the direct

217

results of technique. The problem posed by technique, as Jacques Ellul points out, is something more than the domination of machines over men. It lies in the domination of standardization over spontaneity and means over ends. Yet that very standardization allows the modern hero-maker to turn images into profit. By leaving the studio and invading America's nurseries and bedrooms, Mickey achieved fame and fortune that few flesh-and-blood paragons have ever enjoyed. Entrepreneurs universalized Mickey. By 1940 over two thousand companies were affiliated with the Disney Studios. One of them, Lionel Corporation, sold more than a quarter-million Mickey Mouse toy handcars in a single Christmas season. The Ingersoll Watch Company sent its five-millionth Mickey Mouse watch to Walt as a special gift. (Any person lucky enough still to own one in 1969 could sell it for $150 on the "black market.") Children could spend hours in a Mickey Mouse world, wearing Mickey Mouse clothes, reading Mickey comics, working on Mickey desk outfits. They could play with Mickey toys and games and see Mickey cartoons at the movies. At night they could put on Mickey pajamas and tumble into Mickey beds, to dream of a happy land where cats do not break through and steal.

Technology creates its own sense of values. Whereas other symbolic figures (Uncle Sam, Paul Bunyan) had human origins, Mickey's was mechanical. Mickey had been created by Disney, whom he resembled, but he became himself. When Army Intelligence used "Mickey Mouse" as the password for the Normandy invasion, they were using the mouse as the message. In addition to creating its own fantasy, machine culture engenders its own obsession with time and demand for improvement. Change becomes a religious ritual, a confirmed habit. Thus Disney, creator of happy cartoon-cartoons and Snow White, seemed to Aubrey Menen "a somber man who appeared to be under the lash of some private demon." Cars, cartoons, and heroes are affected by tempo. In America, the swing from thesis to antithesis is played in folk-rock, with no pause for synthesis. Yet man continues to yearn for timeless utopia. Perhaps that is why Walt built Disneyland, an isle of pastoral innocence in a sea of urban sprawl and smog.

"At Disneyland," a full-page 1968 magazine advertisement read, "in the General Electric 'Carrousel of Progress,' is a huge model of a city with automated highways, easy-to-run homes, high-speed electric commuter trains run by computer." Here, in a miniature mirror, is the American dream—Disneyland, popstyle capitol; Carrousel of Progress, model of mythology; a dream city, home of modern man; a computer, his most precious toy. No wonder today's Canterbury Pilgrims head west, not to see the tomb of Beckett, but the mask of Mickey.[3]

Opened in 1955 near Anaheim, California, Disneyland is a unique combination of verisimilitude, vulgarity, and innovation; a monument to a man who sought absolute control of nature in expressing American mass consciousness; who when asked, just before his death in 1966, what was his life's most rewarding experience replied: "The whole damn thing. The fact that I was able to build an organization and hold it."

Walt held it, one can say in retrospect, by being an egomaniac. Intellectually and emotionally he never cast off the Horatio Alger syndrome of his youth—in fact, never grew up. Behind the friendly, smiling fellow was a moody inarticulate man who always had to be "in charge." By producing clever sound cartoons before anyone else, he got the jump on the field and won deserved acclaim; but like Mickey

[3] See Richard Schickel, *The Disney Version—The Life, Times, Art, and Commerce of Walt Disney* (New York: Simon and Schuster, 1968).

Mouse, he became locked into little patterns and situations. Disney's folksy façade masked a virulent personality cult—you *had* to call him Walt.

Like Henry Ford, whose career he strikingly parallels, Disney believed in the small-town America that was disappearing, not the urban nation that was coming into being. Disneyland was his Dearborn Village; Mickey was his Model T. Neither Disney's style nor his technique ever got beyond the 1940s. Only those with much more flexible systems could give us a Mr. Magoo or Gerald McBoing Boing. What Walt Disney held onto, with a death grip, was really yesterday.

Disneyland is a closed autocracy, taking on the guise of a Magic Kingdom. "Disneyland isn't really for children," Edmund Carpenter has pointed out, "but for old folks from Kansas City who yearn for a childhood that never was and never will be." [4]

Nor were his films "good clean fun for kids." They were full of sex, violence, and (as Richard Schickel points out) an anal-fixation. Still Walt had the magic touch, turning things not into art but into money. He was one of the first to experiment with controlled environments, which figure so largely in the world of Marshall McLuhan. In fact, the *ersatz* emporium called Disneyland is a multimillion-dollar controlled environment, with flying elephants, clay *Tyrannosaurus rex,* and a plastic baby elephant that squirts water into the jaws of a crocodile.

What no one can deny is the effectiveness of Disney's technique. Like Henry Ford, he could make things run, even if he could never humanize his compulsion to control. Disney had an enormous influence on pop artists like Roy Lichtenstein and Claes Oldenberg. Canada's Expo 67 owed

[4] Edmund Carpenter in *The New York Times Book Review* (May 5, 1968), p. 5.

much to his genius for technological planning. Disney was responsible for pioneer models in fields of still-unfathomed consequence. He helped turn America on.

For all his popstyle technique, Walt had a strong penchant for folkstyle America. Observe his Audio-Animatronic Abe Lincoln, who not only looks and moves like a real man, but states (helped by an electric console): "Our reliance is in the love of liberty which God has planted in us." With sixteen air lines to his head, ten to his hands and wrists, fourteen hydraulic lines to control his body, and two pairs of wires for every line, Honest Abe makes an unforgettable impression. He can talk, raise one eyebrow quizzically, nod, and fix you with a glance. Instant character!

No one has dramatized instantness and the implications of the Electronic Age like Marshall McLuhan. His formula is the beep heard round the world: $P + C = PC$ (power plus circuitry equals pop culture).

Born in Canada in 1911, son of Baptist parents but later a convert to Catholicism, McLuhan studied engineering and literature in Canada before attending Cambridge University in England. His interest in modern literature (particularly the novels of James Joyce) led him back to the Elizabethan stylist Thomas Nashe, on whom he wrote his 1943 doctoral dissertation. He taught in Wisconsin and St. Louis before returning to Canada in 1946 as Professor of Literature at Toronto. He has published hundreds of articles in "little" magazines, and four major books: *The Mechanical Bride: Folklore of Industrial Man* (1951); *The Gutenberg Galaxy: The Making of Typographic Man* (1962); *Understanding Media: The Extensions of Man* (1964); and *The Medium Is the Message: An Inventory of Effects* (1967). These set off an international *Kulturkampf* and won for the mild-mannered McLuhan such epithets at Metaphysical Wizard, Distorter of Immature Minds, High Priest of Popthink, Oracle of Electronics, and A Belated Whitman Singing the Body Electric with Thomas Edison as Accompanist. McLuhan accepts all of them and none of them: "I have no point of view. I do not stay in one position." His claim was verified by a 1967 anthology in which thirty critics' opinions ranged from adulation to damnation.[5]

"McLuhan has looted all culture from cave painting to *Mad Magazine*," complained elitist Dwight Macdonald, "to shore up against the ruins of his system." Fellow academicians have been skeptical, scolding, or scathing. Arthur M. Schlesinger, Jr., defines McLuhanism as "a chaotic combination of bland assertion, astute guesswork, fake analogy, dazzling insight, hopeless nonsense, shockmanship, showmanship, wisecracks, and oracular mystification." [6] "Suppose he is what he sounds like, the most important thinker since Newton and Einstein?" asks Tom Wolfe. "What if he is right?" No one can tell yet whether McLuhan is right or not, but everyone must admire his cryptic cool.

McLuhan's ideology lends itself to no simple summation, but there is an overall framework. He is multi-media and multi-cultural. Beginning with the phonetic alphabet and the Greeks, he argues, there emerged in Western civilization a mode of detachment and noninvolvement. From this refusal to be involved in the world he lived in, literate man became alienated from his environment, even from his body. He valued the isolated, delimited self, particularly the mind. Today, we have entered a relatively dim, unconscious world in which the electronic extensions of everyone's nerves involve him deeply in all other lives. While writing and print technology tore man out of group-creating and brought on the great misery of psychic alienation, suddenly and with-

5 Gerald E. Stearn, editor, *McLuhan, Hot and Cool* (New York: Dial, 1967). This book has an excellent McLuhan bibliography.
6 New York *World Journal Tribune*, "Book Week" (March 11, 1967), p. 1.

out warning the electronic media hasten him back into the embrace of the group.

Electronic media have created a global village in which all information can be shared, simultaneously, by everyone; where all walls between peoples, arts, thoughts, come tumbling down. In this vastly confusing environment, the problem becomes one of data selection and processing.

Formerly, work was in direct relation to the source of available energy. Man scratched only the earth's surface for resources. Electric energy allows us to create our own environments, as artists create theirs. Suddenly everybody and everything is involved in transforming the environment into a work of art. The world is a throbbing assemblage of *things* that communicate. The Black Age (coal, mines, factories, soot) is gone. The White Age (electricity, air travel, glass houses, computers) is here. With the sense of sight, the idea communicates the emotion.

The Electronic Age is returning oral and tribal culture to the book-oriented West; we are being hurled back into tribal and oral patterns with seamless webs of kinship and interdependence. Speech over writing, primitive over civilized; is McLuhan trotting out that old eighteenth-century hero, the noble savage? Yes—but in a new model, with electronic devices that make writing and rhetoric unnecessary for communication. Despite his own historical and academic training, McLuhan does not defer to great men or exemplars of the past. For him the real heroes of the human drama are not men, but media.

Hence his chapters do not center on Washington, Lincoln, or Kennedy, but Money ("The Poor Man's Credit Card"), Photographs ("Brothels Without Walls"), and Movies ("The Reel World"). For him media do extraordinary things, altering the total social temperature. "Since TV," he writes, "the whole American political temperature has cooled down, down, down, until the political process is almost approaching *rigor mortis.*" This, more than the politicians, is what interests him about American politics.

Nor are the inventors or perfecters of media his special idols. Alexander Graham Bell had no idea how the telephone would change modern life—his personal story does not interest McLuhan. The drama of history is a pageant whose inner meaning is man's metamorphosis through media. The medium is the message, the focus, the hero. When men *do* achieve fame, they ride on technological tides like driftwood thrown up onto the beach. The general level of heroic quality does not impress the iconoclastic professor. "Any phrasemaking yokel can become a world center."

When McLuhan speaks of "Cool Ones" (as we did in an earlier chapter), he refers not to people but to media. To be "cool" is to be poorly defined, low on data—cartoons, telephone, television. To be "hot," on the other hand, is to be highly defined and full of data—photographs, radio, movies. The TV image is of low intensity and does not afford (as does the film) detailed information about objects. So the viewer is forced to participate. Cool!

One should note that for him *hot* and *cool* are not classifications, but structural forms—slang terms from the musical world, where they have high, structural meaning. The hotting up of one sense leads to hypnosis, the cooling off of all senses to hallucination. So one can extend his hot-cool dichotomy over into the real world of people:

HOT	COOL
Phonetic alphabet	Ideogram
City	Hillbilly
Waltz	Bougouloo
Hitler	Stalin
"Hard sell"	"Soft sell"

Occasionally McLuhan does glance directly at our century's heroes and ask oblique questions about them. Is it an accident, he asks, that "the narcissistic heroes like Tarzan, Superman, Cowboys, and Sleuths are weak on social life?" Intrigued by the tart, anti-heroic pose of film star Humphrey Bogart, somewhat reminiscent of the nineteenth-century poetry of A. E. Housman, he asks (with his own brand of "cool"), "Is Bogart America's Shropshire Lad?" These specific hero-directed questions he has never investigated thoroughly or consecutively. "I make probes," he explains. "I don't explain—I explore."

What he *has* explored, quite thoroughly, are the contributions of his *own* literary heroes—James Joyce, T. S. Eliot, Ezra Pound, and Thomas Nashe. Like them, he is fascinated with words, innuendoes, puns. To pun is "to consolidate by pounding or ramming down (as earth or rubble, in making a roadway)." He has never sought popular support or acclaim; like Eliot, he thought writers required not a large but a significant audience. When the *Gutenberg Galaxy* appeared in 1962, McLuhan got both. The scope and originality was breathtaking. For the intellectual, he is master of bigthink in the 1960s.

For McLuhan the hero is a happening. The process by which the hero is created and recognized involves a spontaneous, unrehearsed, often unconnected cluster of events. Instead of thinking of the hero as being on stage, we might think of him as being in a circus, which is the perfect metaphor for a happening. No information structure is implied. Every act in each ring is a thing in itself. Yet taken together, the events make a total performance that is more than the sum of its parts.

Heroes can no longer work or think in isolation, since they confront a group on either side of their message. Everything is interdependent. The heroes' realm today is not spe-

225

cific and private, but open, public, and plural. There is no place for them to hide.

What stands before us seems to some the reawakened Adam; to others, the mind-blown hippie. Consider the "heroes"—if the term applies—in actual "happenings" that have been staged in the last few years. Such "happenings," visual reflections and extensions of what the French call *le McLuhanisme,* should not be compared or confused with the Theater of the Absurd. Paris-centered and best exemplified in the work of Beckett, Ionesco, and Genet, the Absurd Theater faced a world in which God was dead—in which man was more pathetic than tragic. Disgust, not catharsis, is their specialty. Zero times anything equals *zero.* The protagonist (anti-hero rather than hero) is cut off, tongue-tied, dehumanized. The situation is exasperating, pointless, static. In Samuel Beckett's *Waiting for Godot,* purposeful action is paralyzed, as this excerpt indicates:

VLADIMIR: Pull on your trousers.
ESTRAGON: (*realizing his trousers are down*) True.
          (*He pulls up his trousers.*)
VLADIMIR: Well? Shall we go?
ESTRAGON: Yes, let's go.
          (*They do not move.*)

How different is the tone and mood in "happenings," where *everything* moves. Life is fanciful, irrational, cock-eyed—but not absurd.

This becomes quite clear from a specific instance: *Eat,* by Allan Kaprow. We can hardly choose a better example, for Kaprow is generally credited with having coined the word "happening" in 1959. Later on, interestingly enough, he chose to call his productions *environments.* To be accurate, *Eat* is an environment by Allan Kaprow, presented

226

during the mornings and afternoons of the two last week-ends in January 1964. What happened?

First, one had to make reservations, then wend his way to the caves in the Bronx where the environment was created. Having entered a shabby old building the visitor (there were only twenty per hour) walked through several corridors and doorways and finally came to the environment. The rock from which the caves were carved had been incompletely covered with white paint—the place had once been used by the Ebling Brewery. Age and seeping water had created a sense of decay. Black charred wooden beams stood propped against the walls in several places. Here and there water collected in depressions in the floor and trickled in rivulets through the dirt. Soft but steady ticking noises could be heard from several spots in the cave where battery-operated window-display devices had been hidden, and a man's voice called out, "Get 'em! Get 'em! Get 'em! . . ."

As the visitor moved from the antechamber through a stone arch and into the cave itself, he faced several wooden steps that led up to a low platform. At the far end of the platform more steps led down again to the cave floor. (This entrance to the main part of the cave was not mandatory. An unobstructed passage was possible along one wall.) At right angles to the entrance platform and crossing just under it was another platform, at either end of which stood a rectangular wooden tower about seven feet high. On each of these towers a girl sat motionless on a chair facing away from the entrance. The girl on the left had a gallon of red wine, and the girl on the right had a gallon of white wine. If a visitor specifically asked her for wine, she poured some into a paper cup and handed it to him. The girls did not speak and seldom moved, except to pour.

Directly in front of the entrance, apples hung on rough strings from the ceiling. If the visitor wished, he could remove one of the apples and eat it or, if he was not very hungry, merely take a bite and leave it dangling.

To the right and left of the hanging apples, the cave divided into two large branches or bays of equal size. At the far end of the bay on the right, which contained many charred wooden beams, a girl sat at a small electric hot plate frying sliced bananas in brown sugar. If a spectator asked for some, she gave them to him, but she did not speak. Nearby, whole bunches of bananas wrapped in transparent plastic hung from the ceiling. If he wished (although no suggestions or instructions were ever given), the visitor could take a banana and eat it.

In the left bay a square structure about eight feet high had been built of wooden beams. In the spaces between the beams and on a table inside the enclosure were loaves of sliced bread, jars of strawberry jam, and a few table knives. The only way to get inside the structure—and to get at the food—was to climb a tall ladder propped against the side.

At the rear of the bay another ladder leaned against the stone. It led to a small cave high in the wall, in which a man sat with a large pot. "Get 'em! Get 'em! Get 'em!" he called out mechanically over and over, pausing occasionally for a while and then continuing again. If a visitor climbed the ladder, the man cut a piece of boiled potato, salted it, and gave it to him.

In the best McLuhan fashion, all usual "job functions" were abandoned. Visitors were free to wander about through the cave. Some ate and drank; others didn't. "Performers" were replaced by fresh volunteers. The hero was not *in* the happening, but the happening itself. Having been boxed in by the Shakespeare syndrome for centuries, contemporary theater has broken out of the square, into the round, into McLuhanland.

Mickey, media, McLuhan—what do they mean for the

228

hero, American style? As we enter the Age of Circuitry we have no way of knowing—none of the old yardsticks and criteria apply. We can no longer deal with time and men in slices, like well-cured bologna; everything is happening all at once. Information no longer comes in item by item, but in an electronic cascade. Pattern recognition rather than data collection is the key to many things—including heroes. Men great and small no longer have jobs, but roles. If Mc-Luhan is right, we are about to be retribalized; what will that mean to the hero?

Where once only Mickey and Minnie Mouse dared go, thousands of media-made images and characters rush. The world is wired for sound, focused for sight, for myths to provide a new mental and emotional framework. The balance of human senses is being altered. How to make sense out of such changes is the formidable task confronting tomorrow's heroes.

16

Pop Princes

"Kennedy's lively, upstart quality and Pop-Heroic proportions is part of a legend."

ROY LICHTENSTEIN

THEY are gone now, but memories remain—unruly shocks of hair, quick smiles, press conferences, touch football games, incredible, indelible assassinations. There was never a time within memory when people everywhere were so quiet, so forgetful of everyday problems, so united in grief. "We have been cheated, in a moment," Alistair Cooke wrote from London, "of the promise of what we had begun to call the Age of Kennedy." [1] Yet how can we say we were cheated, when we had our pop princes?

The two Kennedys, John and Robert, are the Castor and Pollux of our era. John F. Kennedy was the first "modern" President, born in and molded by the twentieth century, the first man in that office who refused to be "corny." Self-ridicule was his trademark. Like young musicians and comics, he flattened and deflated. "How did you become a war hero?" someone asked. "They sank my boat," the pop prince replied.

Or again: "Why did you give a cabinet position to your

---

[1] Quoted in *Four Days* (ed. by American Heritage staff), "The Assassination" (New York: Simon and Schuster, 1964), p. 138.

brother?" "I see nothing wrong with giving Robert some legal experience as Attorney General before he goes out to practice law." Robert practiced politics, too. As United States Senator from New York, he reflected much of his brother's image and style in his own life. When in 1968 he became an announced Presidential candidate, men wondered if another prince would be crowned, if indeed history would repeat itself. Only a few minutes after he claimed victory in the California primary—an event which moved him a good deal closer to the White House—he was struck down in a Los Angeles hotel. By mid-June 1968, both young princes were resting in Arlington Cemetery graves looking down on the capital they had seemed destined to rule.

Many things could not be taken from them, however. They were the best loved of young American political leaders in this century, the most bona-fide examples of pop heroes. Precisely what is pop? No easy question, this. *Random House Dictionary* lists twenty-six separate definitions, excluding pop-overs, pop-ups, and popsickles. It's *pop*-ular, prankish, visceral, vital: where the action is. Now lifestyle is electrified, extending our central nervous system in a global embrace, outmoding old space-time patterns. After centuries of exploding, Western man is imploding. Everyone participates in the consequences of every action. Circuits bring social and political functions together in a sudden implosion that changes outlooks and responsibilities. We cope not only with words but with non-verbal data— image, sound, look, gesture. The mind is not a debating hall, but a picture gallery.

In place of national culture Americans confront pop circuits. Only local politicians rely on old ethnic and regional clichés. All others have to face the big light, to sandwich themselves in between ads that sell and shape millions of people. The nineteenth century took its toll on workers' bodies, the twentieth on their minds. In place of the illusion of progress is the illusion of technique. Out of focus, out of mind.

The abrasive process of rubbing information against information accelerates. Instead of simple sequence, there is radical juxtaposition. Slow evolution is being turned into instant alchemy. John F. Kennedy was one impressive product. Suddenly we are light-years not only from eighteenth-century swashbucklers, squires, and cavaliers, but from nineteenth-century men, self-made men, and jolly giants as well. The very idea of looking backwards for heroic patterns and meaning is outmoded. New operative words are *now, pop, fluid, action, accidental,* and *cool.* The present instant is the plane upon which signals of all being are projected. The world is neither meaningful nor meaningless. It simply is.

The environment itself has changed, from natural and mechanical to electrical. Things are plugged in, turned on, computed too fast to observe. No one can see the juice jump. Yet, because of changes too fast to see, everything is suddenly visible—the riot in Washington, the hill in Vietnam, the wart on Nasser's nose. The style in politics, always an indicator of heroic opportunity, is experimental. Candidates stroll through ghettoes and used-car lots saying, "You can trust me. I am a neon sign. Turn me on," which is precisely what the princes did for their generation.

The Kennedys' roots went back to that folkstyle paradise, Ireland. Both their grandfather ("Honey Fitz" Fitzgerald, Mayor of Boston) and their father, Joseph Patrick Kennedy, were political powers in Boston's Irish wards. The nation's youngest bank president at twenty-five, autocratic Joseph Kennedy amassed a fortune that assured all nine of his children of a good life. But John Fitzgerald, his second son, was restricted to a skimpy allowance, as this note written in 1929 (when he was twelve) indicates:

> A Plea for a raise
> By Jack Kennedy
> Dedicated to my father
> Mr. J.P. Kennedy

Chapter I

My recent allowance is 40 cents. This I used for areoplanes and other playthings of my childhood but now I am a scout and I put away my childish things ... So I put in my plea for a raise of thirty cents for me to buy scout things and pay my own way more around.[2]

Educated at Brookline's Dexter School, Canterbury School, and Choate, John finished in 1935. Graduated from Harvard in 1940 *cum laude* in political science, he wrote a thesis that was published as a book entitled *Why England Slept*. "If John Kennedy is characteristic of the younger generation," Henry R. Luce wrote in the introduction, "many of us would be happy to have the destinies of this Republic handed over to his generation at once."

By 1941 John was commissioned in the Navy, and in 1943 he had his first command—PT 109. On August 20 of that year *The New York Times* carried a headline which, as far as I can discover, was the first linking of the name of young Kennedy with the world "hero":

KENNEDY'S SON IS HERO IN PACIFIC
AS DESTOYER SPLITS HIS PT BOAT

"He didn't make it any great hero story," his friend Torbert Macdonald wrote. "Jack was an understater, but he also did make the statement that at night, when you don't

[2] Harold Faber, editor, *The Kennedy Years* (New York: Viking, 1964), p. 17.

know what's in the water beside you. . . . He didn't need to draw me a diagram. I knew how he felt." [3]

Even in his twenties John Kennedy was on his way to being a hero. The story after that is not only part of the public record, but of the legend of our times—the bright brash young politician, the eligible bachelor, the junior Senator from Massachusetts, the efficient organizer. His tightly knit political staff (on which his brother Bobby, Ted Sorensen, and Larry O'Brien held key posts) worked incessantly; in the summer of 1960, at forty-three, he won a first-ballot Presidential nomination at the Democratic National Convention.

In the ensuing campaign against Richard Nixon, it was the four national television debates held in September and October that best revealed Kennedy's understanding of new media and opportunities. Cool and apparently nerveless, Kennedy showed an impressive command of facts and the ability to push Nixon into generalization. James Reston observed:

Kennedy started like the underdog who wasn't supposed to be able to stay the course with the champ, but is winding up with more specific information on the tip of his tongue than Mr. Nixon, whose presentation was general and often emotional. Mr. Kennedy was curt and factual. [4]

On a cool medium, Kennedy was ice, Nixon fire. One did not have to be Marshall McLuhan to predict which candidate benefited most from the electronic encounter. Nor was it hard to guess why the Republicans broke off all negotiations for a fifth nationwide television debate. Experts estimated that 120,000,000 people had seen at least one of the

[3] *Ibid.*, p. 136.
[4] Goddard Lieberson, editor, *John Fitzgerald Kennedy: As We Remember Him* (New York: Atheneum, 1965).

four debates. Nothing in the other 43 Presidential campaigns had in any way approximated it. An opinion poll showed that 75 percent of those voters who had made up their minds on the basis of the debates had supported Kennedy. Pop goes the election.

So much has been written about the "Kennedy style" that no clear picture of just what it was, or how it functioned, has emerged. That John abhorred sentiment, purple prose, and trite comments, and yearned to bring art, poetry, and creativity into public places was apparent. His careful exploitation of mass media was a Kennedy hallmark; his press conferences were masterpieces of relaxed, confident exposition. Here was the old Roosevelt "Fireside Chat," made visible, with prince charming doing the chatting. Warm smile, quick jokes, dry wit, hands that stabbed the air; the style was the message.

"He has a mind quite unlike that of any other Democrat of this century," Richard Rovere wrote. "It is not literary, metaphysical and moral, as Adlai Stevenson's is. Whereas Mr. Stevenson's political views derive from a view of life that holds politics to be a mere fraction of existence, Kennedy's primary interest is politics." [5]

This point was developed further by Norman Mailer in his book called *The Presidential Papers*. Eisenhower had been the anti-hero, the regulator; his view was narrow, cautious, and planted in the life-logic of the small town. John Kennedy was the new hero—dynamic, unsettling, accelerating to the psyche of the city. Mailer found in Kennedy "a suggestion of dry pen heat, his eyes large, the pupils gray, the white prominent, almost shocking, his most forceful feature: he had the eyes of a mountaineer."

With the coming of mass media and the big light, politics

[5] Richard Rovere, "The Candidates," *The New Yorker* (July 23, 1960).

235

has also become America's favorite movie, America's first soap opera, America's best seller. To cope with these things, John Kennedy developed a cool grace, almost an indifference. His manner was like the poise of a fine boxer—quick with his hands, neat in his timing, two feet away from his corner when the bell ended the round. Here was a new sense of proportion for a new America. Here in the midst of pop culture was our pop prince.

"What is already evident is that the national pantheon has a new figure and a fine one," Gerald W. Johnson wrote. "It is, above all, the ideal of youth; when a nation has gained a symbol that can release the generous impulses of its young men and women it is fortunate beyond computation." [6]

Instead of destroying the symbol, John Kennedy's assassination transferred it to his brother Robert. Eight years younger than John, Robert became a national figure at thirty-five when he became Attorney General, where his record in the fields of civil rights, crime, and labor legislation won wide respect. Moody and quick-tempered, he was the Celt of the Kennedys. Uncompromising in his honesty, he constantly irritated as well as delighted. He was the "strong right arm" of his brother, the President. Once his brother was gone, and he was the premier prince, he repeated the Kennedy message for the new era: the worst sin is to do nothing. One man can make a difference, government is the worthiest employment, moral idealism is a more powerful force than military weapons.[7] A lot of oldstyle virtues, preached by Emerson and many other spokesmen for the Harvard both Kennedys attended, won their endorsement— self-reliance, self-discipline, self-improvement. After all,

[6] Gerald W. Johnson, "Once Touched by Romance," *The New Republic* (Dec. 7, 1963).
[7] William V. Shannon, "The Kennedy Legend," *The New York Times,* Section 4, E 1 (June 9, 1968).

they were not far removed from one of the most traditional spots in Europe—Ireland. Their family had every reason to praise the open society to which the immigrant Kennedys came in tumultuous pre-pop days. Not from their European heritage but from their national culture did the Kennedy brothers draw their real strength, and it was that culture which made them into heroes.

Circumstances and personality inevitably favored John Kennedy as the brightest star in the pop firmament.[8] Robert's only chance of equaling him came when he decided to run for the Presidency in 1968. But five months before the election was held, he was dead. Eulogizing Robert at the funeral in New York's St. Patrick's Cathedral, a still younger brother, Edward (who may have his own chapter in later books on American heroes) said:

My brother need not be idealized or enlarged in death beyond what he was in life. He should be remembered simply as a good and decent man, who saw wrong and tried to right it, saw suffering and tried to heal it, saw war and tried to stop it.

At that very moment he was being both idealized and enlarged in death throughout the world. This was the hysteria that exalts; when the reverse hysteria would set in, no one could say. But at that moment, death had put him right alongside John Kennedy in Arlington Cemetery. By a heroic symbiosis the two Kennedys had merged into a single symbol of the new generation, ready to meet the revolutions of their time head-on.

The eighteenth century had gained the same type of youthful symbol when William Pitt the Younger became

[8] Could it be that it was the Kennedy family, rather than any member of it, that created the heroic image? Journalists wrote of the "Kennedy-style self-control" and the "interchangeable images." It will be a whole generation before questions like this can be answered.

Prime Minister in 1783, when he was twenty-four. Not a chip off the old block, but the old block itself, the "boy premier" served wisely and well. Across the seas the former English colonies, independent now, also followed youthful leaders like Hamilton and Jefferson. Only twenty-six in 1783, Hamilton had been a Lieutenant Colonel when he was twenty, and an important figure in the Continental Congress a few years later. Thomas Jefferson, who had been in his thirties when he wrote the Declaration of Independence, was approaching forty in 1783, and preparing to go abroad and serve as Minister to France. Pop prince John Kennedy admired no American more than Jefferson. Gathering a distinguished group of intellectuals together in the White House, he said it was the largest collection of brain power to meet there since Jefferson had had dinner alone.

But the best analogy, so far as the pop prince is concerned, is with Teddy Roosevelt. Like John Kennedy, Teddy was in his early forties when he assumed the Presidency in 1901. Having served with distinction in civilian and military posts, and led the Rough Riders in the "bully little war," he reflected the same vigor and confidence that were Kennedy trademarks. But while Roosevelt had years to work out his program, Kennedy was given only a thousand days.

The assassinations of the Kennedys, one in 1963 and another in 1968, took on aspects of a grim, unbelievable happening. The President of the United States killed by an ex-Marine; he in turn killed in front of a mass television audience; a web of circumstances so complex that millions still believe there was a massive conspiracy and "the truth has not been told." The official *Report* of the Warren Commission inflamed rather than ended the controversy. Titles like *Who Killed Kennedy?* (Thomas G. Buchanan); *Un-*

238

answered Questions About President Kennedy's Assassination (Sylvan Fox); *Rush to Judgment* (Mark Lane); *Were We Controlled?* (Lincoln Lawrence); and *Whitewash* (Harold Weisberg) reflect the air surrounding John Kennedy's death. Since Robert Kennedy's assassination involved one of the bitterest international rivalries of our generation (Jew versus Arab), the appearance of books similar in tone following the second assassination was inevitable.

Not since Lincoln's assassination had there been such national trauma as that which came with the deaths of the pop princes. Lincoln's generation saw death on the battlefield; that of the Kennedys saw it hourly on television. Violence had become one of the chief devices, diversions, and commodities in twentieth-century America. At the very time in which a new generation was formulating a doctrine of love and flower power, hate and firepower were everywhere in evidence.

In 1968 Mrs. John Kennedy became Mrs. Aristotle Onassis. She was thirty-nine, he was sixty-two—and had no annulment for his first marriage from the Greek Orthodox church. Why had she left "Camelot" for the world of shipping tycoons?

The world of pop heroes has many other contradictions, many dilemmas. Youth-dominated and frantically optimistic, it harps back nostalgically to the 1920s and '30s, and mourns America's lost innocence. "We'll laugh again," a Kennedy aide was quoted as saying after the pop prince's assassination, "but we'll never be young again." Can heroes and cultures move from adolescence to old age without anything between? Pop goes the image of the All-American Boy. But the Kennedys remain, frozen in death and legend.

17

The Heroic Style in America

"I want to live in a world that is able to get on to the questions that belong to the twentieth century."

DONNA MICKLESON, *A Student Look at America*

AMERICA'S heroic style evades chronology, but not contour. We assign the swashbuckler to the seventeenth century only to have Doug Fairbanks leap onto the twentieth-century scene, sword in hand. We think we've seen the last of the cavaliers who sat proudly on their horses and dashed toward Gettysburg—only to find General Patton atop his tank turret, dashing toward Germany. Fairbanks and Patton inherited their style from earlier epochs of swashbucklers and cavaliers. They reflect contours of an earlier time, as the rear-view mirror reflects the landscape behind.

Other heroes anticipate epochs yet to come. Cool ones dominate the twentieth century; but there was also something wonderfully cool about sixteenth-century Sir Francis Drake, "singeing the beard of the Spanish king" by sailing right into the harbor at Cadiz; or laconic, eccentric, professor-turned-Civil-War-soldier "Stonewall" Jackson, saying quietly to his aides, "If the enemy is still standing at sunset, press them with the bayonet." The history of heroes echoes and re-echoes statements and styles down the corridors of time.

240

In that history, repetition and revolution exist side by side. The red badge of courage for today's youth is long hair; nothing signals popstyle more decisively. Old boys moan the new barbarism and shagginess in the same terms as did Thomas Hall in 1654:

> Go, Gallants, to the Barbers go
> Bid them your hairy Bushes mow.
> God in a Bush did once appear
> But there is nothing of Him here.[1]

What the newly emerging bushy-headed hero stands for, no one can yet say. He is not, Ihab Hassan notes, exactly the liberal's idea of the victim, nor the conservative's idea of the outcast, nor the radical's idea of the rebel. He finally appears as an expression of man's quenchless desire to affirm, despite the pressures of our age, the human sense of life.[2]

Some of America's most colorful paragons were heroes in homespun—products of a genuine, orally transmitted folklore that did not scorn the grass-roots idiom:

> Beefsteak when I'm hungry,
> Corn likker when I'm dry,
> Pretty little gal when I'm lonesome,
> Sweet heaven when I die.

Diligent collectors have found examples of ballads, dance and game lyrics, blues, spirituals, work songs, hymns and white spirituals, Indian chants and prayers, trickster tales, local legends, tall tales, adapted European stories. There is

[1] Thomas Hall, *The Loathesomeness of Long Haire ... With an Appendix Against Painting, Spots, Naked Breasts, Etc.* (London: 1654).
[2] Ihab Hassan, *Radical Innocence: Studies in the Contemporary American Novel* (New York: Harper and Row, 1961), p. 6.

no shortage in America of superstitions, sayings, proverbs, occupational jokes, and an infinite variety of games, dances, riddles, and rhymes. The distilled experience of generations of birth, life, and death are universal themes with local habitations and names.

What changes is locale, personnel, circumstances. In America the hero moved steadily westward, until he reached Hollywood. Later, he went into orbit. Popular favorites advanced from the open forest to the big tent to the nightclub to the discotheque. European oldstyle was left behind as American folkstyle took root in the rich virgin land. Farmer-planters like Thomas Jefferson, George Washington, and William Penn set our pattern in politics. The myth of the garden, summarized at the end of the nineteenth century by Frederick Jackson Turner, coupled with the Jeffersonian ideal of the family farm to provide the chief theme of American history. Karl Marx also used the struggle between country and city as a major theme in *Das Kapital*. Simultaneously, American ballad-makers complained:

> The farmer is the man
> Lives on credit till the fall;
> Then they take him by the hand
> And they lead him from the land
> And the city man's the man who gets it all.

What happened to the country man in a rapidly changing economy is paralleled by the history of one of his best-loved songs, "Home on the Range." Written by Brewster Highley in 1873, it was picked up as a folksong by John A. Lomax in 1908. In the 1930s city people made it into a popular "hit." The state of Kansas declared it the official state song in 1947. In 1954, Kansas politicians turned Brewster Highley's log cabin, where he allegedly wrote the song, into a shrine. By then, rural sociologists acknowledged that their field had virtually ceased to exist.[3]

So had the traditional ballads, full of oldstyle and folk-style heroes. In earlier form they had been handed down from the past without known individual authorship; showed evidence of variation in content; had a compact and concise narrative; made much of repetition and refrain.[4] Instead of going to such native folk material, early American writers preferred to return to European precedents. Washington Irving, the first widely accepted professional American writer, made a fairyland of the Hudson Valley by importing tales from the Rhine, changing distant Otmar into nearby Rip Van Winkle.[5] In so doing he became a founding father of American fakestyle, which eventually overshadowed both oldstyle and folkstyle.

Fakestyle impetus also came directly from Europe, where the "artsy-craftsy" ideas of Neo-Medievalists like John Ruskin and William Morris enjoyed a wide vogue. Hatred of early machine civilization, best exemplified in their native England, caused them to retreat to mythical Camelot—a kingdom John F. Kennedy would covet in the twentieth century. While the English were condemning machines, Americans were using theirs to produce dime novels and give fakestyle an enormous boost. The key date here is June 1860,

[3] Thomas C. Cochran, "The History of a Business Society," *Journal of American History,* LIV (June 1967), p. 9.

[4] The Archives of American Folk Song in the Library of Congress has more than 40,000 pieces of recorded folk music; there are thousands more in state and regional archives, as well as regular commercial issues. In *Folksongs on Records* (1950), Ben Gray Lumpkins lists over 4000 titles.

[5] "Irving pretended both childishness and antiquity for America, then stood back and saw these things fail before an always triumphant broad daylight which existed to celebrate the absence of childishness and antiquity," writes Terence Martin in "Rip, Ichabod, and the American Imagination," *American Literature,* XXI (May 1959), p. 148.

243

when the first example of this new vulgarism, a uniquely American form of popular literature, was published. This sensational "yellowback," written by Ann S. Stephens, was entitled *Malaeska: The Indian Wife of the White Hunter*. Soon Beadle's New Dime Novels, Frank Starr's American Novels, and the Beadle-Adams combination changed the nation's reading habits. Folkstyle is built on facts and real events, fakestyle on images and pseudo-events. We have seen how fakestyle changed America's heroes.

The 1876 Philadelphia World's Fair gave fakestyle another boost. Exhibits stressed the production of bijouterie —"artistic" bronzes, luxurious furniture, and artificial flowers that had (to quote the French critic Simonin) "the veritable stamp of solidity and good taste." A key statistic involves the sale of jigsaw blades in America, chief source of bric-a-brac and fretwork. About 3000 a year were sold in 1875—over 500,000 a month in 1878.[6]

"Americans," William Dean Howells complained, "have cast about for the instruction of someone who professed to know better, and who browbeat wholesome commonsense into the self-distrust that ends in sophistication." As if to illustrate his claim, the lead article in *Harper's Bazaar* for July 1, 1876, urged readers to clip items out of periodicals, then paste them "in a pretty scrap album for the library table. Stick on all sorts of little ornaments: monograms, little gilt devices cut from envelope bands, false flowers— anything at all that is pretty." [7]

While ladies were clipping for scrapbooks and Robber

[6] John A. Kouwenhoven, *The Arts in Modern American Civilization* (New York: Norton, 1967), p. 89. Kouwenhoven's analysis of "bric-a-brac" America provides a good introduction to the subject of fakestyle.

[7] Quoted by John Kouwenhoven, *Made in America* (New York: Norton, 1960), p. 89; reprinted as *Arts in Modern American Civilization* (New York: Norton, 1967).

Barons were bringing home European art objects by the barrel-load, the era's greatest American writer was still drawing from folk material. Born in a sordid frontier town, schooled in mining camps and riverboat pilothouses, Mark Twain created the last genuinely American folk hero, *Huckleberry Finn*. In presenting Huck, he also showed that a novel could be built on dialogue, not rhetoric. But Huck was overshadowed by a new breed of fakestyle jolly giants —reckless, ruthless, chauvinistic. Horatio Greenough was wrong when he complained that America has "no half-fabulous, legendary wealth, no misty, cloud-enveloped background." A more accurate diagnosis might be that America deliberately rejected these elements of her past in order to create a new interpretation of history.

The Greeks used mythological metaphors as the basis for heroic style; the Romans depended on biographical archetypes; the Middle Ages on hagiography. By stressing a few themes and patterns each epoch greatly increased the focus and intensity of meaning. There is no such cohesive force in American culture—hence no such clarity or intensity. We may get it, for the first time, in the new pop iconography.

Meanwhile, we struggle with the aesthetics and heroics of impermanence. To modern critics an art-object is a temporary center of energy, which motivates for a while, then dies. America went into a furor in 1913 over Marcel Duchamp's "Nude Descending a Staircase." Half a century later—as Duchamp himself admitted—the Nude was dead; she had become a tombstone to her still-living creator. The same can be said about heroic acts, such as Lindbergh's 1927 solo crossing of the Atlantic. Today impermanence is not only an observable fact, but a stylistic device.[8]

[8] Harold Rosenberg explores this subject in *The Anxious Object* (New York: Horizon, 1965).

Another key word is *interface*. Originally a chemical term referring to the interaction of substances in a kind of mutual irritation, it has been broadened to deal with the whole culture. In its most natural form interface emerges as random conversation or dialogue—bits and snatches. This is what we see on the avant-garde stage. The interplay of multiple aspects generates insights and discovery. Interface is random contact with the life of forms. One by-product is a new heroic style. The hero becomes a happening. Whatever happens, this style will not be simple or linear. To be contemporary is to give up simple explanations of man and his world, to embrace complexity once and for all, to try both to manage and image it.

Heroic deeds are generally done in mysterious places, where obstacles are as great as imagination unencumbered by fact can make them. This described the Holy Land in the thirteenth century, the brave new world in the seventeenth, the American frontier in the nineteenth. Today, mystery dwells in outer space and on other planets. *What is it like out there?* Will those who go "out there" ever tell us? Perhaps the reign of words will come to an end, along with man's bondage to gravity. Scientists already do things that cannot be made intelligible in words, only in formulae. We may be abolishing speech as the most vital communication between men. This implies that the life of action, the matching of great words with great deeds, might end.

To continue with space-age metaphors, we are all crew members on a single global spaceship, making our way through infinity. The voyage our earth makes is precarious. We depend on a thin layer of soil beneath us, a layer of atmosphere above us, and a hero at the helm—these, and nothing more.

If we are to survive, we must know the other crewmen, even if we don't like them. Entering the final third of the twentieth century, we must invent new systems, symbols, and rituals. They must be born out of processes in which we participate, but over which we may have no conscious control.

Western man lives in a society where most old myths have lost their mana and power. He no longer accepts either the motifs or the materials of Christian mythos, which served him well for centuries. His has been that most terrible of fates—he is demythologized.

When an old mythology disintegrates, a new one originates. To survive is to remythologize. Instead of *discovering* a new mythos, we find ourselves *participating* in it. That is what our pop artists and pop heroes are doing, what our children are seeking with their new tactics, songs, morals, haircuts. They will bury not only us, but our worn-out mythology, too.

When Western demythologizing reached its crest, between the World Wars, a doom boom resulted. Darkness, despair, and doubt spread everywhere. *The Wasteland* that T. S. Eliot described in his 1922 poem was bone-dry:

> He who was living is now dead
> We who were living are now dying
> With a little patience
> Here is no water but only rock
> Rock and no water but only rock.

No place for the hero to thrive here. Other things withered, too—laissez-faire economics, Newtonian physics, stiff-collar diplomacy. The "modern" world, as that term was understood by Locke, Jefferson, Voltaire, and Gladstone, gave way to a post-modern world. Inevitably the heroic style changed radically. The arts pointed the way. Daniel French gave way to Alexander Calder, John Singer Sargent to Jackson Pollock, Stephen Foster to Dizzie Gillespie. We left the world of Descartes and Newton, with closed boxes, for that of Einstein and Wernher von Braun, with infinitely open spaces. The structure of society, the order of ideas, the basic concepts of space and time were up-ended. Where there had been time-honored myth, suddenly there was a void. Even the existence of God, that hero of heroes, was questioned. The church found itself in the embarrassing position of having within its affluent confines everything it needed—except God.

One of the brightest popstyle theologians, Harvey Cox, urges his fellow churchmen to seek God not in the sacred cloisters, but in the secular city. How, he asks, can man separate sacred and secular, when they are both God's? The sacred always goes bad unless it is working with the secular; the word becomes mere vapor unless it becomes flesh. There is no theology without sociology. No matter how pure and ethereal a religion may be at first, it is always converted into something else.

Realizing this, a group of tough-minded thinkers called existentialists have forced us to think about ultimate problems. Are we free? Have we ever been free? What does it mean to exist now, genuinely?

The golden thread of thought goes back to Plato, who pondered essences, and Aristotle, who stressed existence. That to him was reality. Man is as he does; action justifies life. Existence is action and involvement. In today's idiom—are you swinging?

Pop culture, with all its faddish stunts, asks these same questions in a new idiom. New sounds and stagings penetrate the modern condition, ridiculing outworn dogmas and platitudes. There are many different ways and levels on which existential concern can be shown. Our cultural package is all of a piece. Change seems most radical in some areas only because we know more about them, or are more

248

involved with them. The radical common denominator is that we accept change as a normal condition. *Dubito, ergo sum.*

From Descartes through Hegel, Western thought was dominated by rationalism, system-building, and the notion of progress. As in formal theology, house-wrecking has been the order of the day. Dominant themes of twentieth-century philosophy are disillusionment, pessimism, the lure of destruction. Paradox prevails; we live at a moment of economic optimism, and political pessimism. Automation, computerization, nuclear fission, and rocketry should have made us free—but have only tyrannized us to a degree unparalleled in history. Our ancestors thought we would, by now, have built the brave new world. Instead, we seem unable to prevent blowing it up. Here is the overwhelming problem for contemporary heroes to face and solve.

They must learn to cross new bridges, touch new godheads. Think how theology could be enriched by encompassing ecology, which studies the interrelationship of organisms and their environment. Until recently, ecology was largely the bailiwick of biologists concentrating on plant environments. Now ecologists say man's total environment includes not only the physical and biotic, but the cultural and conceptual. Material from the traditional humanities, arts, social sciences—and why not theology?—should be gathered. Only interdisciplinary efforts can focus on the holistic man in his total surroundings. Man is moving into an era of *total environment* and radical new styles. Confronted with that movement, theologians would seem to have three alternatives—change the image they now present, adapt to needs of twentieth-century society, or retreat into pedantic triviality.

If only yesterday's heroes and saints are revered, in the capitol and the cathedral, the government and church will

249

emerge as the safe-deposit box where archaic images are stored. To find new heroes, institutions must make adjustments. In rethinking they may see that new ideas and labels apply admirably to old truths. Christianity as revealed through the Gospels is a kind of happening. Why should He have been conceived of a Virgin, rejected by His own people, hung on a cross? Was ever a story more astounding (to the unbeliever, absurd) than this? While oldstyle theologians mourn the death of God, new media let their light shine on all men. The shining light—epiphany! God is dead only for those who seek Him in a square tomb. He's definitely alive for those watching the tube.

To recognize the absence of myth is the first step toward resurrecting it. By 1960, that recognition was widespread in America. The heroic style is being refashioned. Remythologizing is under way.

America has never been an aristocratic society, but it has aped Europe's for generations. If America was (to quote Mark Twain) "fresh out of kings," it produced scores of kings and queens for sports events, agricultural fairs, and every product on the store shelf. In our ambivalent effort to establish democracy, we first concentrated on politics (during our Revolution), then economics (during the New Deal). Perhaps we can now create an environmental democracy, in which we both accept and improve the twentieth-century world. The March of the Poor on Washington in 1968 showed how far we still have to go. We must not be afraid of America, the things in it, the way it operates. Boredom, frustration, repetition, waste, and delay are all built into the model. A new generation no longer thinks of used-car lots, billboards, and flashing neon signs as part of the Wasteland. Instead they are raw material for visual involvement—the stuff out of which pop heroes are made. The entire environment can be seen as a work of art, a teaching machine designed to maximize perception. For the first time artists can be, in the full sense of the word, popular heroes. But it must be on the people's terms, not the élite's.

When most men lived in the country, folkstyle allowed us to mythologize American culture. By deflating rural values, fakestyle demythologized our lives. The job today is to remythologize them.

Certain distinctions between the main heroic styles in the last three centuries emerge not as factual syllogisms, but as suggestions:

FOLKSTYLE	FAKESTYLE	POPSTYLE
oral	verbal	multisensory
traditional	nostalgic	experimental
realistic	romantic	psychedelic
earthy	sticky	tart
homespun	factory-spun	polyester
continuity	transition	explosion
improvised	ersatz	electronic
cowboy	Buffalo Bill	Bonanzaland
community sing	folk festival	Disneyland

Stylistic changes are reflected in the work of young writers like Susan Sontag and Tom Wolfe, young campus heroes like David Harris. In *Against Interpretation,* Miss Sontag includes an essay "On Style," arguing that style is the principle of decision in a work of art, the signature of the artist's will. She puts her own signature on "Notes on Camp," widely regarded as one of the most influential essays of the decade. "Camp" is love of the unnatural—of artifice and exaggeration. She traces camp's origins to eighteenth-century Gothic novels, chinoiserie, and artificial ruins, and sees it responding to "instant character," thus supplementing the new Age of Circuitry. New style-makers are usually

251

not writers, according to Miss Sontag, but artists, film makers, social planners, TV technicians, neurologists, electronics engineers, and sociologists. Basic texts for this new cultural alignment are found in the writings of Marshall McLuhan, Buckminster Fuller, John Cage, Siegfried Gidieon, Norman O. Brown, and Gyorgy Kepes. "Sensations, feelings, the abstract forms and styles of sensibility count. It is to these that contemporary art addresses itself." [9] The way of camp is not in terms of beauty, but of stylization. Are we to witness the rise of campstyle in America?

If so, Tom Wolfe must be accounted a Daniel Boone who led us across its frontier. Touring the country to find out about postwar teen-age culture, Wolfe chose the name for his full-length report from the incredibly stylized custom cars California kids design and produce—*Kandy-Kolored Tangerine-Flake Streamline Baby*. In the "Introduction" style is central to his whole thesis:

Since World War II classes of people whose styles of life had been practically invisible had the money to build monuments to their own styles. This took the form of custom cars, the twist, the jerk, the monkey, the shake, rock music generally, stretch pants, decal eyes. All these things, like Inigo Jones's classicism, have started having an influence on the life of the whole country.

To Wolfe, Baby Jane Holzer, the society girl who went pop, is "the hyper-version of a whole new style of life in America." She is a symbol, just as is Las Vegas—"the Versailles of America, the only architecturally uniform city in the Western World." Gangsters built it in an isolated spot, just as Louis XIV went outside Paris to create his fantastic baroque environment. The Las Vegas hoods celebrated, very early, the new style of life of America—"using the

[9] Susan Sontag, *Against Interpretation* (New York: Dell, 1967), p. 300.

money pumped in by the war to show a prole vision of style."

Wolfe's special hero—"The Last American Hero"—is Junior Johnson, the Carolina country boy who learned to drive by running whisky for his bootlegging father and grew up to be a famous stock-car racing driver. "Junior Johnson is one of the last of those sports stars who is not just an ace at the game itself, but a hero a whole people or class of people can identify with." [10] He "turns on" the white Southerner the way Jack Dempsey stirred up the Irish and Joe Louis the Negroes. Johnson is a modern popstyle hero, involved with car culture and car symbolism; Wolfe is his Boswell.

His images are as hard-edged, clear, objective, precise as pop paintings, or as the two-minute summaries by a master popstyle TV journalist like Eric Sevareid. Here is Wolfe's description of the IRT subway station at 50th and Broadway at 8:45 on a Thursday morning:

All the faces come popping in clots out of the Seventh Avenue local, past the King Size Ice Cream machine, and the turnstiles start whacking away as if the world were breaking up on the reefs. Four steps past the turnstiles everybody is already backed up haunch to paunch for the climb up the ramp and the stairs to the surface, a great funnel of flesh, wool, felt, leather, rubber and steaming alumicron, with the blood squeezing through everybody's old sclerotic arteries in hopped-up spurts from too much coffee and the effort of surfacing from the subway at the rush hour.

The tendency here, and in most pop prose, is not to pontificate, but to probe, to twist the cultural kaleidoscope, to

[10] Tom Wolfe, *The Kandy-Kolored Tangerine-Flake Steamline Baby* (New York: Farrar, Straus, 1965), p. 131 (paperback ed., Pocket books, 1967).

travel without a road map. And that, you may be sure, the Old Boys can never approve. No wonder they have trouble with Barbara Garson's *MacBird!* This gay, gaudy play, most widely heralded political parody in the 1960s, goes its own outrageous way, toward no particular point. MacBird's outcry sums it up: "Unity, Unity, wherefore art thou, Unity?" Lyndon B. Johnson has the distinction of being the first Presidential anti-hero in American history. Other Presidents (including an earlier Johnson) have been attacked and scorned, but only popstyle could have done it in this manner.

Once the beatnik witches have assured Johnson (alias MacBird) that he can be President if Kennedy (alias John Ken O'Dunc) is assassinated, our shotgun parody is off and popping. The Egg of Head (Adlai Stevenson), the Earl of Warren, the Wayne of Morse, and Lord MacNamara get into the act. Everyone does his thing. Riots, sit-ins, foreign interventions, demonstrations, and skullduggery play their part in the creation of a new Pox Americana. In the words of MacBird:

> We mean to be the firemen of peace
> Dousing flames with freedom's forceful flow.

Paradoxically, the mediocrity of the play serves a purpose. The more it puts us on, the clearer becomes the message. What can you do with a parody that parodies straw men and falsehoods rather than real men and foibles? Will the real catharsis please stand up?

MacBird is a minor play pointing to a major tendency— to ridicule not only people, but art-forms. The line between "impure life" and "pure art" is no longer considered valid. Not only Happenings but public events and demonstrations become theater. In a real sense, the various riots, marches, and protests of the 1960s were means for dramatic expression and catharsis in American life. The TV screen became Everyman's theater. Everyone had a box seat.

In this setting no one can *plan* to be a hero, the way a general plans a battle or an architect a building. No one knows when he is "on stage" or "off stage"—which camera is focusing on which person now? (No wonder President Nixon avoided campaign television debates.) Or, if there are six cameras, which button is the studio technician pushing to put one image into 100,000,000 minds, and keep the other five out? If we leave mass media, do we move *into* the action or *away* from it?

Such questions open up the whole area of leisure in pop-style America. Just what we can anticipate is explored in the Spring 1968 issue of *TDR, The Drama Review*. The day of the Fun Palace is upon us, where Gala Days and Nights will be filled with:

Instant Cinema	Juke Box Information
Genius Chat	Adult Toys
Clownery	Star Gazing
Fireworks	Concerts
Battles of Flowers	Rallies
Science Gadgetry	Learning Machines
Kunst Dabbling	Theater

All for your delight! New wealth, mobility, flexibility, and social interdependence demand an awareness of the vast range of influences and experiences open to all at all times. Since the Fun Palace Foundation was registered as a Charitable Trust in 1966, some of these dreams-on-paper may be realities within a few years.[11]

Already the search is on for new modes of expression; new discoveries are on display. Thus, a single issue of the

[11] Preliminary drawings and a "Non-Program" for a Laboratory of Fun appear in *TDR, The Drama Review*, T 39 (Spring 1968), pp. 127 f.

avant-garde popstyle newspaper *Village Voice,* for April 11, 1968, advertises:

"The Space Music of Sun Ra"—A Freeform Excursion into the Far Reaches of Sound and Sight

"Alice, Through the Glass Lightly"—A Turn on For Kids and Adults Who Never Believed Alice Was 9 Feet High

"Hair—The American Tribal Love-Rock Musical."

"An Electric Easter—A Total Theater, The Art Form, the Gesamtkunstwerk of the Future"

"The Groove-Tubers, Regular TV With Hair"—It Discovers an Example of What Television Could Be; or Could Have Been."

Ads such as these, plus the staccato prose of Stephanie Harrington, Leticia Kent, Don McNeill, Michael McDonald, and Sally Kempton, made the *Village Voice* one of the best barometers of style-change, and proof that sensitive reporting comes in any style, any idiom.

They also suggest that in their newstyle involvement with popular culture, young Americans are discovering new modes of experience, new ways to achieve depth and total involvement. Old walls of snobbery and élitism are tumbling down. The "highbrow" seems more and more ridiculous as he preens his own feathers. In an incredibly varied and altering culture, we find a priceless artistic and stylistic pluralism. If we can separate the real from the phony, the serious from the pseudo, we may move into one of man's most creative epochs. This calls for skillful and interdisciplinary criticism, which will "both confront the implications of the new sensibility and build on the substantial achievements of the mass culture critics." [12] This is indeed a major responsibility of the new intellectual generation.

[12] John G. Cawelti, "Reviews," *American Quarterly,* XX (September 1968), p. 259.

Recent activities within the historian's camp indicate that this confrontation is taking place. The "consensus school" of the 1950s, which held that most of the heated controversies of America's past were hyperbolic, a kind of ritual warfare associated with politics, has been challenged and in some instances discredited.[13] America is not "one nation under God, indivisible." Tension, not consensus, is the dominating theme. A "New Left" school of radical historians will have nothing to do with consensus and the Establishment. Chief among their heroes is Herbert Marcuse, who calls for intolerance against movements from the right and toleration of movements from the left—since the left alone is the agent of history. To avoid the "systematic moronization" of America we must resist goods and services that render us incapable of achieving an existence of our own and make us "one dimensional men." Living in what another able young historian, Michael Harrington, calls *The Accidental Century,* we must move *Toward a Democratic Left.* We must have more democratic debate and more effective popular control over huge government programs if our democracy is to endure, he argues. One hears the echoes of the old Jeffersonian line: "Give the people light and they will find their way."

As the writings of men like Harrington show, the fear of apathy and automation that saturated the 1950s has changed to violence and the fear of revolution in the 1960s. Students, linked together as never before in the Age of Circuitry, are revolting everywhere. No more talk of the "Silent Generation." Obviously young people are turned on—engaged in an intense search for personal commitment. Seeking a prototype, Gina Berriault chose David Harris, 1967 student presi-

13 See John A. Garraty, "A Then for Now," *The New York Times* (May 12, 1967), Section 7, p. 1.

dent at Stanford University.[14] Harris has pale-blue eyes, rimless glasses, a substantial mustache that makes him appear older than twenty-one, and large photos of Charlie Chaplin and Mahatma Gandhi on his wall. The books on his shelf are Nietzsche, Kierkegaard, A. J. Muste, and the *Upanishad*. He talks with a fast mixture of beat jargon, academic terms, and words in common usage. Meeting for the first time with Stanford's President Wallace Sterling, Harris wore a work shirt, Levis, and moccasins. He doesn't dress oldstyle, one presumes, because he doesn't think oldstyle; in the words of Thoreau (a popstyle favorite), he listens to the music of a different drummer.

So do his contemporaries whose student lectures were published under the title *A Student Look at America* (1967). One of them, twenty-five-year-old Louis Cartwright, said that the new hero is one who "knows nobody knows—and isn't afraid of not knowing." The key to the heroic personality is not achievement, but potential, since "we are a potential world of men who require no corrals." The New Reality, says twenty-eight-year-old Phil Baumgartner, is "the power of courage to bring the individual so immediately in contact with the here-and-now that all expectation or possibility of death is wiped out." [15]

Despite their infinite varieties, new student heroes have one platform in common—the determination to prove to themselves and to others that there are ways to live where no *They* is ever blamed, where no rule is ever made that can't be unmade or changed, and where the exceptions make up the reality and beauty of being human.

All around us in the 1960s we see the "failure of suc-

[14] Gina Berriault, "The New Student President, David Harris of Stanford," *Esquire* (September 1967).
[15] Otto Butz, editor, *To Make a Difference* (New York: Harper & Row, 1967), p. 231.

258

cess." Studies of alienated youth who will make and be to-morrow's heroes indicate they will not settle for the bag of toys that fascinated devotees of Horatio Alger. Typical of the times was Jan Myrdal's *Confessions of a Disloyal European*. Son of the great Swedish economist whose book *An American Dilemma: The Negro Problem and Modern Democracy* helped shape a whole generation of liberal thinking, Jan sings not a hymn, but a eulogy to revolution. Our civilization is full of promises that are never fulfilled—reeking with bad faith. Prejudice and hatred are wrong, war is madness, massive inequality is intolerable. Suddenly the world seems filled with young people who are neither ideologues nor psychological misfits, but pragmatists who had no recourse but to become radicals. Not only their politics but their programs are radical. There is no vaccination against the "malaise of affluence." Thus Jan Myrdal describes himself lying in a bed he has not made or left for three weeks, practicing yoga breathing with his legs up against the wall.[16] Young people around the world seem on the same wavelength. What does this imply for the hero, American style?

Young men and women who formulate this lifestyle reflect the mood of the 1960s. They also remind us, after our survey of several centuries, that man is the only being who asks questions about being—about power and potential beyond himself. Power plus structure equals a life of being. America is searching for a new ontology. Cultural relocation and heroic transformation are radical interests of a new generation.

Image-makers are engaged in a worldwide scavenger hunt involving African sculpture, Zen fables, Indian music, the

[16] Jan Myrdal, *Confessions of a Disloyal European* (New York: Pantheon, 1968). See also Kenneth Keniston, *Young Radicals: Notes on Committed Youth* (New York: Harcourt, Brace and World, 1968).

camp style of Victoria, the click-clack of computers, the primitive masks of Mali. By telescoping time, tradition, and geography the first universal heroic tradition may emerge. All world history is its past; all the world's its stage. The arts may be one before the church is one. The atelier is more ecumenical than the altar.

Yet it is not in the church but in the laboratory that the germs of this culture will best flourish. Science is the foundation of the new mythos. There are indications that biology may be grasping the lead from physics. The whole psychedelic spectrum, like work with DNA and RNA, points to revolutionary ideas. They will be dramatized in new heroes. We are on the verge of what the twentieth century's greatest poet, William Butler Yeats, called a *Second Coming:*

> The darkness drops again; but now I know
> That twenty centuries of stony sleep
> Were vexed to nightmare by a rocking cradle,
> And what rough beast, its hour come round at last,
> Slouches towards Bethlehem to be born?

Bibliographical Note

For further information consult volumes and articles mentioned in chapter footnotes, and in the author's *Bibliography of the American Hero,* published by the Bibliographical Society of the University of Virginia (1950; reprinted 1968).

Below is a list of an essential small library of books and articles for the student of the hero, American style; but one should also study the films, ads, billboards, and graffiti all around him to round out the heroic picture.

Baker, Carlos, ed. *Hemingway and His Critics: An International Anthology.* New York: Hill and Wang, 1961.

Basler, Roy. *The Lincoln Legend.* Cambridge, Mass.: Houghton Mifflin Co., 1935.

Bentley, Eric. *A Century of Hero-Worship.* Boston: Beacon Press, 1957.

Bergonzi, Bernard. *Heroes' Twilight: A Study of the Literature of the Great War.* New York: Coward-McCann, 1966.

Boorstin, Daniel. *The Image, Or What Happened to the American Dream.* New York: Atheneum, 1962.

Brustein, Robert S. "America's New Culture Hero," *Commentary,* February 1958, 123–129.

Burns, Walter Noble. *The Saga of Billy the Kid.* Garden City, N.Y.: Doubleday, Page and Co., 1926.

Campbell, Joseph. *The Hero with a Thousand Faces.* New York: Meridian Books, 1956.

Camus, Albert. *The Myth of Sisyphus and Other Essays.* New York: Vintage Books, 1960.

———. *The Rebel.* New York: Vintage Books, 1956.

Carlyle, Thomas. *On Heroes, Hero-Worship and the Heroic in History* (1841).

Coblentz, Stanton A. *The Paradox of Man's Greatness*. Washington: Public Affairs Press, 1966.

Cohn, Ruby. "Four Stages of Absurdist Hero," *Drama Survey*, Winter 1965, 195–208.

Cooke, Alistair. "Epitaph for a Tough Guy," *Atlantic Monthly*, May 1957, 31–35.

Cunliffe, Marcus. *George Washington, Man and Monument*. Boston: Little, Brown and Co., 1958.

Davis, Kenneth S. *The Hero: Charles A. Lindbergh and the American Dream*. Garden City, N.Y.: Doubleday & Co., 1959.

Dorson, Richard M. "Davy Crockett and the Heroic Age," *Southern Folklore Quarterly*, VI, 1942, 95–102.

Emerson, Ralph Waldo. *Essays, Second Series* (1844).

———. *Representative Men* (1850).

Feldman, Gene, and Max Gartenberg, eds. *The Beat Generation and the Angry Young Men*. New York: Dell, 1958.

Fiedler, Leslie. "War, Exile, and the Death of Honor," and "The Death of Old Men," *Waiting for the End*. New York: Stein and Day, 1954.

Fishwick, Marshall W. *American Heroes: Myth and Reality*. Washington: Public Affairs Press, 1954.

———. *Gentlemen of Virginia*. New York: Dodd, Mead, 1961.

Galloway, D. D. "Clown and Saint: the Hero in Current American Fiction," *Critique*, 7, Winter 1964–65, 18–35.

Giraud, Raymond. *The Unheroic Hero in the Novels of Stendhal, Balzac and Flaubert*. New Brunswick, N.J.: Rutgers University Press, 1957.

Glicksberg, Charles I. *The Tragic Vision in Twentieth-Century Literature*. Carbondale: Southern Illinois University Press, 1963.

Gurko, Leo. *Heroes, Highbrows and the Popular Mind*. Indianapolis, Ind.: Bobbs-Merrill, 1953.

Heilbrun, C. "Woman as Hero," *Texas Quarterly*, Winter 1965, 132–141.

Hoffman, Daniel G. *Paul Bunyan, Last of the Frontier Demigods*. Philadelphia: University of Pennsylvania Press, 1952.

Hoffman, Daniel G. "Davy Crockett and the Self-Defeating Dream," *Form and Fable in American Fiction*. New York: Oxford University Press, 1961.

Holbrook, Stewart. *Dreamers of the American Dream*. Garden City, N.Y.: Doubleday & Co., 1957.

————. *Lost Men of American History*. New York: Macmillan Co., 1946.

Hook, Sidney. *The Hero in History*. New York: Humanities Press, Inc., 1943.

Kennedy, John F. *Profiles in Courage*. New York: Harper & Row, 1961.

Kerényi, C. *The Heroes of the Greeks*. London: Thames and Hudson, 1959.

Klapp, Orrin E. *Heroes, Villains and Fools*. Englewood, N.J.: Prentice-Hall, Inc., 1962.

Lehman, B. H. *Carlyle's Theory of the Hero*. Durham, N.C.: Duke University Press, 1928.

Lowenthal, Leo. "Biographies in Popular Magazines," in *American Social Patterns,* ed. William Peterson. New York: Doubleday Anchor Books, 1956.

Lubin, Harold, ed. *Heroes and Anti-Heroes*. San Francisco: Chandler Press, 1968.

Mailer, Norman. *The Presidential Papers*. New York: G. P. Putnam's Sons, 1963.

————. *The White Negro*. San Francisco: City Lights Books, 1957.

Mathewson, Rufus. *The Positive Hero in Russian Literature*. New York: Columbia University Press, 1958.

Mayo, Bernard. *Myths and Men.* Athens. University of Georgia Press, 1959.

Myers, Henry. "Heroes and the Way of Compromise," *Tragedy: A View of Life*. Ithaca, N.Y.: Cornell University Press, 1956.

O'Faolain, Sean. *The Vanishing Hero: Studies in Novelists of the Twenties*. London: Eyre and Spottiswoode, 1956.

"On the Difficulties of Being a Contemporary Hero." *Time,* June 24, 1966, 32–33.

263

Panichas, George A., ed. *Promise of Greatness: The War of 1914–1918*. New York: John Day, 1968.

Raglan, Lord. *The Hero: A Study in Tradition, Myth and Drama*. New York: Vintage Books, 1956.

Rank, Otto. *The Birth of the Hero, and Other Essays*. New York: Vintage Books, 1964.

Rischin, Moses, ed. *The American Gospel of Success: Individualism and Beyond*. Chicago: Quadrangle Books, 1968.

Rosenberg, Harold. "The Heroes of Marxist Science," *The Tradition of the New*. New York: Horizon Books, 1959.

Schickel, Richard. "Raymond Chandler, Private Eye," *Commentary*, February 1963, 158–161.

Steckmesser, Kent L. *The Western Hero in History and Legend*. Norman, Okla.: University of Oklahoma Press, 1965.

Thorsler, Peter L. *The Byronic Hero: Types and Prototypes*. Minneapolis: University of Minnesota Press, 1962.

Warshow, Robert. *The Immediate Experience*. Garden City, N.Y.: Doubleday & Co., 1962.

Wecter, Dixon. *The Hero in America, A Chronicle of Hero-Worship*. New York: Charles Scribner's Sons, 1941.

Williams, William Carlos. *In the American Grain*. Norfolk, Conn.: New Directions, 1925.

Wolfe, Thomas. *The Electric Kool-Aid Acid Test*. New York: Farrar, Straus and Giroux, 1968.

————. *The Pump House Gang*. New York: Farrar, Straus and Giroux, 1968.

Index

Catastrophe, 33
Cavalier, 54f., 65, 137; *see also* Gentlemen.
Celebration, 37, 39, 49, 57, 63, 67, 182, 207
Chaplin, Charlie, 38
Christ, 7f., 209f.
Christian, 8, 11, 60, 86, 177, 209f., 236, 246
Church, 59, 87, 236
Cinema, 3, 38, 60, 64, 158, 163f., 209, 214f.
City, 42, 62, 69, 82, 84
Civil War, 54, 55f., 122, 138, 198
Clark, Joe, 134f.
Clothing, 68
Classics, 6, 44f., 117, 154, 230
Code, 67, 208
College, 31, 60, 221
Colonial, 43
Comic book, 114f.
Comic figure, 81, 114, 230
Confederacy, 49, 58f., 128, 196
Cool Ones, 146f.
Coolidge, Calvin, 50
Cosmos, 29, 198
Cowboy, 61, 91
Crockett, Davy, 81f., 110, 124

D.A.R., 46
Darwinism, 86, 99, 133, 153
Dean, James, 157
Death, 17, 28, 36, 50, 79, 158, 237
Debunker, 50
Demigods, 5, 18, 65, 105f., 136; *see also* Jolly Giants
Democracy, 110, 145
Detroit, 93
Dime Novel, 84, 121, 128, 150

Disc Jockey, 129
Disney, Walt, 214f.
Disneyland, 69, 129, 217f.
Drama, 5, 17, 71, 117, 123, 142, 185, 209, 254
Drugs, 2, 156, 192
DuBois, W. E. B., 204f.
Dylan, Bob, 24, 145, 177f., 195

Economics, 71, 84, 91, 127, 183, 250, 259
Edison, Thomas A., 100, 222
Education, 81, 137, 233
Eisenhower, Dwight, 51f.
Electronics, 49, 67, 68, 213, 221, 241
Emerson, Ralph W., 5, 13, 59, 70, 106, 236
England, 16, 29, 34, 39, 45, 85, 175, 243
Environment, 49, 57, 73, 82, 84, 143, 159, 222, 226, 232, 246, 254, 260
Establishment, 155, 241, 258
Ethnic, 71, 126, 140, 205, 206
Europe, 18, 25, 36, 39, 67, 70f., 81, 98, 250
Existentialism, 69, 155, 185, 248

Fairbanks, Douglas, 38
Fairfax, George, 47
Fakestyle, 15, 67, 69, 89, 118, 214f.
Family, 57, 71, 75, 80, 119
Fantasy, 39, 77, 114f., 169, 196, 198, 215, 218
Feud, 138f., 201
Finn, Huck, 46, 77, 245
Folk culture, 1, 71, 205f., 221, 243

Folklore, 6, 11, 43, 68, 70f., 84, 85, 93, 108, 135f., 143, 150, 193, 196, 207, 214
Folkstyle, 13, 15, 57, 68, 71, 78, 79, 89, 196, 214f., 221, 243
Food, 44, 47, 196
Ford, Henry, 93f., 220
Ford jokes, 95f.
Franklin, Ben, 45, 75, 86, 101, 217
Freaklore, 160
Frontier, 45, 50, 71, 74, 86, 129, 161, 246

Gable, Clark, 163f., 216
Gangster, 90f., 152, 252
Gentlemen, 30, 43, 48, 124; see also Cavalier.
Gilded Age, 118f.
Gospel of Success, 85, 204, 216, 220, 235
Greece, 23, 37, 153, 181, 214, 222, 245
Guthrie, Woody, 144f.

Happening, 2, 226f., 246
Harris, Joel C., 196f.
Hefner, Hugh, 164f.
Hemingway, Ernest, 180
Henry, John, 18, 198
Henry, Patrick, 121
Hero, theory of, 1, 5, 19, 57, 68, 207f., 255f.
Hero, uses of, 1, 24, 68, 74, 79f., 91, 135, 182, 206, 258f.
Hero-maker, 10, 20, 208f., 234f., 259
Hillbilly, 140f.
Hippie, 90, 155f., 182, 226

Historic interpretation, 22, 31, 77, 85, 92, 97, 118, 135, 148, 207, 257, 260
History, theory of, 5f., 77, 259
Hitler, Adolf, 10, 97
Hobo, 190
Horse, 55f., 63, 66
"Hot stuff," 163

Ideology, 9f., 17, 222, 251
Image, 64, 75, 85, 162, 167, 176, 219, 250
Indian, 16f., 32, 44, 63, 70f., 73f., 117, 135, 151, 195, 209, 259
Industrialism, 39, 68, 114, 141, 201
Ingraham, Prentiss, 128
Innovation, 2, 19, 201, 217, 255
Isolation, 71, 76, 157, 193, 225

Jackson, "Stonewall," 56, 240
Jamboree, 83
James, Jesse, 149f.
Jamestown, 55
Jay, John, 45
Jazz, 167, 177
"Jeb" Stuart, 56, 64
Jefferson, Thomas, 45, 55, 58, 74, 211, 217, 242, 247
Jet Age, 39, 69, 102, 234
Johnson, Lyndon B., 254
Jolly Giant, 105f.; see also Demigod
Journalism, 50, 63, 79, 100, 117, 127, 204, 216, 256
Judson, Edward, 120f.

Kafka, Franz, 184
Kansas, 51

267

268

Pocahontas, 32
Poetry, 17, 23, 26, 40, 46, 72, 74, 78, 106, 150, 155, 225, 241, 260
Politics, 6, 22, 42, 48, 52, 64, 71, 81, 104, 192, 223
Poor whites, 134f.
Pop art, 162, 167, 220
Popstyle, 15, 178, 219, 223, 231f., 250
Popular culture, 2, 25, 114, 141, 168, 250
Portrait, 48, 50
Pragmatism, 34
Presentism, 3
Private Eye, 129f.
Psychiatry, 65, 147
P.T. 109, 12, 233
Puritan, 73, 85, 100, 115, 132

Queen, 70f., 164

Racism, 63, 71, 84, 112
Raleigh, Walter, 28f.
Rear-view mirror, 57, 69
Religion, 10f., 84, 184, 221, 258
Resurrection City, 145
Revere, Paul, 68
Revolt, 2, 35, 49, 56, 134
Revolution, 5, 20, 41, 48, 61, 145, 211, 250, 259
Rhetoric, 35f., 48, 90, 92, 109, 125
Robber Baron, 85f., 168, 244
Rockefeller, John D., 101
Romanticism, 73, 74f., 132, 209
Rome, 8, 23, 41, 93
Roosevelt, Franklin, 52, 74, 103, 116, 172, 216
Roosevelt, Theodore, 66f., 197

Russia, 97, 216
Ruth, Babe, 169f.

Science, 5, 11, 77, 206, 217f., 246, 260
Secret agent, 129f., 154
Self-made man, 84f.
Sex, 65, 72, 87, 132, 142, 153, 162
Slavery, 31, 203
Smith, John, 1, 9, 30f., 64, 74
Sports, 3, 23, 51, 169f.
Spotswood, Alexander, 37
Status, 43, 71, 90, 230
Stereotype, 7, 9, 53, 61, 86, 110, 137, 142, 165, 231
Stuart, Gilbert, 48
Stuyvesant, Peter, 36
Style, 3, 5, 12, 25, 48, 53, 67, 74, 83, 91, 144, 191; *see also* Fakestyle, Folkstyle, Lifestyle, Oldstyle, Popstyle
Superman, 114, 225
Super-star, 3, 67, 234
Sweetheart, 47, 66
Symbol, 2, 20, 21, 48, 60, 64, 83, 162, 206, 236, 252

Technology, 77, 93, 98, 201, 222, 248
Teen culture, 156f., 160, 179, 252, 259
Television, 63, 68, 115, 144, 168, 175, 234f., 250, 255f.
Theology, 64, 98, 132, 184, 221, 250
"Toby," 141f.
Tough guy, 131f., 157
Travel, 44, 68, 205
Truman, Harry, 103f.

Ulysses, 74, 159, 207
Unilinear, 66, 160, 208, 221
U-2 plane, 52

Valentino, Rudolph, 163f.
Van Dyke, 54
Vernacular, 99, 207f.
Versailles, 72
Village Voice, 256
Villain, 116, 148, 154, 192
Violence, 62, 65, 74, 75, 79, 121, 132, 142, 146, 152
Virginia, 29f., 44f., 54f., 87, 134

War, 66f., 117
War of 1812, 134f., 150
Washington, Booker T., 203f.
Washington, George, 20, 45f., 55, 58, 74, 121, 166, 242
Washington Monument, 46f.
Webster, Daniel, 81
Weems, Parson, 20f.
Weltanschauung, 144

Western, 65, 73
White House, 71, 104, 236
White Man's Burden, 63, 112
Whitman, Walt, 13, 78
Wild West, 82, 123, 198, 210
William, Old Bill, 14, 71, 79
Williamsburg, 43f.
Witchcraft, 43
World War I, 51f., 90, 180f., 216
World War II, 51f., 66, 97, 116, 153, 163, 173

Xerxes, 46

Yahweh, 50, 57, 132
Yankee, 55, 70f., 87, 150, 169, 198
York, Alvin C., 139f.
Young, Arthur, 46

Ziegfeld's Follies, 67
Zionist, 184
Zorro, 39